BARE METAL C

Embedded Programming for the Real World

by Steve Oualline

no starch
press

San Francisco

Printed in the United States of America

First printing

26 25 24 23 22   1 2 3 4 5

ISBN-13: 978-1-7185-0162-1 (print)
ISBN-13: 978-1-7185-0163-8 (ebook)

Publisher: William Pollock
Managing Editor: Jill Franklin
Production Manager: Rachel Monaghan
Production Editor: Jennifer Kepler
Developmental Editors: Jill Franklin and Frances Saux
Cover Illustrator: Gina Redman
Interior Design: Octopod Studios
Technical Reviewer: Frank Duignan
Copyeditor: Bart Reed
Compositor: Ashley McKevitt, Happenstance Type-O-Rama
Proofreader: Rachel Head

For information on distribution, bulk sales, corporate sales, or translations, please contact No Starch Press, Inc. directly at info@nostarch.com or:

No Starch Press, Inc.
245 8th Street, San Francisco, CA 94103
phone: 1.415.863.9900
www.nostarch.com

Library of Congress Cataloging-in-Publication Data

Names: Oualline, Steve, author.
Title: Bare metal C : embedded programming for the real world / Stephen Oualline.
Description: San Francisco : No Starch Press, [2022] | Includes index.
Identifiers: LCCN 2021049830 (print) | LCCN 2021049831 (ebook) | ISBN 9781718501621 (paperback) |
    ISBN 9781718501638 (ebook)
Subjects: LCSH: C (Computer program language) | Embedded computer systems--Programming.
Classification: LCC QA76.73.C15 O835 2022 (print) | LCC QA76.73.C15 (ebook) | DDC 005.13/3--dc23/
    eng/20211105
LC record available at https://lccn.loc.gov/2021049830
LC ebook record available at https://lccn.loc.gov/2021049831

About the Author

Steve Oualline has been writing reliable, low-bug programs for embedded systems for over 50 years. He has a master of science from the University of Southern California and has written many books for both No Starch Press and O'Reilly. He is currently a volunteer at the Southern California Railroad Museum, where his most recent project was debugging the computer controller for their Acme Traffic signal. (Ants built a nest inside it and had to be removed.) His website can be found at *http://oualline.com*.

About the Technical Reviewer

Frank Duignan graduated as an electrical engineer in 1988. Since then he has worked mostly at the interface between hardware and software. He is currently lecturing in electrical/electronic engineering at Technological University Dublin. Frank's blog can be found at *https://ioprog.com*.

BRIEF CONTENTS

CONTENTS IN DETAIL

3
PROGRAMMING THE MICROCONTROLLER   33

4
NUMBERS AND VARIABLES   53

12
THE PREPROCESSOR
207

PART II: C FOR BIG MACHINES
221

13
DYNAMIC MEMORY
223

14
BUFFERED FILE I/O
237

INTRODUCTION

This book is called *Bare Metal C* because it's for people who get close to the hardware. It's not for people who buy their computer in a box and never see the inside. The computer used in this book doesn't even have a box. If you want to use it, you're going to have to connect something to the "bare metal" of the board.

This book teaches embedded programming. An *embedded computer* is one that sits inside the machine and you never know it's there. It's the device that runs your garage door opener, your microwave, your car, or even your greeting card. But before it can do any of those things, it needs to be programmed. And that is what this book teaches you: how to program an embedded system.

Why C? C gives you precise control over what your program is doing, whereas other languages, such as C++, can do a great deal of things behind your back. Consider the following statement:

```
a = b;
```

In C++, this could call a class's assignment operator function, which might result in heap memory being allocated and freed as well as an exception being thrown. What all that means is unimportant right now; the point is that you don't know exactly what's going to happen.

In C, this statement assigns the value b to the variable a with no side effects; it's just an assignment, nothing more. This example is simple, but you'll see other ways that C does exactly what you tell it throughout the book.

Precise control is important because we are using C to program a low-end *system on a chip (SOC)* system based on the STM32F030x4 processor (a cheap ARM Cortex-M0-based system) that has 8KB of RAM. Memory management is very important with limited RAM, so we can't afford to have a high-level language like C++ play with memory behind our backs. Precise control is also important because an embedded system doesn't have an operating system and you need to tell the hardware what to do directly. High-level languages don't always let you talk to the hardware, but C does.

The book is designed for people who have a basic knowledge of computers and hardware, but have a limited knowledge of programming. It is for the hardware designer who wants to connect a new piece of hardware to a microcontroller and use it for the first time. It is for the programmer who is interested in low-level programming and wants to get the most out of a 38¢ chip.

NOTE *The ARM Cortex-M0 is very popular with low-end products because it costs 38¢ in quantities of 10,000 at the time of writing. Given that we hope to sell millions of whatever embedded system we are making, the difference between a 38¢ chip and a 56¢ chip is significant.*

To get the most out of your programs, you'll need to know what goes on under the hood. The book shows you not only how to write a program, but also how your program is translated into machine code that's used by the ARM chip. That's important for maximum efficiency. For example, you'll learn how much of a performance hit you'll get if you change your program from using 16-bit integers to using 32-bit integers. The answer, surprisingly, is that 32-bit integers are *more efficient* and *faster* (32 bits is the natural number size for the ARM, and if it's forced to do 16-bit arithmetic, it does 32-bit calculations and then throws away 16 bits).

To program and debug an ARM chip, you'll need some extra tools: a flash memory programmer (to get your code into the machine), a USB-to-serial converter (because we use the serial line for debugging), and a JTAG debugger. Since almost all developers need this combination of tools, STMicroelectronics makes a board that provides all the hardware you'll need, called the NUCLEO-F030R8. As of this writing, a chip shortage has made some boards hard to find. See *https://nostarch.com/bare-metal-c* for alternate boards. You'll also need a mini USB cable (the one that doesn't fit your phone) so you can plug the board into your computer.

Your first task is to order a NUCLEO-F030R8. Then start reading Chapter 1. By the time the board arrives, you will be ready for it.

PART I

EMBEDDED PROGRAMMING

Let me describe a "simple" embedded system. It is a battery-powered processor housed in a pendant worn around someone's neck. When the end user has an emergency, they press the button and the computer sends a radio signal to a receiver that makes an emergency call.

Sounds simple . . . except you have to send a precise set of pulses to the radio so it will generate the proper signal. The system must periodically check the battery and send battery information to the base station as well, which serves two purposes. First, when the battery starts to get a little low, the alarm company is notified and sends the end user a new pendant. Second, if the base station doesn't receive a periodic signal, the alarm company knows that something is wrong with the pendant.

This type of program is typical in the embedded world. It's small, must be precise, and doesn't use a lot of outside resources.

In this section of the book, you'll learn about basic C syntax and programming. We also go through in detail what the C compiler does so you can precisely control what your program does. To have this precise control, you need to know what the compiler is doing behind your back.

Embedded programming presents its own unique debugging challenges. Fortunately, tools like the JTAG debugging interface make things easier, but still, debugging an embedded system can be quite difficult.

One of the most basic and common debugging methods is to put `printf` statements in your code. This is somewhat difficult when doing embedded programming, as there's no place to send printed output. We'll cover how to use serial I/O to get printed data out of the embedded system for debugging and logging.

And finally, in this part of the book, you'll learn about interrupt programming. Interrupts allow you to perform I/O efficiently, but they also allow you to create race conditions and other random bugs if not done right. Design is extremely important here because interrupt problems can be quite debug-resistant.

Welcome to the world of embedded programming. Have fun.

1

HELLO WORLD

In this chapter, you'll create and execute your first program, "Hello World." This is about the simplest program you can make and the first program in almost all C books. But you'll go beyond just creating it: you'll learn what's actually going on behind the scenes during its creation.

The tools you'll use are designed to make things quick and easy, which is good for regular programming but can be bad for embedded programming. The compiler, GCC, is actually a wrapper that runs a whole bunch of other tools. We'll look at what each tool does to get your program from code to execution. In the process, you'll discover that the GCC optimizer has a surprise for us. Although our program is very simple, the optimizer will decide to rewrite part of it to make it more efficient—*and it won't tell us about the rewrite!* In fact, we would never know about it if we didn't look under the hood to see what's going on. (I won't tell you what it will do to us; you'll have to read the rest of the chapter to find that out.)

Installing GCC

In order to run the program in this chapter, you'll need to download and install the GNU C compiler (GCC) on your system, along with related tools. The instructions for doing so vary based on your operating system.

On Windows, install Minimalist GNU for Windows (MinGW), which can be found at *http://www.mingw.org*. See *https://nostarch.com/bare-metal-c* for detailed instructions.

On macOS, the GCC compiler is part of the developer packages that can be accessed with the following command:

```
$ xcode-select --install
```

Select the **Command Line Tools** option for installation.

Linux installation instructions depend on which distribution you are using. For Debian systems such as Ubuntu and Linux Mint, use the following commands:

```
$ sudo apt-get install build-essential
$ sudo apt-get install manpages-dev
```

For Red Hat–based systems (such as Fedora or CentOS), use the following command:

```
$ dnf groupinstall "Development Tools"
```

For any other Linux-based system, use the package manager that came with the system or search online to find the command needed for installation.

After installing the software, open a terminal window and issue the command **gcc**. If you get a "no input files" error, you've installed successfully.

```
$ gcc
gcc: fatal error: no input files
compilation terminated.
```

Downloading System Workbench for STM32

System Workbench for STM32 is an IDE we'll use to write C programs for our embedded devices. We won't use it until Chapter 2, but the download will take some time, so I recommend you start it now. By the time you finish reading this chapter, the download should be complete.

Go to *http://openstm32.org/HomePage*, locate the link for System Workbench for STM32, and click it. Register (it's free), or log in if you have an account, and then follow the links to the installation instructions. Install the IDE from the installer and not from Eclipse. When the download starts, return here and continue reading.

Tools and installation procedures may change over time. If you encounter any issues, visit *https://nostarch.com/bare-metal-c* to check for updated instructions.

Our First Program

Our first program is called *hello.c*. Begin by creating a directory to hold this program and jump into it. Navigate to the root directory of your workspace, open a command line window, and enter these commands:

```
$ mkdir hello
$ cd hello
```

Using a text editor such as Notepad, Vim, or Gedit, create a file called *hello.c* and enter the following code:

```
#include <stdio.h>
int main()
{
    printf("Hello World!\n");
    return (0);
}
```

We'll walk through this program in detail in the following sections. First, though, we have to run it.

Compiling the Program

The file you just created is known as a *source file*, and it contains code in human-readable format. (Yes, really; this is supposed to be human readable.) It's the source of all the other files we are going to produce. The content of the file is called *source code*. The computer does not understand source code; it only understands *machine code*, a set of instructions in a numeric format. So, we need to transform our source code into machine code, a process called *compiling*.

To do this, we execute the following compiler command on macOS or Linux:

```
$ gcc -o hello hello.c
```

On Windows, we execute the following command:

```
$ gcc -o hello.exe hello.c
```

If you get no output, just a command prompt, the command was successful. Otherwise, you'll get error messages.

This command tells the program *GCC* to *compile* and *link* the program, putting the output in a file called *hello* on macOS and Linux or *hello.exe* on Windows. We can now run our program using the following command on macOS or Linux:

```
$ ./hello
Hello World!
```

On Windows, run the following:

```
$ hello
Hello World!
```

Making Mistakes

Let's introduce a mistake and see what happens. Change the second line so that it looks like this:

```
intxxx main()
```

Now let's try to compile the program:

```
$ gcc -o hello hello.c
hello.c:2:1: error: unknown type name 'intxxx'
 intxxx main()
 ^
```

The output tells us that there is a problem in line 2 of the program and that the error was discovered at character position 1. In this case, where the compiler was expecting a type, it got something different—namely, the garbage we deliberately put in. Fix the program by changing the line back.

Next let's take something out—specifically, the semicolon on the fourth line:

```
    printf("Hello World!\n")
```

This gives us a different error message:

```
$ gcc -o hello hello.c
hello.c: In function 'main':
hello.c:5:5: error: expected ';' before 'return'
 return (0);
 ^
```

You'll notice that the compiler pointed to line 5 when issuing the error message. That's because although we made a mistake on line 4, the compiler didn't detect it until it looked at line 5.

Sometimes errors on a previous line will not be detected for one or more lines, so don't look just at the line specified by the error; look above it as well.

Understanding the Program

Now let's go through our program line by line to see what it is doing. Take a look at the first line:

```
#include <stdio.h>
```

In order to build our program, we are using components that come with the compiler—namely, the standard input/output (I/O) package. The functions in this package are defined in the */usr/include/stdio.h* file. (Windows may use a slightly different directory.) Specifically, we use the standard I/O function printf later in the program.

Next, we define the starting point for our program:

```
int main()
```

The name main is special and indicates the main body of the program. All programs start at main. This is followed by a set of statements enclosed in curly brackets:

```
{
...
}
```

The curly brackets denote the body of main. In other words, they're used to group the statements that follow. We indent the statements inside the curly brackets by four spaces for readability, but you are free to use other indentation sizes. In fact, the C compiler doesn't care how much whitespace we use. We could have used no indentation at all, but no indentation makes the program hard to read, so most C programmers indent their code.

Inside the curly brackets is our first executable statement:

```
printf("Hello World!\n");
```

This tells the program to use the standard I/O function printf to output a string to the standard output location (our terminal). The \n is a special character in this string. The backslash (\) is called the *escape character*. It tells C that the following character should be treated as code. In this case, the n tells C to output a "newline," which means the next character will be printed on a new line. Some of the more common escape characters are shown in Table 1-1.

Table 1-1: Common Escape Characters

Escape character	Result
\n	Newline (also known as *line feed*)
\t	Tab
\"	"
\\	\
\r	Carriage return

Finally, the program ends with this statement:

```
return (0);
```

This causes the program to stop and exit, returning an exit code of 0 to the operating system, which indicates that the program terminated normally. A nonzero exit code indicates an error.

Adding Comments

So far we've confined ourselves exclusively to writing code. In other words, everything we've seen is designed to be read by the computer and processed. Programs can also contain *comments*, which aren't seen by the compiler; instead, they're designed to be read by the person viewing the program. Comments commonly begin with /* and end with */. For example, the following is a comment:

```
/* Hello World - A nothing program */
```

It tells you what the programmer who wrote this thought of the program. Let's put some comments at the beginning of our program:

```
/*
 * Hello World -- not the most complicated program in
 *      the universe but useful as a starting point.
 *
 * Usage:
 *      1. Run the program.
 *      2. See the world.
 */
```

Another style of comment starts with // and goes to the end of the line. As you see more programs, you'll be able to determine for yourself which is better to use.

Always add comments to your code when you write a program, because that's when you know what you are doing. Five minutes later, you might forget. Five days later, you *will* forget. For example, I once had to do a complex bitmap transformation in order to translate a raster image into a firing command for an inkjet nozzle. The transformation involved taking a horizontal raster image, turning the row data into column data for the nozzles, and then, since the nozzles were offset, shifting the data left to match the nozzle location. I wrote out a page of comments describing every factor that affected the firing order. Then I added half a page of ASCII art diagramming what I had just described. Only after doing this and making sure I understood the problem did I write the code. And because I had to organize my thoughts in order to document them, the program worked on the first try.

When creating the answers to the programming problems presented in this book, get in the habit of writing comments. The really good programmers are fanatical comment writers.

Improving the Program and Build Process

When it comes to our little "Hello World" program, manually compiling it isn't a problem. But for a program with thousands of modules in it, keeping track of what needs to be compiled and what doesn't can be quite difficult. We need to automate the process to be efficient and avoid human error.

In this section, we'll tweak our program to improve it and automate the build process. Ideally, you should be able to build a program using a single command and no parameters, which would indicate you have a consistent and precise build process.

The make Program

One problem with our build process is that we have to enter the compilation command each time we build the program. This would be tedious for a program with several thousand files in it, each of which would need to be compiled. To automate the build process, we'll use the make program. It takes as its input a file called a makefile, which tells make how to build a program.

Create a file called *Makefile* containing the following on macOS or Linux:

```
CFLAGS=-ggdb -Wall -Wextra

all: hello

hello: hello.c
        gcc $(CFLAGS) -o hello hello.c
```

On Windows, the makefile should contain the following:

```
CFLAGS=-ggdb -Wall -Wextra

all: hello.exe

hello.exe: hello.c
        gcc $(CFLAGS) -o hello.exe hello.c
```

It's important that the indented lines begin with a tab character. Eight spaces won't work. (Horrible file design, but we're stuck with it.) The first line defines a macro. As a result of this definition, whenever we specify $(CFLAGS) in the makefile, the make program will replace this with -ggdb -Wall -Wextra. Next, we define the target all, which is the default target by convention. When make is run with no parameters, it tries to build the first one it sees. The definition of this target, all: hello, tells the make program, "When you try to build all, you need to build hello." The final two lines of the makefile are the specification for hello (or hello.exe on Windows). These tell make that hello is made from *hello.c* by executing the command gcc $(CFLAGS) -o hello hello.c. This command contains the macro we defined, $(CFLAGS), which expands to -ggdb -Wall -Wextra. You'll notice that we added a couple of extra flags to our compilation. We'll discuss those in the next section.

Now let's make the program using the make command:

```
$ make
gcc -ggdb -Wall -Wextra -o hello hello.c
```

As you can see, the program ran the commands to build the executable. The make program is smart. It knows that hello is made from *hello.c*, so it will check the modification dates of these two files. If hello is newer, then it does not need to be recompiled, so if you attempt to build the program twice, you'll get the following message:

```
make: Nothing to be done for 'all'.
```

This is not always the correct behavior. If we change the flags in our makefile, we've changed the compilation process and should rebuild our program. However, make doesn't know about this change and won't rebuild the program unless we edit *hello.c* and save the file or delete the output file.

Compiler Flags

The GCC compiler takes a number of options. In fact, the list of options for this compiler exceeds eight pages. Fortunately, we don't have to worry about them all. Let's take a look at the ones we used for our program:

-ggdb   Compiles the program so we can debug it. Mostly, this adds debugging information to the output file that allows the debugger to understand what is going on.

-Wall   Turns on a set of warnings that will flag correct but questionable code. (This book will teach you not to write questionable code.)

-Wextra   Turns on extra warnings in an effort to make our code more precise.

-o hello   Puts the output of our program in the file *hello*. (This option is -o hello.exe for Windows users.)

How the Compiler Works Behind the Scenes

In order to best make use of the compiler, you need to understand what goes on behind the scenes when you run it. That's because when you're writing software for embedded devices, you'll often need to circumvent some of the operations the compiler performs automatically, which consist of a number of steps:

1. The source code is run through a *preprocessor*, which handles all the lines that begin with #, called *directives*. In our original source file, this is the #include statement. Later, you will learn about additional directives.

2. The compiler proper takes the preprocessed source code and turns it into *assembly language* code. C code is supposedly machine-independent and can be compiled and run on multiple platforms. Assembly language

is machine-dependent and can be run on only one type of platform. (Of course, it is still possible to write C code that will work on only one machine. C tries to hide the underlying machine from you, but it does not prevent you from directly accessing it.)

3. The assembly language file is passed through an *assembler*, which turns it into an *object file*. The object file contains just our code. However, the program needs additional code to work. In our case, the object file for *hello.c* needs a copy of the printf function.

4. The *linker* takes the object code in the object file and combines (links) it with useful code already present on your computer. In this case, it's printf and all the code needed to support it.

Figure 1-1 illustrates the process. All these steps are hidden from you by the gcc command.

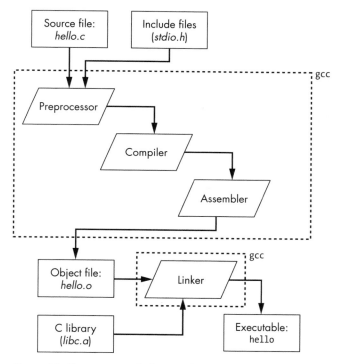

Figure 1-1: The steps needed to produce a program

You'll notice that the gcc command is acting as both compiler and linker. In fact, gcc is designed as a sort of executive program. It looks at the arguments and decides which other programs it needs to run in order to do its job. This might include the preprocessor (cpp), the C compiler (cc1), the assembler (as), the linker (ld), or other programs as needed. Let's walk through these components in more detail.

The Preprocessor

The first program run is the preprocessor, which is a *macro processor* (a type of automatic text editor) that handles all the lines that begin with #. In our program, it processes the #include line. We can get the output of the preprocessor with this command:

```
$ gcc -E hello.c >hello.i
```

The output of this command is stored in the *hello.i* file. If we look at this file, we see that it's more than 850 lines long. That's because the #include <stdio.h> line causes the entire *stdio.h* file to be copied into our program, and because the *stdio.h* file has its own #include directives, the files included by *stdio.h* get copied in as well.

We needed *stdio.h* for the printf function, and if we look through *hello.i*, we find the definition of this function, which is now included in our program:

```
extern int printf (const char *__restrict __format, ...);

extern int sprintf (char *__restrict __s,
    const char *__restrict __format, ...) __attribute__ ((__nothrow__));
```

The preprocessor also removes all the comments and annotates the text with information indicating what file is being processed.

The Compiler

Next, the compiler turns the C language code into assembly language. We can see what's generated with this command:

```
$ gcc -S hello.c
```

This should produce a file that starts with the following lines:

```
        .file   "hello.c"
        .section        .rodata
.LC0:
        .string "Hello World!"
```

Notice that the compiler translated the C string "Hello World!\n" to the assembly language .string command. If you have sharp eyes, you'll also notice that the \n is missing. We'll discover why a little later.

The Assembler

The assembly language file goes into the assembler, where it is translated into machine code. The gcc command has an option (-Wa) that lets us pass flags to the assembler. Since it's impossible to understand the machine code unless you're a machine, we will use the following command to ask for an assembly language listing that prints the machine code in human-readable format, with the corresponding assembly language statements that generated that code:

```
$ gcc -Wall -Wextra -g -Wextra -Wa,-a=hello.lst -c hello.c
```

The -Wa option tells GCC that what follows is to be passed to the assembler. The -a=hello.lst option tells the assembler to produce a listing called *hello.lst*. Let's take a look at that file. It begins as follows:

```
4                               .section      .rodata
5                 .LC0:
6 0000 48656C6C                 .string "Hello World!"
6      6F20776F
6      726C6421
6      00
```

Assembly language differs on each machine. In this file, you're looking at x86 assembly language. It might seem like a confused mess, even in comparison to other assembly languages. You probably won't understand it completely, and that's okay; this chapter should only give you a sense of what assembly language looks like. In later chapters, when we get to the ARM processor, you'll see a much saner and easier-to-understand assembly.

The first column is a line number from the assembly language file. The second column, if present, indicates the address of the data being stored. All computer memory slots have a numerical address. In this case, the string "Hello World!" is being stored at address 0000 relative to the section that is currently being used (in this case, a section titled .rodata). When we discuss the linker in the next section, we'll see how this relative address is translated into an absolute one.

The next column contains the numerical values to be stored in memory in hexadecimal format. Then comes the text of the assembly language code itself. In the file, we can see that the .string directive tells the assembler to generate the codes for a text string.

Later in the file, we find the code for main:

```
15 0000 55                      pushq   %rbp
16                              .cfi_def_cfa_offset 16
17                              .cfi_offset 6, -16
18 0001 4889E5                  movq    %rsp, %rbp
19                              .cfi_def_cfa_register 6
12:hello.c        ****         printf("Hello World!\n");
20                              .loc 1 12 0
21 0004 BF000000                movl    $.LC0, %edi
21      00
22 0009 E8000000                call    puts
22      00
```

On line 15, we can see the assembly language instruction 55, which will be stored at location 0 in this section. This instruction corresponds to pushq %rbp, which does some bookkeeping at the start of the procedure. Also notice that some machine instructions are 1 byte long and others as long as 5 bytes. The instruction at line 21 is an example of a 5-byte instruction. You can see that this instruction is doing something with .LC0. If we look at the top of our listing, we see that .LC0 is our string.

As a C programmer, you're not expected to fully understand what the assembly language does. Complete understanding would require absorbing several thousand pages of reference material. But we can, sort of, understand the instruction at line 22, which calls the function puts. This is where things get interesting. Remember that our C program didn't call puts—it called printf.

It seems that our code has been optimized behind the scenes. In embedded programming, "optimized" can be a dirty word, so it's important to understand what happened here. Essentially, the C compiler looked at the line printf("Hello World!\n"); and decided it was identical to the following:

```
puts("Hello World!");
```

The truth is that these functions aren't actually identical: puts is a simple, efficient function, whereas printf is a large, complex one. But the programmer isn't using any of the advanced printf features, so the optimizer decided to rewrite the code to make it better. As a result, our printf call became puts and the end-of-line character (\n) was removed from the string, as the puts call adds one automatically. When you get especially close to the hardware, little things like this can make a big difference, so it's important to know how to view and sort of understand assembly code.

The output of the assembler is an object file containing the code we wrote and nothing more. In particular, it does not contain the puts function, which we need. The puts function resides, along with hundreds of other functions, in the C standard library (*libc*).

The Linker

Our object file and some of the components of *libc* need to be combined to make our program. The linker's job is to take the files needed to make up the program, combine them, and assign real memory addresses to each component. As we did with the assembler, we can tell the gcc command to pass flags to the linker using this command:

```
$ gcc -Wall -Wextra -static -Wl,-Map=hello.map -o hello hello.o
```

The -Wl tells GCC to pass the option that follows (-Map=hello.map) to the linker. The map tells us where the linker put things in memory. (More on this later.) We've also added the directive -static, which changes the executable from dynamic to statically linked so that the memory map will look more like what we will see with our embedded systems. That way, we can avoid having to discuss the complexities of dynamic linking.

Object files such as *hello.o* are relocatable. That is, they can go anywhere in memory. It is the job of the linker to decide exactly where in memory they go. It is also the linker's job to go through the libraries used by the program, extract any needed object files, and include them in the final program. The linker map tells us where things went and what library components were included in our program. For example, a typical linker entry might look like this:

```
.text      0x000000000040fa90      0x1c8 /usr/lib/gcc/x86_64-linux-gnu/5/../../../
           x86_64-linux-gnu/libc.a(ioputs.o)
           0x000000000040fa90              puts
           0x000000000040fa90              _IO_puts
*fill*     0x000000000040fc58      0x8
```

Remember that we didn't write puts, even though it appears in this linker entry. As mentioned, it came from the standard C library file (*libc.a*). We can see here that the code for this function is located at 0x000000000040fa90. This information could be useful if, say, our program crashed somewhere between 0x40fa90 and 0x40fc58. In that case, we would know that puts caused the crash.

We also know that puts takes up 0x1c8 bytes (40fc58–40fa90). This is 456 decimal bytes, or a little under .5K. The amount of memory will concern us when we start programming our microprocessor, which has limited memory.

You should now have a good idea of every element of a C program and what these various pieces do. Most of the time, you can let the compiler take care of these details without worrying about what's going on under the hood. But when you're programming small chips with limited resources, you do need to worry about what's going on inside.

Adding to Your Makefile

Explore the various aspects of the GCC compiler, assembler, and linker on your own by amending your makefile to generate all the files described in the previous section:

```
CFLAGS=-Wall -Wextra -ggdb

all: hello hello.i hello.s

hello.o: hello.c
        gcc $(CFLAGS) -Wa,-a=hello.lst -c hello.c

hello: hello.o
        gcc $(CFLAGS) -static -Wl,-Map=hello.map -o hello hello.o

hello.i: hello.c
        gcc -E hello.c >hello.i

hello.s: hello.c
        gcc -S hello.c
```

```
# Type "make verbose" to see the whole command line
verbose:
        gcc -v $(CFLAGS) -Wextra -c hello.c

clean:
        rm -f hello hello.i hello.s hello.o
```

As described earlier, the first non-blank line defines a macro that tells make to replace $(CFLAGS) with -Wall -Wextra -ggdb everywhere in the rest of the file. Next, we define a *target* (an item that needs to be built) named all. Since this is the first target in the file, it is also the default one, which means you can build it simply by entering the following:

```
$ make
```

This target is what we call a *phony target*, as it doesn't result in a file named *all*. Instead, every time you execute the make all command, make will check whether it needs to re-create its dependencies. You can see these dependencies listed in the makefile after the keyword all and the colon. In order to make the target all, we need to make the targets hello, hello.i, and hello.s. The following lines clarify how to make those targets. For example, to make the target hello.i, we must use the target hello.c. If hello.i is newer than hello.c, then make will do nothing. If hello.c has undergone recent changes and hello.i is not up to date, make will produce hello.i using the following command:

```
gcc -E hello.c >hello.i
```

Thus, if you edit hello.c and then execute the command make hello.i, you'll see make do its job:

```
$ (Change hello.c)
$ make hello.i
gcc =E hello.c > hello.i
```

Another target in our makefile, clean, removes all the generated files. To get rid of the generated files, execute the following command:

```
$ make clean
```

GNU make is a very sophisticated program with a manual that is more than 300 pages long. The good news is you need to deal with only a very small subset of its commands in order to be productive.

Summary

Making a "Hello World" program is one of the simplest things a C programmer can do. However, understanding everything that happens behind the scenes to create and run that C program is a bit more difficult. Luckily, you don't have to be an expert. But while you don't need to master every bit of the assembly language generated by the program, any embedded programmer should understand enough to be able to spot potential problems or unusual behavior, such as puts showing up in a program that calls printf. Paying attention to these details will allow us to get the most out of our small machines.

Questions

1. Where does the documentation for GNU make reside?
2. Is C code portable between different types of machines?
3. Is assembly language code portable between different types of machines?
4. Why does a single statement in assembly language code generate just one machine instruction when one statement in C can generate many?

2

INTRODUCTION TO THE INTEGRATED DEVELOPMENT ENVIRONMENT

So far, we've used individual tools such as GCC, make, and a text editor to build our program. This has allowed you to see what each tool does and learn about the details of software development. Now you'll learn about using an integrated development environment (IDE). The IDE is a program designed to take all those tools (and some others) and hide them behind one integrated interface.

The main advantage of this approach is that you can use one GUI-based tool to do everything. The major disadvantage is that it works well only if you behave the way the IDE expects you to behave. Also, it hides a great deal from you. For example, to get a linker map, you have to go through several layers of GUI and enter the map option in an obscure customization box.

The IDE we'll use in this book is the System Workbench for STM32 IDE. From its name, you can tell it was created for the STM32 microprocessors. An enhancement to a very popular IDE called Eclipse, it includes an editor, debugger, and compiler. It is especially powerful when it comes to debugging, because remotely debugging on a microcontroller involves a lot of tools, and the IDE makes them work together seamlessly.

To practice using the IDE, you'll write the same "Hello World" program you wrote in Chapter 1, only this time you will wrap every step of the process in a unified GUI. In one respect, the IDE makes things simpler by hiding the compiler and other tools from you. In other ways, it makes things more complex, because accessing those tools to tune them is more difficult. For example, if I want to add the flag -Wextra to the compiler command line without an IDE, all I do is edit the makefile. When using an IDE, I have to find the magic box in which I can enter this value (spoiler: it's Project ▸ Properties and then C/C++ Build ▸ Settings ▸ Tool Settings ▸ GCC Compiler ▸ All Options).

Using System Workbench for STM32

So far, we've used a text editor, a compiler called GCC, and a program called make to run the compiler. As we get into more complex programs, we'll need a debugger as well.

The STM32 Workbench bundles all these tools into one integrated development environment that is built on the Eclipse IDE. In fact, it *is* Eclipse, with lots of special STM32 stuff added, and I'll refer to it as such in the following discussion. We'll get deeper into the STM32 side of things in Chapter 3. For now, let's explore the IDE by writing a "Hello World" program.

Starting the IDE

If you followed the advice at the beginning of Chapter 1, you've already downloaded System Workbench for STM32. Install it using the instructions from the website. The standard installation creates a desktop icon and a startup menu item, so you should be able to start the IDE in the same way as any other program.

When first started, Eclipse asks for the location of your workspace. Enter the directory that will contain all the projects for this book. Next, Eclipse should display the Welcome screen. Dismiss the screen by clicking the close icon (the little X next to the tab).

A window should pop up indicating that the system is downloading additional tools for the ARM processor. When the system finishes, you should get a C/C++ view of an empty project, as shown Figure 2-1.

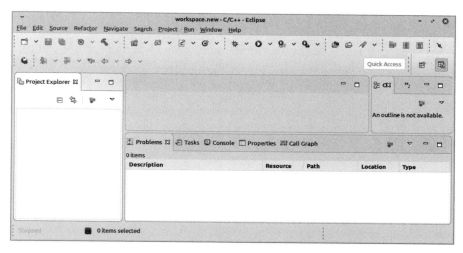

Figure 2-1: An empty project screen

Eclipse is the frontend for a *lot* of tools. Displaying them in an organized manner is quite a challenge. To cope with this, Eclipse uses the concept of views. A *view* is a window layout that is designed for a particular task. For example, a Java programmer might have a different view than that of a C programmer. Likewise, debugging requires a different view than coding.

The default view in this version of Eclipse is that of a C/C++ project. (You can change the view at any time by using the Window ▸View menu.) On the left of the view is the Project Explorer (currently empty), which allows you to view your projects and their details. In the upper middle, you have a text editor. On the right is a window with three tabs: Outline, Build Targets, and Task List. We'll go into them when we get to more complex projects.

At the bottom is a small, wide window with the tabs Problems, Tasks, Console, Properties, and Call Graph. The Problems window contains a list of the errors and warnings generated by the code in your current project. The Console window contains the output of the build process. The other tabs we'll worry about when we start generating more complex programs.

Creating Hello World

We will now create another "Hello World" project. You must take certain steps whenever you create a native C project (*native* means the program runs on the machine on which it was compiled; if you compile it on one machine and run it on another, that's called *cross-compilation*), and this chapter goes through them in detail. You will be going through these steps a lot; so that you don't have to remember them all, refer to the checklist in the appendix.

Start a new project by selecting **File ▸ New ▸ C Project** from the menu bar. This brings up the C Project dialog.

I've chosen the name *02.hello-ide* for our project, as it's unique and descriptive. Project names can contain any character except spaces and special characters such as a forward slash (/), backslash (\), colon (:), and other characters that have special meaning for your filesystem. Letters, digits, dashes, dots, and underscores are okay.

Eclipse will let you create a project with a space in the name and then fail to properly build it, so don't use spaces.

For the project type, select **Hello World ANSI C Project**. For toolchains, select the toolchain for your operating system, as shown in Figure 2-2. Click **Next**.

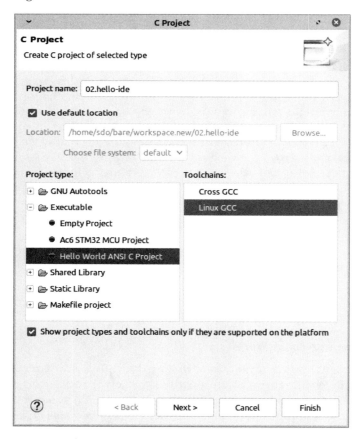

Figure 2-2: The project creation dialog

We now see the Basic Settings dialog. Leave these settings alone and click **Next**.

The next dialog is Select Configurations (see Figure 2-3).

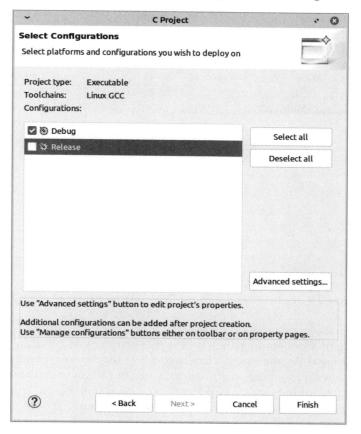

Figure 2-3: The Select Configurations dialog

You have a lot of different options for building your project. Eclipse groups these into project configurations. The two defined by default are Release and Debug. Release produces highly optimized code that is difficult if not impossible to debug. Debug produces unoptimized, easy-to-debug code and generates debug symbols. Since you are learning, we'll stick with the Debug configuration. Deselect the **Release** configuration, leaving only **Debug** selected, and click **Finish**.

The IDE creates our project and generates a number of files. One of these is our source code, already filled in with its version of a "Hello World" program (see Figure 2-4).

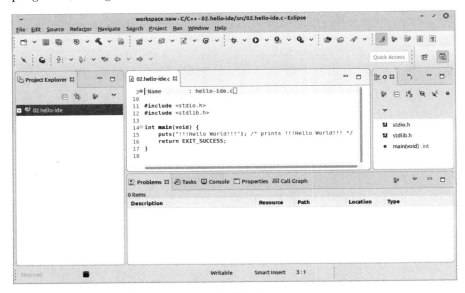

Figure 2-4: The result of creating our "Hello World" project

If you enter any code yourself, note that the Eclipse editor uses a tab size of 4 by default, which means that when you use a tab to indent a line in source code, the tab will have a width of four spaces. Practically every other editor and tool uses eight spaces. You can fix this with one of the configuration items in Window ▸ Preferences. (Telling you how to further customize Eclipse would take a whole book, and this is not that book.)

At this point we would be done—if we were writing in Java. Eclipse was designed for Java. C is an add-on that *almost* completely works. We have to do one more fix-up.

First, compile the project by choosing **Project ▸ Build Project**. Then select **Run ▸ Run Configurations**, which should bring up the Run Configurations dialog. Next, click **C/C++ Application** on the left side, and then click the small icon on the left of the icon row to create a new configuration. Finally, under C/C++ Application, click **Browse**, as shown in Figure 2-5.

Use the file browser to find your executable in the *Debug* directory. The IDE has created a project directory for you in your workspace (the location of which is system-dependent) that has the same name as your project. All the files for your project are in this directory. Within the project directory, a *Debug* directory contains all the files built as part of the Debug build (the only type of build we are doing). Within that directory, you'll find *02.hello-ide* on macOS and Linux or *02.hello-ide.exe* on Windows. Select this file, as shown Figure 2-6, and then click **OK**.

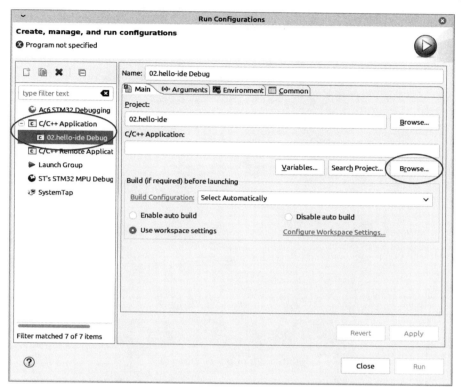

Figure 2-5: The Run Configurations dialog

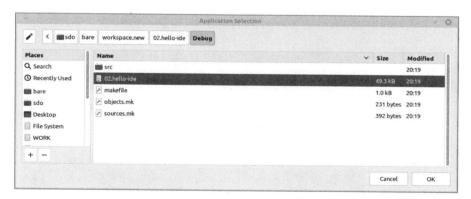

Figure 2-6: The Application Selection dialog

Next, click **Apply** and **Close** to finish the run configuration. This setup tells the IDE where your program is actually located. (Since it decided where to put it, you'd think it would know where it went, but for some reason it doesn't.)

Now let's actually run the program. Select **Run ▸ Run**. The results should appear in the Console window, as shown in Figure 2-7.

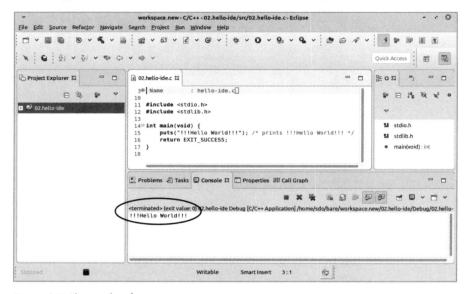

Figure 2-7: The results of our program

Debugging the Program

Now for a quick introduction to the *debugger*, which watches our program execute and lets us see what's going on inside it. First, let's generate a little more code to debug by duplicating line 15 (puts("!!!Hello World!!!");) and then save the project by choosing **File ▸ Save All**.

It is important to choose File ▸ Save All after each edit. If you were to run the program now, before saving all files, the compiler would see the old, unsaved file on disk and compile it. The resulting program would print !!!Hello World!!! only once instead of twice, which could get very confusing. The code we have in front of us is correct; the code we are running is not. Until you choose File ▸ Save All, the files are not the same. (End of soapbox mode.)

Now let's start the debugger with **Run ▸ Debug** (see Figure 2-8).

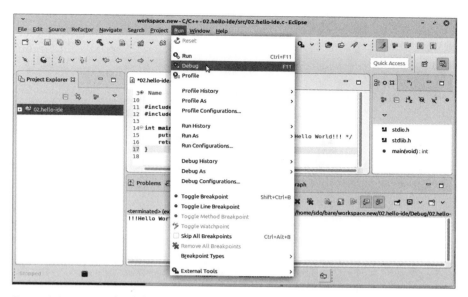

Figure 2-8: Starting the debugger

The IDE is about to switch into debugging mode, which changes the perspective from development to debugging. This means a whole new window arrangement. The system warns you that this is about to happen, as shown in Figure 2-9. (Remember that you can always switch perspectives with the command Window ▸ Perspective ▸ C/C++ or Window ▸ Perspective ▸ Debug.)

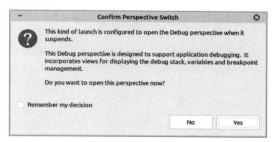

Figure 2-9: The debug perspective warning

Click **Yes** in the warning. The debug perspective should open, as shown in Figure 2-10.

Stack Trace   Variables/Breakpoints/Registers/I/O Registers/Modules

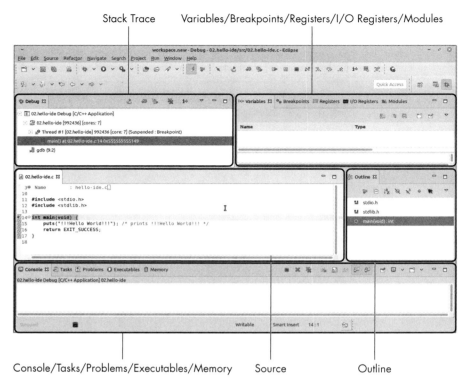

Console/Tasks/Problems/Executables/Memory   Source   Outline

Figure 2-10: The debug perspective

In the upper left is the Stack Trace window, which shows the program being executed and how far into it you are. This information will become more useful when we discuss stack usage in Chapter 7.

Next to that is the Variables/Breakpoints/Registers/I/O Registers/ Modules window, which contains the following:

Variables   Information about the program's variables. (More on this starting with Chapter 4.)

Breakpoints   A *breakpoint* is a location in your program at which the program stops and lets the debugger examine it. You can set a breakpoint by double-clicking the line number of an executable line in your program. We'll start using them in Chapter 3.

Registers   Information about the current state of the processor's registers. (Discussed in Chapter 10.)

Modules   The dynamically linked modules. Since this feature is not available to embedded programmers, we won't be discussing it.

In the middle of the screen, the Source window displays our program. The highlighted line of code indicates that the debugger has run the program up to this line and stopped.

Next to the Source window is the Outline panel. This is like a table of contents indicating which files go into our program. I've included the files *stdio.h* and *stdlib.h* so that they show up here.

Across the bottom is the Console/Tasks/Problems/Executables/Memory window. The Console window displays the output from the program. All the other tabs contain information we're not interested in.

Now we'll *step through* the program, meaning we will execute one statement at a time using the debugger. Click the Step Over icon at the top of the screen (see Figure 2-11) or press F6 to step over the current line.

Figure 2-11: Step Over (F6)

The highlighted line in the Source window advances one line, and !!!Hello World!!! appears in the Console window (see Figure 2-12).

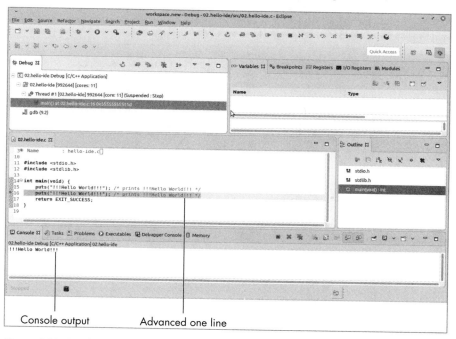

Figure 2-12: Single-step results

If you keep stepping, you'll see the second puts executed, followed by the return statement. After that, the program goes into the system library to do cleanup work. Since we don't have the source code for this library, the debugger can display no information about it.

There are two other significant icons on the toolbar (see Figure 2-13). The Resume icon (or F8 key) runs the program until it finishes or hits a breakpoint. The Debug icon restarts debugging.

Figure 2-13: Debugging commands

We'll make use of the debugger a lot in coming chapters. It will provide a very useful way of getting information out of our running program and seeing what's going on. To return to the original C/C++ perspective, select **Window ▶ Perspective ▶ Open Perspective ▶ C++**.

What the IDE Did for Us

The IDE generated the C source file, including the puts functions, to print "Hello World." It also generated a file called *Debug/makefile*, which is used as input to the make program. Listing 2-1 contains an excerpt from this file.

```
############################################################################
# Automatically-generated file. Do not edit!
############################################################################

-include ../makefile.init

RM := rm -rf

# All of the sources participating in the build are defined here
-include ❶ sources.mk
-include src/subdir.mk
-include subdir.mk
-include ❷ objects.mk

ifneq ($(MAKECMDGOALS),clean)
ifneq ($(strip $(C_DEPS)),)
-include $(C_DEPS)
endif
endif

-include ../makefile.defs

# Add inputs and outputs from these tool invocations to the build variables
```

```
# All Target
all: 02.hello-ide
```

Listing 2-1: An excerpt from Debug/makefile

This makefile is located in the *Debug* directory. The IDE supports multiple build configurations and generates a makefile in a different directory for each of them. (For this project, we created only a Debug configuration. Other projects may also use a Release configuration.)

The makefile is more complex than the one we generated ourselves in Chapter 1 because the IDE uses lots and lots of advanced make syntax. The IDE also generated the files *sources.mk* ❶ and *objects.mk* ❷, which are included in the makefile. What we can see from these files is that computer-generated stuff is designed to be very flexible at the cost of making the thing nearly impossible to read.

As it stands now, the IDE does not generate or download a lot of data. But when we start to do embedded programming, this will change dramatically.

Importing the Book's Programming Examples

The programming examples used in this book can be downloaded at *https://nostarch.com/bare-metal-c*. To use the downloaded programming examples, you'll need to import them. (You can't just stick the files in your workspace; that would be too easy.) To perform an import, use the following steps:

1. Select **File ▸ Import**.
2. In the Import dialog, select **General ▸ Existing Projects into Workspace**.
3. Click **Next**.
4. Select the radio button **Select Archive File** and then click **Browse** after the blank space to select the file containing the project (the one you downloaded from the website).
5. Click **Finish**.

Summary

The IDE is a mixed blessing. On the one hand, you don't have to worry about all the tools that it takes to create a program. You didn't have to create the makefile, manually perform the build, or run the debugger.

But this hands-off approach comes with a price. To add a compile-time flag to your program from Chapter 1, you just add the flag to the makefile. With the IDE, you can't do this, because the IDE generates the makefile on its own. You have to find the right configuration item to do it in the IDE, and, as we will discover, the IDE has a lot of options.

In this book I try to keep things as simple as possible through the use of checklists (like the one in the appendix) and standard procedures. Eclipse tries to take care of everything, but you will occasionally need to tweak things under the hood.

Programming Problems

1. Find out what happens when you put \t in a string to be printed.
2. In Chapter 1, we used printf to print the message. In this chapter, Eclipse uses puts. Look up the documentation of these functions to see how they are different.

Questions

1. What is an IDE?
2. What are the files generated by our IDE, and what do they contain?
3. Where can you get help with using C and Eclipse?

3

PROGRAMMING THE MICROCONTROLLER

Now that we've written and run a "Hello World" program in the IDE, we'll do the same on the STM32 NUCLEO-F030R8 development board, which contains the STM32F030R8 processor and several other components needed to use the processor. On an embedded system, the equivalent of "Hello World" is a program that makes an LED blink. By making an LED blink, you'll learn the steps needed to make a complex program at a smaller scale.

In the process, you'll learn how to use the System Workbench for STM32, which we explored in the last chapter, to create an embedded program. To assist us, we'll use STMicroelectronics software called the hardware abstraction layer (HAL), which hides some of the more annoying details of the hardware from you. (However, the details aren't hidden very deep, and you can examine the source code to see what was done.) We'll also get into what the IDE is doing behind the scenes with a detailed explanation of the options it's using to compile the code.

Finally, like we did in Chapter 2, we'll run the debugger to see our program execute one statement at a time, which will prove extremely useful when we start to make larger and larger programs.

The NUCLEO-F030R8 Development Board

Development boards are circuit boards that contain a processor chip and various other components required to develop applications for that processor, including a lot of useful items for developing programs and circuits that use the chip. In addition to programming and debugging support, the development board includes numerous *connectors*, which allow you to hook up your prototype hardware. It also includes a few *peripherals* such as a serial port, a push button switch, and an LED, although some of the fancier boards will have additional peripherals.

Thus, the development board provides you with an instant prototype for developing the initial software with breadboarded hardware. Microprocessor manufacturers generally sell development boards with all that stuff included to get people to use their chips.

The STM32 NUCLEO-F030R8 board bundles the STM32F030R8 chip with a clock circuit, a power supply, and some devices to talk to, including an LED, a button, and a serial I/O device. Figure 3-1 shows the basic building blocks of our processor board.

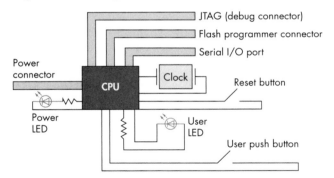

Figure 3-1: The processor board

The power and clock drive the CPU, the reset button restarts the CPU, the user LED and push button are for user interaction, and the serial port and connectors are for programming and debugging.

Programming and Debugging the Board

The development board contains three devices useful for programming and debugging the chip—a flash programmer, a JTAG pod, and a serial I/O device—all of which connect to your computer through a single USB cable. (One cable, three devices.)

To program the chip, we use the *flash programmer*, a device that allows our PC to reprogram the memory of the chip. Reprogramming memory is how we get our program into the machine.

To facilitate debugging, the chip has a JTAG port. JTAG, which stands for Joint Test Action Group, is a standard debugging interface. Before this standard came out, everyone created their own debugging interface or, more often, left it out, leaving programmers to get very creative when it came to debugging programs. To debug with the JTAG port, we need to connect it to our computer. This is done through a *debug pod*, which has a connection to the JTAG port on our development board on one end and a connection to our computer's USB port on the other.

Another very useful debugging and maintenance tool is the printing of diagnostic messages. The problem when it comes to embedded programs is where to print them. You don't have a screen, so printing to the screen is out. Printing the messages in a logfile is difficult because you don't have a filesystem. What most device designers do is put a *serial port*, a simple three-wire communication interface, on the board. Chapter 9 goes into the details of this device.

Setting Up the Board

The bottom half of the Nucleo board contains the chip and support circuitry, with lots and lots of pins broken out to connectors on the sides of the board (for connecting peripherals). Above that is the support board containing a programmer, a debugger, a serial-to-USB device, and a USB storage device.

Figure 3-2 shows how the board is put together.

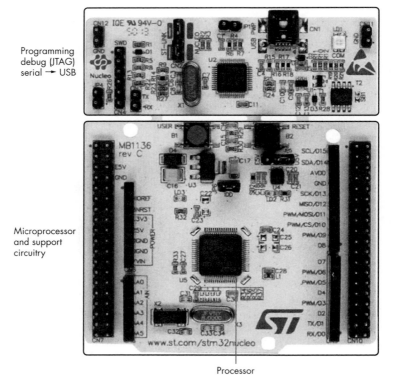

Programming debug (JTAG) serial → USB

Microprocessor and support circuitry

Processor

Figure 3-2: The NUCLEO-F030R8 board

The board also contains several jumpers and LEDs. *Jumpers* are small plastic devices that short two pins together. They are used to select hardware options, such as enabling the onboard debugger (ST-LINK), and should be installed as shown in Figure 3-3. Follow these steps to do so:

1. Install the ST-LINK with two jumpers (CN2). Doing so configures the onboard debugging pod (ST-LINK) to debug the onboard microcontroller. If you remove these two jumpers, you can use the ST-LINK pod to debug other boards instead.

2. Do not install the power supply jumper (JP1). This configuration allows the Nucleo board to draw up to 300mA of power through the USB port, letting you power the device using the USB port. If you connected lots of power-hungry peripherals to the board, you could use JP1 to enable an external power supply. This book doesn't use any external hardware, so leave JP1 out.

3. Do not install RX-TX, a debug option that shorts the input and output of the serial port together. We'll use the serial port as an actual serial port later, so leave this jumper off.

4. Install the JP5 jumper to the right position (U5V). Doing so ensures the board will be powered through the USB port instead of through an external power source.

5. Power the measurement jump (JP6). This is a lower-power device. The two pins shorted by JP6 supply power to the chip. Remove the jumper and connect an amp meter to measure power consumption.

CN11 and CN12 are places to store jumpers when not in use. Installing jumpers there won't affect the circuitry.

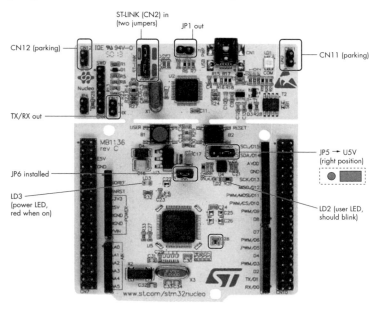

Figure 3-3: Jumper and LED locations

Now plug the device into your computer using a mini USB cable. LD1 should turn red, indicating the programmer has power. LD2 should blink, because the board comes with a preinstalled program that blinks LD2. (This is true assuming you bought the board new. If, like me, you got your first board from your buddy down the hall, it will contain your buddy's last experiment.) LD3 should also turn red, indicating that the chip has power.

Setting Up an Embedded Project

Before you begin programming, close any open editing windows in System Workbench for STM32. The editing window identifies the filename, not the project name, which causes a problem; all our projects will have a *main.c* file, and things would get pretty confusing with half a dozen *main.c* editing windows open.

Next, create an embedded project by selecting **File ▸ New ▸ C Project**. (A checklist detailing these steps can be found in the appendix.) The C Project dialog should appear (see Figure 3-4).

Figure 3-4: The C Project dialog

For the project name, enter **03.blink**. For the project type, select **Ac6 STM32 MCU Project**. On first startup, the IDE downloads the GCC ARM toolchain to the directory where you installed the IDE, as well as the entire STM32 firmware library, a portion of which will get copied to your project. If you'd like to explore this library's code and examples further, the cache directory it uses is *~/.ac6* on Linux and macOS and *C:\Users\<username>\AppData\Roaming\Ac6* on Windows. Be warned, however, that these examples are designed to show off the STM chips and aren't easily understood by novice programmers.

Click **Next**. The Select Configurations dialog, shown in Figure 3-5, should appear.

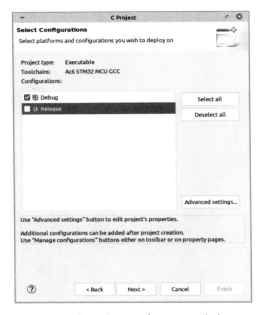

Figure 3-5: The Select Configurations dialog

Leave **Debug** selected and deselect **Release**. To keep things simple, we'll perform only one type of build. Click **Next**.

Next is the Target Configuration dialog (see Figure 3-6).

Figure 3-6: The Target Configuration dialog

For the series, select **STM32F0**, and for the board, select **NUCLEO-F030R8**. Click **Next**.

This brings us to the Project Firmware Configuration dialog (see Figure 3-7).

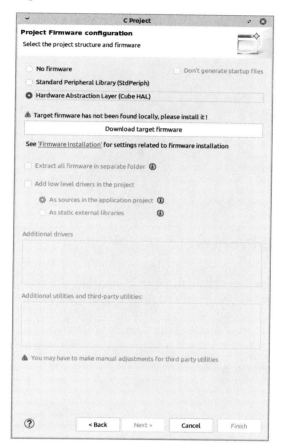

Figure 3-7: The Project Firmware Configuration dialog

The project firmware configuration options let us use free standard code available from STMicroelectronics and other suppliers. Since someone else has written most of the hard stuff, let's use their work. Select **Hardware Abstraction Layer (Cube HAL)** and then click the button labeled **Download Target Firmware** when it appears. Accept the license agreement, and the IDE will download the firmware library.

After the long download completes, the system displays additional options. Leave them to the default values and click **Finish**.

Back in the C/C++ Project view, you should see an entry in the project list for *blink*. Click the triangle next to *blink* to see a list of directories that make up the project, and click the triangle next to *src* to expand that directory. Double-click *main.c* to make it appear in the editing window, as shown in Figure 3-8.

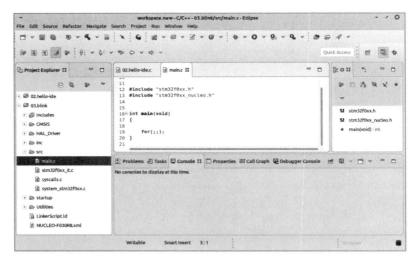

Figure 3-8: The editing window, showing main.c

Your First Embedded Program

The IDE has conveniently supplied you with a main file that has the minimal features of your program filled in: a comment, the code libraries for the Nucleo board, and a generic main function. The + icon next to line 3 indicates that some program lines have been *folded*, or hidden from view. Click the + icon to expand the long comment describing the file:

```
1 /**
2   ******************************************************************
3  * @file    main.c
4  * @author  Ac6
5  * @version V1.0
6  * @date    01-December-2013
7  * @brief   Default main function.
8   ******************************************************************
9 */
```

You may wish to update this comment with your name and information. The keywords that begin with @ are designed to work with *Doxygen*, a complex and full-featured system that extracts documentation out of large programs. We won't be using this tool for our small programs, so you can edit the comment any way you want.

The main function doesn't have a return statement because the return statement returns control from the program to the operating system, but a bare metal system doesn't have an operating system. One of the jobs of the operating system is to start and stop programs (among other things). Since we don't have an operating system, the processor halts whenever our program stops and does absolutely nothing. So we don't stop. Ever. To see how we accomplish this, notice the for(;;); on line 19. This is C code for "loop forever" (for(;;)) and "do nothing" (the closing semicolon).

But without an operating system, how do we start? Our program starts when the processor is turned on or is reset (hence the need for a big black reset button on the board).

As it stands now, our program doesn't do anything and takes forever to do it. Let's put in some code to do something.

Initializing the Hardware

First, we need to initialize the hardware. To do so, we'll make our first use of the HAL library. The HAL software layer is designed to hide all the ugly details involved with getting the chip to work. For example, we have to initialize the on-chip clock before we can use it to time the blinks of an LED. Doing this ourselves would require programming specific *I/O registers* that directly control how an I/O device acts. They are part of the hardware.

Although we could go through the chip's 700-page reference manual to determine what registers to program, and then do all the calculations to figure out what values to program them with, this would take a lot of work.

Instead, we can use the HAL software, and specifically the HAL_Init function, to do all that work for us. The HAL_Init function programs the system clock so we can use it later to time our LED. Insert a call to HAL_Init just after the first curly bracket in the main function, as follows:

```
int main(void)
{
    HAL_Init();
```

In general, it's best practice to indent by four spaces for every set of curly brackets you use. The C language does not require this, but it makes understanding the program easier. (There's nothing magical about four spaces. Some programs use two, some eight, and a few strange people use three.)

That takes care of the basic hardware.

Programming a GPIO Pin

The chip has a number of *general-purpose input/output pins*, referred to as *GPIO pins*, which we can program to either receive input or send output for a variety of things. For example, we can program a pin for output and connect it to an LED (which is exactly what we'll do in this program). Alternatively, we can program a pin for input and connect it to a switch (which we'll do in the next chapter).

Some of the microcontroller's pins can be used as analog input or output. Most GPIO pins can be either on or off. Analog pins can handle voltages between on and off, such as 32765/65536 on. Others can be connected to a *USART* (serial I/O controller) or an *I2C bus* (simple I/O bus) to communicate with I2C peripheral chips. The good news is that these pins can do a lot of things. The bad news is that we have to program our chip to tell it, "Don't do all that fancy stuff. Just turn on when I want you to turn on and turn off when I want you to turn off."

We will program the GPIO pin that is connected to the user LED (LED2). We need to tell the chip that we are using this pin for output; then we must tell it a lot about how we are going to use it. This includes setting up a GPIO clock, which controls how fast it reacts. The HAL firmware can do most of this work, but we have to tell the HAL what to do by passing a structure of configuration information to the `HAL_GPIO_Init` function (C's structure concept is covered in more detail in Chapter 7):

```
// LED clock initialization
LED2_GPIO_CLK_ENABLE();

// Initialize LED
GPIO_InitTypeDef GPIO_InitStruct;
GPIO_InitStruct.Pin = LED2_PIN;
GPIO_InitStruct.Mode = GPIO_MODE_OUTPUT_PP;
GPIO_InitStruct.Pull = GPIO_PULLUP;
GPIO_InitStruct.Speed = GPIO_SPEED_FREQ_HIGH;
HAL_GPIO_Init(LED2_GPIO_PORT, &GPIO_InitStruct);
```

NOTE   *The STM hardware guys labeled this LED "LD2" on the board, but the software guys call it "LED2." Therefore, if you set the control bit LED2_PIN, LD2 lights up. Consistency is wonderful.*

We set the pin on in order to transmit data to `LED2_PIN`, which is the one connected to the user LED. Next, we specify that the pin will be used for output because we're sending data to the LED rather than retrieving data, and we set the mode to push/pull. This mode is determined by what you connect to the output pin. In this case, our circuit needs push/pull. This option controls the internal hardware used to drive the GPIO pin. The STM chip reference shows you how this circuit is organized (or, better put, it shows your hardware person how the chip is organized, and they can tell you which mode to use).

The pullup flags configure the GPIO pin so that, in input mode, a pullup resister is part of the circuit. This is irrelevant for output pins, but it still needs to be set. We set it to `GPIO_PULLUP`, which means absolutely nothing. Finally, we set the speed to high with `GPIO_SPEED_FREQ_HIGH`.

Toggling the LED

Now remove the final ; after the `for(;;)` statement. Remember that this semicolon essentially means "do nothing." To introduce code that the `for` loop should execute, add these new lines:

```
for(;;) {
    // Toggle LED2
    HAL_GPIO_TogglePin(LED2_GPIO_PORT, LED2_PIN);
    HAL_Delay(400); // Delay 400 ms
}
```

The function `HAL_GPIO_TogglePin` toggles the `LED2` GPIO pin. On our chip, GPIO pins are organized into groups of 32 bits, collectively called a *GPIO register*. Our pin is in register `LED2_GPIO_PORT`. To tell the function which of the 32 GPIO pins to toggle, we specify `LED2_PIN`.

After we toggle the pin, we need to do nothing for a while; otherwise, the LED will blink so fast we can't see it. We use the HAL_Delay function to delay for 400 milliseconds (ms).

Building the Completed Program

Our full program looks like this:

```c
/*
 * Blink the user LED on the board.
 *
 * A simple program to write, but getting it
 * working is going to require learning a
 * lot of new tools.
 */

#include "stm32f0xx.h"
#include "stm32f0xx_nucleo.h"

int main(void)
{
    HAL_Init();
    // LED clock initialization
    LED2_GPIO_CLK_ENABLE();

    // Initialize LED
    GPIO_InitTypeDef GPIO_InitStruct;
    GPIO_InitStruct.Pin = LED2_PIN;
    GPIO_InitStruct.Mode = GPIO_MODE_OUTPUT_PP;
    GPIO_InitStruct.Pull = GPIO_NOPULL;
    GPIO_InitStruct.Speed = GPIO_SPEED_FREQ_HIGH;
    HAL_GPIO_Init(LED2_GPIO_PORT, &GPIO_InitStruct);

    for(;;) {
        // Toggle LED2
        HAL_GPIO_TogglePin(LED2_GPIO_PORT, LED2_PIN);
        HAL_Delay(400); // Delay 400 ms
    }
}
```

Now build the project by selecting **Project ▸ Build Project**. If everything went okay, you should see no problems in the Problems window. If there are problems, fix them and try again.

In the Console window, you'll see that the IDE invoked make, which then invoked the GCC compiler named arm-none-eabi-gcc. This is the compiler for our embedded chip.

Start the program by selecting **Run ▸ Run**. (Be sure to click **Run** on the main menu. You can also right-click the project, but that runs a slightly different command.) The Run command hides a lot of work. First, the IDE checks whether the project needs to be built. Then it runs a program that takes the program file and communicates with the flash programmer on our development board to flash the program in memory. Finally, the programmer tells the chip to reset and start our program.

As a result, you should see the green LED blink slowly.

Exploring the Build Process

The Console window shown in Figure 3-9 contains the output of the build process. (If this window is empty, you can re-create the contents with **Project ▸ Clean** followed by **Project ▸ Build Project**.)

NOTE   *If the menu item Build Project is not enabled, select the top-level project directory in the Project Explorer and try again.*

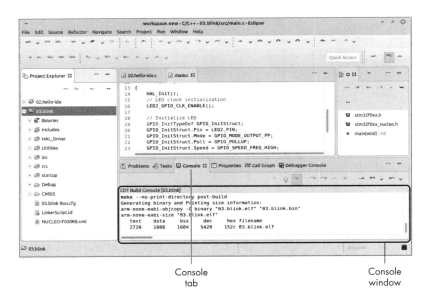

Figure 3-9: The Console window

Let's scroll up and look at one line in the build process, a typical invocation of the GCC compiler:

```
arm-none-eabi-gcc -mcpu=cortex-m0 -mthumb -mfloat-abi=soft \
-DSTM32 -DSTM32F0 -DSTM32F030R8Tx -DNUCLEOF030R8 -DDEBUG
-DSTM32F030x8 \
-DUSEHALDRIVER \
-I"/home/sdo/bare/workspace/blink/HALDriver/Inc/Legacy" \
-I"/home/sdo/bare/workspace/blink/Utilities/STM32F0xx-Nucleo" \
-I"/home/sdo/bare/workspace/blink/inc" \
-I"/home/sdo/bare/workspace/blink/CMSIS/device" \
-I"/home/sdo/bare/workspace/blink/CMSIS/core" \
-I"/home/sdo/bare/workspace/blink/HALDriver/Inc" \
-O0 -g3 -Wall -fmessage-length=0 -ffunction-sections \
-c -MMD -MP -MF"HALDriver/Src/stm32f0xxlltim.d" \
-MT"HALDriver/Src/stm32f0xxlltim.o" \
-o "HALDriver/Src/stm32f0xxlltim.o" "../HALDriver/Src/stm32f0xxll_tim.c"
```

This is a single line in the Console window, broken apart for formatting. As you can see, the compiler is being given a lot of additional options. The following are the key items on this command line:

arm-none-eabi-gcc This is a GCC compiler, but unlike the native GCC, which compiles for your computer, it is a cross-compiler producing code for the ARM processor. There is no underlying operating system (hence the none option), and the system is designed for an embedded application binary interface (eabi), which defines how pieces of the program communicate with one another and with the outside world.

-mcpu=cortex-m0 This produces code for the cortex-m0 version of the CPU. ARM has multiple processor variations, and this flag tells GCC which version to use.

-mthumb Some ARM processors can execute two different instruction sets. There is the full 32-bit RISC instruction set, which executes very quickly but uses lots and lots of memory, and there is the *thumb* set, which is slower but far more compact. This directive tells GCC that we want thumb code (a good idea if you are using a cheap chip with limited memory, which we are).

-mfloat-abi=soft Our processor does not have floating-point hardware, so this flag tells GCC to fake it with software. (More on floating point can be found in Chapter 16.)

-O0 Specifies level 0 (that is, no) optimization. This turns off a compiler feature where the compiler analyzes your code and performs all sorts of tricks to make it go faster. These tricks make the underlying code harder to understand and debug.

-g3 Turns on debugging.

-Wall Turns on the set of warnings named all, which contains almost all of the useful warnings.

-c Compiles a single source file into a single object file.

-o"HALDriver/Src/stm32f0xx11_tim.o" Stores the object file in the given file.

"../HALDriver/Src/stm32f0xx11_tim.c" Specifies name of the source file.

The other options tell the compiler where the included files are for the library and how these files should be configured. (We discuss the -D directive in Chapter 12.) The -I directive tells the compiler to search for include files in the specified directory in addition to the standard include file directories.

In addition to the compilation commands, we can see the linker command:

```
arm-none-eabi-gcc -mcpu=cortex-m0 -mthumb -mfloat-abi=soft \
-T"/home/sdo/bare/workspace/blink/LinkerScript.ld" \
-Wl,-Map=output.map -Wl,--gc-sections \
-o "blink.elf" @"objects.list" -lm '''
```

The key directive, -T"/home/sdo/bare/workspace/blink/LinkerScript.ld", tells the linker to use *LinkerScript.ld* to tell it where to put the various pieces of the program. (This is discussed in detail in Chapter 11.)

The build process ends with the following two commands:

```
arm-none-eabi-objcopy -O binary "blink.elf" "blink.bin"
arm-none-eabi-size "blink.elf"
   text       data        bss      dec      hex filename
   2620       1088        1604     5312     14c0 blink.elf
```

The arm-none-eabi-objcopy command takes the *.elf* file and turns it into a raw binary image. ELF is a complex file format that tells the loader where to place various things. The raw binary image is exactly what's going into your flash memory.

Finally, arm-none-eabi-size prints out the size of the resulting program (Table 3-1).

Table 3-1: Program Memory Section Sizes

Segment	Description
text	Size of read-only data (goes into flash)
data	Size of read/write data that requires initialization (goes into RAM)
bss	Size of read/write data that is initialized to zero (goes into RAM)
dec	Total size in decimal
hex	Total size in hexadecimal

We will explore the different types of memory, like flash and RAM, in later chapters. For now, understand that this step is done to answer the question, "If I keep programming, when will I run out of memory?"

Exploring the Project Files

System Workbench for STM32 has created and downloaded a lot of files for our project. Let's go through the key files.

We can view our *src* directory by clicking the triangle next to the directory name. It contains the files listed in Table 3-2.

Table 3-2: The *src* Directory Files

File	Description
main.c	The main program, where all our code goes.
stm32f0xxit.c	The interrupt service routines. You will learn about interrupts in Chapter 10. For this simple program, the only interrupt we care about is the system clock, and even then, we don't see the details of it directly. It's used by HAL_Delay.
syscalls.c	Dummy functions that are not used.
Systemstm32f0xx.c	Code that supports the system clock (explained in later chapters).

The *startup* directory contains one file: *startup_stm32f030x8.S.* This is an assembly language file that performs just enough initialization that the processor can run C code; it then jumps to the C startup code. This program contains the first instruction executed when you press the reset button.

The *inc* directory contains one file, *stm32f0xx_it.h*, which is used to tell other programs about the interrupt handlers in *stm32f0xx_it.c.* It's a very small and boring file.

Now we come to the *HAL_Driver* directory. This directory contains approximately 130 files that provide a HAL library for use in the program. The HAL hides (abstracts) the fact that different ARM CPUs have different capabilities. For example, the function `HAL_Init` will initialize all the hardware. If you have a Cortex-M0 processor, the Cortex-M0 version will initialize all the Cortex-M0 hardware. If you have a Cortex-M4 processor, all the Cortex-M4 hardware will be set up. There are so many files in this directory because the board we are using has lots of hardware. (And this is the simple version of the system.)

The *CMSIS* directory contains low-level code designed to support the HAL layer.

Finally, the *Debug* directory contains all the files related to our Debug build. In particular, it contains a `make` input file called *Makefile* and some generated files (see Table 3-3).

Table 3-3: Generated Files in the *Debug* Directory

File	Description
blink.elf	Our program in ELF format (a file format for executables)
blink.bin	Our program as a memory image (raw code)
output.map	The memory map for the program

NOTE *Unlike the makefile we wrote in Chapter 1, this makefile is machine-generated and uses tons of very advanced make features. If you really want to understand everything that goes on in this file, search online for "GNU Make Manual" and spend a few hours with it.*

The last file on our list is at the top level: *LinkerScript.ld.* It tells the linker what the memory layout of our chip looks like and where to load the various pieces of the program. More on this in Chapter 11.

Debugging the Application

Our blink program is simple and it works, but later we're going to make more complex programs, and they will have bugs in them. Since the board we are programming has such a good debugger, we might as well get started learning how to use it. Start the debugger by selecting **Run ▶ Debug**, as shown in Figure 3-10.

Figure 3-10: Starting the debugger

The IDE will then ask you for what type of debugger to run, as shown in Figure 3-11. Select **Ac6 STM32 C/C++ Application**.

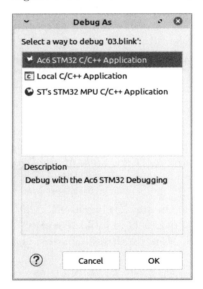

Figure 3-11: Debugger selection

The system will ask if you want to "Switch to the Debug Perspective." Answer **Yes**. The system then goes through a number of steps automatically:

1. It builds the software.
2. The IDE downloads the program to the chip using the flash programmer.

3. A debugger is attached to the device through the JTAG interface.

4. The debugger sets a breakpoint at the first line of main.

5. The breakpoint tells the chip to stop just before the first line of main is executed.

6. The microprocessor resets, and the program runs up to main.

7. The debugger regains control when the program reaches the breakpoint at main.

Once the debugger reaches the breakpoint, you are ready to debug the program, as seen in Figure 3-12. At this point, the program has executed until the first statement of the main function and is paused before the call to HAL_Init.

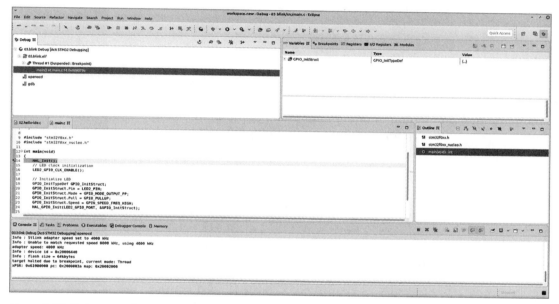

Figure 3-12: Debugging the program

NOTE *The light in the corner of the Nucleo board flashing red and green indicates that the board is under the control of the external debugger.*

Now that we've got control, let's use it. Use the command **Run ▸ Step Over** to start executing the program one line at a time. We'll do this a number of times, so remember the shortcut key F6. Keep stepping over lines using F6 until you get into the for loop.

Notice that every time you execute the HAL_GPIO_TogglePin(LED2_GPIO_PORT, LED2_PIN) function, the LED turns on or off. Since you are in the for loop, you ping-pong back and forth indefinitely between the toggling and the delay. If you are really observant, you'll notice that it takes a little over 400 ms (two-fifths of a second) to execute the call to HAL_Delay. You can change this value to something really big if you would like to better observe the delay.

Stepping Through the Program

Now we'll get into some of the details of this program. Most of the concepts are covered in more depth in future chapters, but I'll give you a taste of them now. First, let's abort the current debugging session with **Run ▸ Terminate**. Now let's start all over again, with **Run ▸ Debug**. You should be back to the line that calls HAL_Init. To step through the program, use a different command, **Run ▸ Step Into** (or shortcut key F5).

All of a sudden, the file *stm32f0xx_hal.c* appears in our editing window (see Figure 3-13). Where did this file come from?

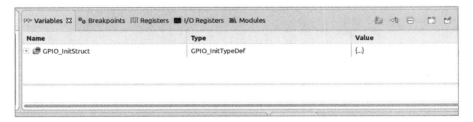

```
[c] 02.hello-ide.c    [c] main.c    [c] stm32f0xx_hal.c ⊠
  159        HAL_FLASH_PREFETCH_BUFFER_ENABLE();
  160  #endif /* PREFETCH_ENABLE */
  161
  162        /* Use systick as time base source and configure 1ms tick (default clock after Reset is HSI) */
  163
  164  HAL_InitTick(TICK_INT_PRIORITY);
  165
  166        /* Init the low level hardware */
  167  HAL_MspInit();
  168
```

Figure 3-13: Debugging stm32f0xx_hal.c

Well, we called the procedure HAL_Init. That procedure is defined in *stm32f0xx_hal.c*, so the debugger automatically opened that file when we stepped into the call to HAL_Init. Alternatively, the Step Over command would treat the statement (in this case, HAL_INIT();) as a single unit and step over the function, hiding all the details.

The Step Into command knows we are calling a function and steps into its code. As you can see, it takes a lot of extra code to support our little program. When you program on a PC, the code is hidden from you, and it's very difficult to get its source. The STM32 Workbench supplies all that code for you in the *HAL_Driver/Src* directory.

In addition to showing the code inside functions, the debugger can show us the status of all program variables. To see this in action, select **Run ▸ Step Over** (or press F6) about half a dozen times until you wind up back in *main.c* at the line that selects the pin to use. In the upper-right corner of the screen, you'll see a panel titled Variables (see Figure 3-14).

Name	Type	Value
⊞ GPIO_InitStruct	GPIO_InitTypeDef	{...}

Figure 3-14: The Variables panel

In our program, we've defined a variable called GPIO_InitStruct. In the Variables panel, the + before the name indicates that GPIO_InitStruct is a *complex* variable, which means that it contains more than a simple integer, Boolean, or other single value. To see the all the components inside, expand it by clicking the + icon (see Figure 3-15).

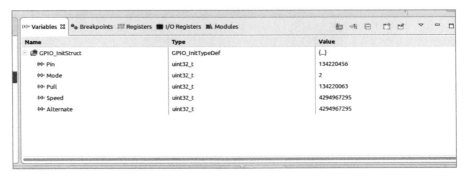

Figure 3-15: An expanded variable

You'll learn about the components of GPIO_InitStruct, and how to create variables yourself, in later chapters. The GPIO_InitStruct variable was created by a programmer who read the 700-page reference manual on our chip and designed a variable to hold this information. Believe it or not, this variable significantly simplifies what's presented in the manual: about 30 pages of compressed technical information on just the GPIO subsystem.

Now step through the next few statements to see the values of the components of this variable.

Summary

I've tried to make this program as simple as possible, but as you can see, with today's complex chips, even the simplest operation takes a bit of work. Getting a program running requires a lot of support.

In the first chapter, our "Hello World" program required pretty much the same number of files mentioned here, but they existed behind the scenes. For example, the initialization file was installed as part of the GCC package. In our blink project, the file *startup_stm32f030x8.S* must be explicitly included.

This chapter threw a ton of new concepts at you. Don't worry if you don't understand them all yet. We'll dive deeper into them in future chapters.

Programming Problems

1. Experiment with changing the delay in the Hal_Delay(); statement to make the blink frequency longer and shorter.

2. Examine *LinkerScript.ld* to find the answers to the following questions:

    a. How much flash (read-only) memory do you have?

    b. How much RAM (read/write memory) do you have?

3. Examine the file *output.map* and determine the actual address of Reset_Handler.

4. For intermediate readers: Change the program so it turns the LED on for a short time, then off for a longer time.

Questions

1. What files are generated by the IDE, and what do they contain?

2. Where on your system did the IDE stash the compiler?

3. What does a commercial JTAG debugger look like? How much does it cost? What does it take to hook it up to a typical development board? (And be glad you got an integrated system!)

4

NUMBERS AND VARIABLES

Now that we have written a trivial program or two, it's time to get the machine to do some real work. In this chapter you will learn how to manipulate numbers.

As embedded programmers, we are concerned with exactly what the numbers are doing. For example, the number 32 could represent the number of sheep in a barnyard, or it could energize GPIO pin #4, which turns on the big red warning light. What's worse, our STM32 groups up to 32 different GPIOs into a single number, so while 32 might tell the device to "turn on the big red light," 34 could tell it to "turn on the big red light and sound the klaxon." To control our devices, we need to know precisely what these numbers are doing. Thus, we will take a deep dive into the numbers as seen by the computer.

Once you know what a number is, you will learn how to work with it by using variables to store the information in our program. Next, you'll practice manipulating the bits in the hardware's I/O registers to turn various functions on or off. In the process, you'll see how the program in Chapter 3 worked behind the scenes.

Working with Integers

We'll start with integers, or whole numbers. These are numbers without a decimal point, such as 37, 45, –8, and 256.

Table 4-1 lists the operations you can do with numbers in C.

Table 4-1: Number Operators in C

Operator	Description
+	Add
-	Subtract
*	Multiply
/	Divide (truncates to a whole number)
%	Modulus (returns the remainder after division)

The following listing illustrates how these operators work:

```
#include <stdio.h>

int main()
{
    printf("3 + 2 is %d\n", 3 + 2);
    printf("3 - 2 is %d\n", 3 - 2);
    printf("3 * 2 is %d\n", 3 * 2);
    printf("3 / 2 is %d\n", 3 / 2);
    printf("10 / 9 is %d\n", 10 / 9);
    printf("3 %% 2 is %d\n", 3 % 2);
    return (0);
}
```

We demonstrate each operation inside a `printf` statement that prints the result. To print the result of a calculation using `printf`, put a `%d` in the string where you want a number to appear and then list the calculation as a second argument to `printf`. Notice that if you want to print a % to represent the modulus operation, you need to specify it twice.

To view this program's output, let's get it into our IDE. Start System Workbench for STM32 and then go through the list of steps in Chapter 2 to create a program. (A checklist in the appendix summarizes these steps.) This time, however, instead of creating a "Hello World" program, we'll create an empty native C/C++ project, so select **C Managed Build** as the template.

Under Project Type, choose **Executable ▸ Empty Project**. Next, create the program file by selecting **File ▸ New ▸ Source File**.

Enter the program text into the editing window and then save the file. Build the binary and run it as you did in Chapter 2. The program should display its output at the bottom of the Console window (see Figure 4-1).

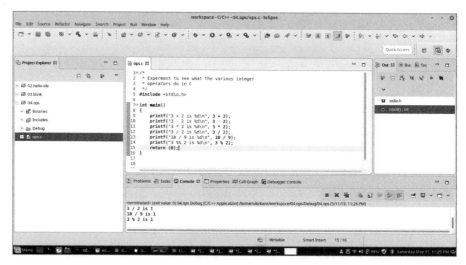

Figure 4-1: The run result

As you can see, the program should print the result of each calculation it performs.

Declaring Variables to Hold Integers

Our program performed operations on fixed numbers, but we can also use variables to store information that can change. Before any variable can be used, it has to be *declared*. The format of a variable declaration is as follows:

```
type variable_name; // Comment explaining what this variable does
```

For example, using int as the type would indicate that the variable is an integer. To be precise, it is the type of integer that the computer can most easily handle. We will get into other types of integers later in this chapter.

Variable names begin with a letter and must contain only letters, digits, and the underscore. The STM32 firmware library uses the camel case variable naming style, where words within the name are capitalized, so to be compatible, we use camel case throughout this book:

```
startTime    currentStation    area
```

While names can begin with an underscore, such names are considered reserved for system functions and should not be used in ordinary programming. Also, never use l (lowercase *L*) or O (uppercase *O*) as a variable name. In case the reasons aren't obvious, consider the following code:

```
O = l + 1 + 0 * o;  // This sort of programming will get you shot.
```

Technically, you can omit the comment from your variable declaration. However, including a comment gives the people who work with the code after you an idea of why you declared the variable and what it does. In other words, it helps you create a mini-dictionary or glossary.

Assigning Values to Variables

Once we've declared a variable, we can assign it a value with an assignment statement. The general form of an assignment statement is as follows:

```
variable = expression;
```

This tells the computer to compute the value of the expression and store it in the variable. Variables can then be used anyplace we put an integer, such as a printf statement. The following program demonstrates variable declaration, assignment, and use:

---

var.c
```
/*
 * A program to sum two variables
 */
#include <stdio.h>

int main()
{
    int aNumber;        // Some number
    int otherNumber;    // Some other number

    aNumber = 5;
    otherNumber = 7;

    printf("Sum is %d\n", aNumber + otherNumber);
    return (0);
}
```

This program creates two variables, aNumber and otherNumber, and then assigns them each a value and prints the sum. Enter this program into System Workbench for STM32 now.

Initializing Variables

When you declare a variable in your program, you tell the C compiler to allocate memory space for an integer (int). But before you specify a value for it, this variable is considered *uninitialized*; it may contain any random garbage value left over from the last time the memory was used.

To see this at work in the program we just wrote, open the debugger and take a look at the Variables panel as you step through the program. Before you assign them values, our two variables, aNumber and otherNumber, have values of zero. But uninitialized variables could have any value; the fact that they're zero here is pure luck.

We can initialize a variable at declaration time by adding an assignment to it:

```
int aNumber = 5;          // Some number
```

This is a good idea in most cases, as it makes sure our program is working with an expected value. Let's rewrite our program to add these initializers:

```
/*
 * A program to see if we can sum two variables
 */
#include <stdio.h>

int main()
{
    int aNumber = 5;        // Some number
    int otherNumber = 7;    // Some other number

    printf("Sum is %d\n", aNumber + otherNumber);
    return (0);
}
```

Once we've made that change, we can delete the lines that initialize the variables later in the program.

Integer Sizes and Representations

C has integer types other than int that it uses to represent numbers of different sizes.

As computers evolved, people discovered that the most efficient way to organize memory is in 8-bit groups called *bytes*. The computer lets you combine multiple bytes into 2-byte, 4-byte, and 8-byte values, and the int type tells C to define an integer using the most efficient number of bytes for the computer you are using. This may be a 16-bit (2-byte) integer or a 32-bit (4-byte) integer, depending on the system. The compiler for our chip, the ARM Cortex-M0 CPU, uses a 32-bit integer.

To make programs even more efficient, C lets you select the type of integer you want. For example, you may wish to store numbers in the range of 0 to 100. You don't need a full-size integer for that, so you can use a short int, which is like an integer but takes up less space. (Technically, the C standard only states that a short int is no larger than a regular int, but in most implementations it is smaller.)

The following declares a short int:

```
short int shortNumber;  // A shorter-than-normal integer
```

A longer-than-normal integer can be declared with the modifier long:

```
long int longNumber;    // A longer-than-normal integer
```

When computers gained the ability to efficiently process even longer numbers, people needed an integer type that could contain even more bits than a long does. The result was the (somewhat silly) long long integer:

```
long long int veryLongNumber;   // An even longer integer
```

The C standard does not define the size of each type of integer. They could all be the same size, and you'd still have a standard compiler. However, it does guarantee the following:

```
sizeof(short int) <= sizeof(int) <= sizeof(long int) <= sizeof(long long int)
```

The sizeof operator returns the number of bytes it takes to store a variable or type.

Let's see how much space each type of integer takes for the compiler on our system using a short program to print the sizes of the various flavors of integer:

size.c
```c
/*
 * Show different number types.
 */
#include <stdio.h>

int main()
{
    short int aShortInt;        // Short integer
    int aInteger;               // Default integer
    long int aLongInt;          // Long integer
    long long int aLongLongInt; // Long long integer

    printf("Size of (short int) = %ld (bytes) %ld bits\n",
            sizeof(aShortInt), sizeof(aShortInt)*8);

    printf("Size of (int) = %ld (bytes) %ld bits\n",
            sizeof(aInteger), sizeof(aInteger)*8);

    printf("Size of (long int) = %ld (bytes) %ld bits\n",
            sizeof(aLongInt), sizeof(aLongInt)*8);

    printf("Size of (long long int) = %ld (bytes) %ld bits\n",
            sizeof(aLongLongInt), sizeof(aLongLongInt)*8);

    return (0);
}
```

Earlier, we used %d to print a number. In this program, we use %ld, because sizeof returns a long int and %ld is used to print long int numbers.

The program produces the following output on my system:

```
Size of (short int) = 2 (bytes) 16 bits
Size of (int) = 4 (bytes) 32 bits
Size of (long int) = 8 (bytes) 64 bits
Size of (long long int) = 8 (bytes) 64 bits
```

From this, we can see that the size of a long int is the same as a long long int. However, that is true only for this compiler on this system (GNU GCC on an x86_64 processor). Different compilers might implement things differently.

Number Representations

Let's say we have five cows. In English, we could represent that number as "five," "5," or "V." Likewise, in C, you can use four number representations: decimal, binary, octal, and hexadecimal.

People typically use decimal (base 10), but computers store numbers in binary (base 2) because it's cheap and easy to make binary circuits. For example, we might write the following assignment statement using decimal:

```
aNumber = 5;
```

This same statement could be written in binary like this:

```
aNumber = 0b101;    // 5 in binary
```

The prefix 0b indicates a binary number follows. (We could use 0B too, but it's harder to read.)

Or, we could use octal (base 8):

```
aNumber = 05;    // 5 in octal
```

Finally, we can use hexadecimal (base 16):

```
aNumber = 0x5;   // 5 in hexadecimal
```

Binary numbers take up a lot of room to write, so to make things more compact, we often use hexadecimal notation in programming to represent exact binary values. Each single hex digit translates into four binary bits, as shown in Table 4-2.

Table 4-2: Converting Between Binary and Hex

Binary	Hex	Binary	Hex
0000	0	1000	8
0001	1	1001	9
0010	2	1010	A
0011	3	1011	B
0100	4	1100	C
0101	5	1101	D
0110	6	1110	E
0111	7	1111	F

As you can see, 1111 1100b is the equivalent of the hex value 0xFC. Similarly, 0xA5 is 1010 0101b. Using this table, you can quickly and easily translate between binary and hexadecimal.

While the computer stores a number as a set of bits, the meaning of those bits is entirely up to us. For example, the bit pattern 0000 0101 could mean 5 if we interpret it as a binary number. But 0000 0101 could also mean 10,005. How did I get that number? I made it up. In this case, I arbitrarily picked a strange value. Other arbitrary meanings could include "May," the letter "E," and "LED0+LED2."

One less common but still useful bit pattern mapping is shown in Table 4-3.

Table 4-3: A Bit Pattern to Number Mapping

Bit pattern	Meaning
000	0
001	1
011	2
010	3
110	4
111	5
101	6
100	7

At first glance, it looks random. But if you look closely, you'll see that only one bit changes between each number. This makes it ideal for use in encoders (see Figure 4-2). It is, in fact, a standard bit pattern encoding called *Gray code*.

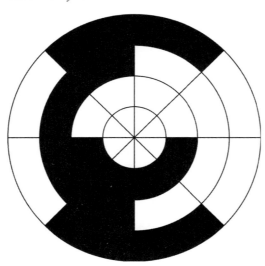

Figure 4-2: A Gray code encoder

Remember that C has no idea how to interpret a bit pattern until you tell it how.

Standard Integers

The big problem with the integer types is that nothing in the standard tells you how big they are, just their relative sizes. If you want to write to a 32-bit device, you have to guess which type of int will be the size you want.

Guessing and programming do not mix well together, so people devised systems using a technique called *conditional compilation* (see Chapter 12) and other tricks to define new types that hold a precise number of bits: int8_t, int16_t, int32_t, and int64_t. The name of the type specifies the size of the integer. For example, the type int32_t has 32 bits in it no matter what size the int is. Like most good ideas, these new types became widely used—so widely used that the C standards committee decided to add them to the language with the stdint library. They are not part of the built-in C types, so you have to include them by using the following statement:

```
#include <stdint.h>
```

Listing 4-1 shows our new integer types in action.

```
/*
 * Demonstrate different sizes of integers.
 */
#include <stdio.h>
#include <stdint.h>

int main()
{
    int8_t   has8bits = 0x12;                  // 8-bit integer
    int16_t has16bits = 0x1234;                // 16-bit integer
    int32_t has32bits = 0x12345678;            // 32-bit integer
    int64_t has64bits = 0x123456789abcdef0; // 64-bit integer

    printf(" 8 bits %x\n", has8bits);
    printf("16 bits %x\n", has16bits);
    printf("32 bits %x\n", has32bits);
    printf("64 bits %lx\n", has64bits);
    return (0);
}
```

Listing 4-1: Integer demonstration

In this program, we use the formatting character %x to print the numbers in hexadecimal. Specifically, the %x format character prints an int in hexadecimal, but we can also use it for int8_t, int16_t, and int32_t because of some behind-the-scenes stuff called *argument promotion*.

C is a somewhat lazy language. Because it's hard to pass a 16-bit integer to printf when your processor has 32-bit registers, C takes the int16_t and converts, or *promotes*, it to an int32_t for this one operation, which lets us get away with using %x for an int16_t. Similarly, we can use %x for an int8_t because it will get promoted to an `int32_t` as well. (Strictly speaking, the C standard states that promotion *may* occur. It does not require it. This code works on our x86_64 machine with this compiler, but it is not portable to other systems.)

Now we come to `int64_t`. If C were to change this into an `int` (`int32_t`), we'd lose half our number. C can't do anything to it, so it passes an `int64_t` argument as an `int64_t` argument. The format had to change from `%x` (`int`) to `%lx` (`int64_t`) to print the longer value.

Investigation for the reader: try changing `%lx` to `%x` in the example and see what you get.

Unsigned Integer Types

In the last section, we used signed integer types, which can be either positive or negative. Unsigned integer types hold only positive values and are simpler than their signed counterparts. The standard unsigned types are `uint8_t`, `uint16_t`, `uint32_t`, and `uint64_t`. The type `uint8_t` is an unsigned 8-bit integer that can hold numbers from 0 (0000 0000b) to 255 (1111 1111b). The ranges of the unsigned integer types are shown in Table 4-4.

Table 4-4: Unsigned Integer Type Ranges

Type	Low	High
uint8_t	0000 0000 (0)	1111 1111 (255)
uint16_t	0000 0000 0000 0000 (0)	1111 1111 1111 1111 (65,535)
uint32_t	0000 0000 0000 0000 0000 0000 0000 0000 (0)	1111 1111 1111 1111 1111 1111 1111 1111 (4,294,967,295)
uint64_t	0000 0000 0000 0000 0000 0000 0000 0000 0000 0000 0000 0000 0000 0000 0000 0000 (0)	1111 1111 1111 1111 1111 1111 1111 1111 1111 1111 1111 1111 1111 1111 1111 1111 (18,446,744,073,709,551,615)

Here's a simple example of using a `uint8_t` variable. This program prints three different representations for `smallNumber` without changing its value:

```
/*
 * Simple use of uint8_t
 */

#include <stdio.h>
#include <stdint.h>

int main()
{
    uint8_t smallNumber = 0x12; // A small number

    printf("0x12 is %u decimal\n", smallNumber);
    printf("0x12 is %o octal\n", smallNumber);
    printf("0x12 is %x hex\n", smallNumber);
    return(0);
}
```

The %u printf specification tells C we want to print an unsigned int (the default unsigned integer type). We use the format specification %o to print in octal and %x to print in hexadecimal.

The output of this program looks like this:

```
0x12 is 18 decimal
0x12 is 22 octal
0x12 is 12 hex
```

Overflow

Now we will explore the limits of our machine. Actually, we will exceed them. The biggest uint8_t number is 255 (0b1111 1111). What happens when we go beyond that and try to print 255 + 1? Let's try it:

```
/*
 * See what happens when we exceed the maximum number.
 * (Contains a mistake)
 */

#include <stdio.h>
#include <stdint.h>

int main()
{
    // Very small integer, set to the maximum
    uint8_t smallNumber = 255;

❶   printf("255+1 is %u\n", smallNumber + 1);
    return (0);
}
```

According to this program, the result of adding 1 to the 8-bit unsigned integer 255 is 256, but the number 256 in binary is 0b1 0000 0000, or 0x100, which can't fit in 8 bits. Either we've warped the laws of the universe or something went wrong with our program.

To understand what's going on, let's take a look at the print statement ❶. The type of smallNumber is uint8_t; however, on most 32-bit computers, it's hard, if not impossible, to add two 8-bit integers. Because of the way the computer is constructed, you have to add two 32-bit numbers. So, to compute an expression, the C compiler does the following:

1. Converts shortNumber to a unit32_t value
2. Adds 1 to the result (of type uint32_t)
3. Prints the result (256) as a uint32_t

The result is a uint32_t that can hold the value 256, and that's what's printed. So, we did not cause an 8-bit overflow (which we wanted to demonstrate). Instead, we demonstrated automatic promotion, which we discussed earlier in this chapter.

To get the result we want, we need to make a slight adjustment to the program to store the result in a uint8_t value (I've highlighted the changes to our program in bold):

```
/*
 * See what happens when we exceed the maximum number.
 */

#include <stdio.h>
#include <stdint.h>

int main()
{
    uint8_t smallNumber;
    uint8_t result;

    smallNumber = 255;
    result = smallNumber + 1;
    printf("255+1 is %d\n", result);
    return (0);
}
```

Now the result is 0. Why? Because our calculation returned 0b1111 1111 + 0b000 0001 = 0b1 **0000 0000**. Only the bold portion was stored due to the limited space in which to store the variable.

Overflow occurs when the result is too big for the machine to handle. In this case, the 9-bit result won't fit in an 8-bit value. Think of a car's odometer. It can display mileage to 999,999. What happens if someone drives a million miles?

Understanding how the compiler is manipulating the numbers is key to making good embedded programs. For example, I once had a GPS that kept altitude as an unsigned number. (It was not designed to work on submarines.) I took it on a trip to Death Valley, and it died. That's because when I reached Badwater Basin, elevation –282 feet, it couldn't handle the negative altitude. The GPS's designers had assumed that all altitudes would be greater than zero. After all, the GPS was not designed to work underwater. Therefore, using an unsigned integer for altitude was not an unreasonable decision—except for users in locations like Badwater Basin, where the altitude is negative, causing the GPS to die. This mistake shows why it's important to know the limitations of your numbering system.

Two's Complement Representation in Signed Integer Types

Signed numbers are represented by using one bit (the leftmost) as a sign bit: if the bit is 1, the number is negative. Thus, 8-bit signed integers (int8_t) can represent numbers from 127 to –128.

Almost all computers today use two's complement numbers to represent negative values. *Two's complement representation* stores a number as that number pre-subtracted from 0.

For example, –1 can be determined by the following calculation:

```
  0000 0000
 -0000 0001
  ---------
  1111 1111
```

This works because the computer adds a magic "borrow" bit to the left of the number, making the arithmetic look like this:

```
1 0000 0000
-   0000 0001
    ---------
    1111 1111
```

Two's complement is similar to a mechanical car odometer. Let's say you buy a brand-new car and its odometer reads 000,000. If you drove backward, your odometer would read 999,999, which is the ten's complement of –1.

You may have noticed that the biggest number a uint8_t can hold is 255, whereas an int8_t can store only values up to 127 (half that). That's because one bit is used as the sign bit, leaving only seven bits to store the number part.

What happens when we exceed the boundaries with 8-bit signed numbers? I'm going to let you investigate that yourself. See what happens with the operations 127 + 1 and –128 – 1. Also see what happens with –(–128), the negation of –128.

Shorthand Operators

You've learned about integers and the simple operations that can be done on them, but to let you do arithmetic faster, C provides a number of shorthand operators.

For example, consider adding a value to a number, like this:

```
aNumber = aNumber + 5;
```

You can shorten this operation to the following:

```
aNumber += 5;
```

You can perform similar shortcuts for all the other arithmetic operators. Additionally, you can condense the operation of adding 1 to a number:

```
aNumber += 1;
```

It can be shortened to this:

```
++aNumber;
```

To decrement numbers by 1, use the -- (minus minus) operator.

There is a caveat. C lets you combine the increment (++) and decrement (--) operations with other statements:

```
result = ++aNumber;    // Don't do this.
```

Please don't do this, as it can cause the program to have undefined behavior. For example, consider the following statements:

```
aNumber = 2;
result = ++aNumber * ++aNumber + ++aNumber;
```

The second statement tells C to increment aNumber, then increment aNumber again. It then multiplies aNumber with itself and increments aNumber a third time. Finally, it adds this to the result.

Unfortunately, nothing tells C that these operations have to occur in the order I've listed here. For example, all the increments could come at the beginning, making the result (5 × 5 + 5) = 30. Or they could come one at a time, and we would have (3 × 4 + 5) = 17. For those reasons, be sure to put ++ and -- on lines by themselves.

One more thing: there are two forms of increment and decrement operations. You can place the operator either before or after the variable you would like to increment:

```
aNumber = 5;
result = ++aNumber;
aNumber = 5;
result = aNumber++;
```

These do slightly different things. I leave it to the reader to write a small program to print the results of the preceding code and figure out what they do—and then please never again use ++ combined with another statement.

NOTE   *In C, the following two statements are equivalent:*

```
++aNumber;
aNumber++;
```

For operations on simple numbers, there is no difference between these two operations. The good news is that C only lets you do ++ on simple numbers.

However, C++ allows you to define your own data types and, through operator overloading, define your own ++ and -- operations. When you are dealing with a complex C++ object, the prefix version is much more efficient in most cases, so it is a good idea to get into the habit of using the first form just in case you need to step into the world of C++.

Controlling Memory-Mapped I/O Registers Using Bit Operations

We can organize eight bits into a single number, but these bits can also represent eight different things. For example, they can be wired to eight different LED lights. In fact, when you place values in special memory locations called *memory-mapped I/O registers*, these values turn on or off I/O pins. Since there are eight bits to the register's byte, a single register can control eight LEDs. (Or, in our case, one LED and seven pins on which we can add more LEDs.)

Bits are normally numbered from 7 to 0, with 7 being the leftmost, or most significant, bit. Let's say our LED register is set up as follows:

Bit 7	Bit 6	Bit 5	Bit 4	Bit 3	Bit 2	Bit 1	Bit 0
Out 7	Out 6	Out 5	Out 4	Out 3	Out 2	Out 1	LED 0

Say we want to turn on LED #0. As each LED is off, our register has the value 0000 0000 in it. To turn on LED #0, we need to flip the final bit to a value of 1. To do that, we just add 1 to the register to get 0000 0001. LED #0 turns on and all the others stay off.

But what if the LED was already on? Then our register would contain 0000 0001, and when we add 1, we'll get 2, which in binary is 0000 0010. Thus, LED #0 turns off and OUT #1 turns on. Not what we wanted.

The problem here is that the arithmetic operators we've been using treat our 8-bit integer as a single integer. The *bitwise operators* treat the number as a set of individual bits, each of which can be turned on, turned off, and tested independently.

OR

The first bitwise operator is *OR* (|). The single-bit version of OR gives a true (or 1) result if either of its two operands is set to 1. I'm going to show how it operates using a *truth table*. It's like the addition and multiplication tables you used in first grade, only it shows the operation of Boolean operators such as OR.

The truth table for OR looks like this:

OR (|)	0	1
0	0	1
1	1	1

OR is a bitwise operator, which means that to "OR" two 8-bit values together, you perform the operation for each pair of bits in the two values. For example:

```
  0010 0101
| 0000 1001
  ---------
  0010 1101
```

To set bit 0 (that is, to turn on LED #0), we use the following C code:

```
ledRegister = ledRegister | 0x01;
```

Alternatively, we can use the following shorthand operator:

```
ledRegister |= 0x01;
```

AND

The *AND* (&) operator returns a true (1) only if both of its operands are true. The following is the AND truth table:

AND (&)	0	1
0	0	0
1	0	1

Like OR, the AND operator works on each pair of bits:

```
  0010 0101
& 0000 1001
  ---------
  0000 0001
```

To turn off LED #0, we can set bit 0 to a value of 0 with the following operation:

```
ledRegister &= 0b11111110;
```

This command "ANDs" our register with a bit pattern that has every bit set *except* bit 0, so bit 0 will be cleared and all the other bits will be unchanged. (ANDing a bit with 1 keeps its value.)

NOT

The *invert*, or *NOT*, operator (~) takes one operand and inverts it. Thus, if the bit is 0, it becomes 1, and if it's 1, it becomes 0. The truth table for the NOT operator is rather simple:

	0	1
~	1	0

The following example demonstrates how this operator works:

```
~ 0000 0001
  ---------
  1111 1110
```

Using the bitwise operators we've covered so far, we can already write some code to turn off all registers and then turn on and off the LED:

```
const uint8_t LED_BIT = 0b0000001;

// Turn off everything.
ledRegister = 0;

// Turn on the LED.
ledRegister |= LED_BIT;

// Wait a while.
sleep(5);

// Turn off the LED.
ledRegister &= ~LED_BIT;
```

This is exactly what the blink program from Chapter 3 was doing, except that the STM library hid these details from us.

Exclusive OR

The result of the bitwise operator *exclusive OR* (^) is true if one or the other bit is set, but not both. Here is its truth table:

Exclusive OR (^)	0	1
0	0	1
1	1	0

To see how it works, consider the following example:

```
  0010 0101
^ 0000 1001
  ---------
  0010 1100
```

Exclusive OR is useful if we want to invert the value of the LED in our ledRegister, like this:

```
ledRegister ^= LED_BIT; // Toggle the LED bit.
```

Inverting an LED makes it blink slowly.

Shifting

The *left shift* operator (<<) shifts the contents of a variable to the left by a given number of bits, filling in zeros for the missing bits. For example, consider the following operation:

```
uint8_t result = 0xA5 << 2
```

This causes the computer to move the bits two places to the left so that the following:

```
1010 0101
```

becomes this:

```
1001 0100
```

The *right shift* operator (>>) is a little more tricky. For unsigned numbers, it works just like the left shift, except it shifts the bits in the rightward direction. Again, the computer fills in zeros for the missing bits. Thus, `uint8_t result = 0xA5 >> 2;` would be computed so that the following:

```
1010 0101
```

becomes this:

```
0010 1001
```

But when the number is signed, the computer uses the sign bit to supply the missing bits. For example, consider the following operation:

```
int8_t result = 0xA5 >> 2;  // Note the lack of "u"
```

This would be computed such that the following:

```
1010 0101
```

becomes this:

```
1110 1001
```

Because it's a signed number shifting right, the missing bits on the right side are filled in with copies of the sign bit, so the result is 0xE9, which is −23.

Defining the Meaning of Bits

Hardware people love defining things in terms of bits. That's because when the signals come out of the chip, they leave from single pins on the hardware that have names like GPIO A-3 (which means GPIO register A, bit 3). As the signal on a single pin is either *high* (1) or *low* (0), you can represent it with a single bit.

But by the time the programmer sees the signal, it has been bundled with a bunch of others into an 8-bit, 16-bit, or 32-bit register. Therefore, we need a way of easily translating hardware speak (like "bit 3") into software speak (such as "0x04"). The shift operators, properly used, can be a big help with this translation.

For example, let's say we have a light board whose hardware specification is the following:

```
+----+----+----+----++----+----+----+----+
|  7 |  6 |  5 |  4 || 3  |  2 |  1 |  0 |
| MF | DF | OL | OP || PW | PF | AP | CF |
+----+----+----+----++----+----+----+----+
```

MF (bit 7)   Master fail: Lights when any other failure light gets lit.

DF (bit 6)   Data fail: Incoming data is inconsistent or corrupt.

OL (bit 5)   Oil low: The oil level in the accumulator is low.

OP (bit 4)   Oil pressure: The accumulator oil pressure is low.

PW (bit 3)   Power failure: The main power supply has failed.

PF (bit 2)   Position fault: The position frame has hit a limit switch and is not where it is supposed to be.

AP (bit 1)   Air pressure: The air compressor has failed.

CF (bit 0)   Clean filter: The filter to the air compressor needs cleaning.

Each of these bits is connected to a light. The light circuit is wired to the GPIO pins of our controller. For example, if we set bit 0 of the GPIO device, the "Clean Filter" light will come on:

```
ledRegister = 1;  // Turn on clean filter.
                  // (Turn all others off.)
```

Even so, it's still not easy to remember which number goes with which bit. Bit 0 is the first value, bit 1 is the second value, and so on. Quick: Which bit is represented by the 6th value? There is a nice way of making this easier. Bit 0 holds value 1, which is equivalent to the expression (1 << 0). Bit 1 is value 2, which is (1 << 2), and bit 3 is (1 << 3), and so on. From this, it's easy to see that bit 5 is (1 << 5). Using this system, we can define constants to represent each bit:

```
const uint8_t MASTER_FAIL     = (1 << 7);
const uint8_t DATA_FAIL       = (1 << 6);
const uint8_t OIL_LOW         = (1 << 5);
const uint8_t OIL_PRESSURE    = (1 << 4);
const uint8_t POWER_FAILURE   = (1 << 3);
const uint8_t POSITION_FAULT  = (1 << 2);
const uint8_t AIR_PRESSURE    = (1 << 1);
const uint8_t CLEAN_FILTER    = (1 << 0);
```

Let's once again turn on the CLEAN_FILTER LED and leave all the others alone, this time using our new constant to reference the relevant bit:

```
ledRegister |= CLEAN_FILTER; // Turn on clean filter.
```

Notice here that we also used the |= shorthand operator introduced earlier in this chapter.

Setting the Values of Two Bits at Once

Now let's say we want to set the values of both POWER_FAILURE and MASTER_FAIL. We can accomplish that with the following statement:

```
ledRegister |= MASTER_FAIL |, POWER_FAILURE;
```

Since MASTER_FAIL has a value of 1 in bit 7, and any nonzero value results in a value of 1, the MASTER_FAIL bit will be set in the panel.

Turning Off a Bit

We use the following pattern to turn off a bit:

```
bitSet &= ~bitToTurnOff;
```

To understand how this operation works, let's go through it in detail using the following statement:

```
ledRegister &= ~(MASTER_FAIL | POWER_FAILURE);
```

Let's start with the result of (MASTER_FAIL | POWER_FAIL):

```
1000 1000 (MASTER_FAIL | POWER_FAIL)
```

Now we apply the invert or NOT (~) operator:

```
0111 0111 ~(MASTER_FAIL|POWER_FAIL)
```

Next, we take a look at the existing value of ledRegister. For this example, it has MASTER_FAIL and CLEAN_FILTER set.

```
1000 0001 (ledRegister: MASTER_FAIL, CLEAN_FILTER)
```

Now we "AND" the results together:

```
0111 0111 ~(MASTER_FAIL|POWER_FAIL)
1000 0001 (ledRegister: MASTER_FAIL, CLEAN_FILTER)
Result:   0000 0001 (CLEAN_FILTER)
```

Checking the Values of Bits

The following program shows a typical use of *bit-banging*, the art of turning on and off individual bits. It also contains logic to check the values of the different bits:

```
/*
 * Program to demonstrate the use of bit operations
```

```c
 */
#include <stdio.h>
#include <stdint.h>

//< Master fail -- shows if any other error is present.
const uint8_t MASTER_FAIL    = (1 << 7);
//< Indicates that inconsistent data was received.
const uint8_t DATA_FAIL      = (1 << 6);
//< Oil container is low.
const uint8_t OIL_LOW         = (1 << 5);
//< Oil pressure is low.
const uint8_t OIL_PRESSURE    = (1 << 4);
//< Main power supply failed.
const uint8_t POWER_FAILURE   = (1 << 3);
//< We told the position to go to x and it didn't.
const uint8_t POSITION_FAULT  = (1 << 2);
//< Air compressor stopped.
const uint8_t AIR_PRESSURE    = (1 << 1);
//< Air filter has reached end of life.
const uint8_t CLEAN_FILTER    = (1 << 0);
/*!
 * Prints the state of the bits
 * (Substitutes for a real LCD panel)
 *
 * \param ledRegister Register containing the LED bits
 */
static void printLED(const uint8_t ledRegister)
{
    printf("Leds: ");
    if ((MASTER_FAIL & ledRegister) != 0)
        printf("MASTER_FAIL ");
    if ((DATA_FAIL & ledRegister) != 0)
        printf("DATA_FAIL ");
    if ((OIL_LOW & ledRegister) != 0)
        printf("OIL_LOW ");
    if ((OIL_PRESSURE & ledRegister) != 0)
        printf("OIL_PRESSURE ");
    if ((POWER_FAILURE & ledRegister) != 0)
        printf("POWER_FAILURE ");
    if ((POSITION_FAULT & ledRegister) != 0)
        printf("POSITION_FAULT ");
    if ((AIR_PRESSURE & ledRegister) != 0)
        printf("AIR_PRESSURE ");
    if ((CLEAN_FILTER & ledRegister) != 0)
        printf("CLEAN_FILTER ");
    printf("\n");
}

int main()
{
    uint8_t ledRegister = 0x00;        // Start with all off.

    printLED(ledRegister);

    // Power went out.
```

```
        ledRegister |= POWER_FAILURE | MASTER_FAIL;
        printLED(ledRegister);

        // Now the air went out.
        ledRegister |= AIR_PRESSURE;
        printLED(ledRegister);

        // Power back, air out, so master is on.
        ledRegister &= ~POWER_FAILURE;
        printLED(ledRegister);
        return (0);
}
```

Let's start by looking at the `printLED` function, which contains a bunch of lines that test each individual bit and print a message if it is set. (You'll learn about the `if` statements used to do this in Chapter 5.) To understand the logic of the test, take a look at the following statement:

```
if ((MASTER_FAIL & ledRegister) != 0)
    printf("MASTER_FAIL ");
```

The message will print if the expression on the first line is not equal to 0. Because the expression uses the AND operator, each bit in `ledRegister` must match the corresponding bit in `MASTER_FAIL` for that bit to have a value of 1. If at least one set of bits both have a value of 1, the `printf` is executed. In other words, behind the scenes, the operation looks something like this:

```
  1000 0000 (MASTER_FAIL)
& 1000 0001 (ledRegister with MASTER_FAIL and CLEAN_FILTER set)
  ---------
= 1000 0000 (Since this is not zero, print "MASTER FAIL")
```

The entire function will perform a similar test and print every bit that's set in the register. This function is used here because we don't have a hardware light panel and we want to see what's happening.

Later in the program, we play with the bits. For example, we simulate a power failure by turning on the `POWER_FAILURE` and `_MASTER_FAIL` bits. Thus, when we print the LEDs now, we get the following message:

```
Leds: MASTER_FAIL POWER_FAILURE
```

The rest of the program sets and clears the various bits to produce the following messages:

```
Leds:
Leds: MASTER_FAIL POWER_FAILURE
Leds: MASTER_FAIL POWER_FAILURE AIR_PRESSURE
Leds: MASTER_FAIL AIR_PRESSURE
```

Summary

This chapter covered what you can do with simple integers. There's the usual add, subtract, multiply, and divide, but you also saw how a computer stores the data and, most importantly, what happens when you run into problems like overflow.

You also learned about bit manipulation, where you treat an integer as a group of 8, 16, or 32 bits. This is very important because embedded programmers frequently deal with bitmapped registers. For example, the GPIO register we used to turn on and off our LED contains bits for 31 other GPIOs. The other 31 pins are entirely unrelated to our LED and have other functions (or they would have if we wired them to anything).

In the next chapter, you'll learn how to make decisions based on those computations.

Programming Problems

1. The largest `int16_t` value is 32,767. Write a program to find out what the `int16_t` value of 32,767 + 1 is.

2. There is a serial I/O register that contains a 2-bit value for the parity, as specified here:

    ```
    +----+----+----+----++----+----+----+----+
    | 7  | 6  | 5  | 4  || 3 .  2 | 1 .  0 |
    | IE | TE | RD | BR || Parity  | X Bits |
    +----+----+----+----++----+----+----+----+
    ```

    a. Write an expression to extract the parity-checking number (in the range 0 to 3) from the register. The parity is stored in bits 2 and 3 as a 2-bit unsigned binary number.

    b. Write code to set the value to 2 (binary 0x10).

5

DECISION AND CONTROL STATEMENTS

A computer is a powerful instrument because it can make decisions based on the data it receives. For example, a computer can turn on an LED if a button is being pressed and turn off the LED if it isn't. In this chapter we will see how C's various decision and control statements operate. Then we'll apply them to embedded programming by making our device respond to button presses.

The if Statement

We use the if statement to execute some code only if some condition is true. Here is the general form of this statement:

```
if (condition)
    statement;
```

To conditionally execute more than one statement, enclose the set of statements affected by the condition inside curly brackets ({}), as shown next. C will treat the set of statements as a single block:

```
if (condition) {
    statement;
    statement;
    statement;
    // ...
}
```

C considers anything nonzero as true and zero as false. Therefore, if the condition is nonzero, the statements will execute. If the condition is zero, they will not.

Table 5-1 lists the other comparison operators.

Table 5-1: The Comparison Operators

Operator	Description
==	Equals
<	Less than
<=	Less than or equal
!=	Not equals
>	Greater than
>=	Greater than or equal

For example, if you wanted some code to execute only if a variable had a value of 5, you could use the equals (==) operator, as follows:

```
if (aNumber == 5) {
    printf("The number is 5\n");
}
```

A word of warning: C allows assignment inside conditionals. For example, the following code, which assigns a variable a value of 7 within the if statement, is legal:

```
if (aNumber = 7) {
    printf("Something happened\n");
}
```

This is the equivalent of the following code, which tests whether the variable is equal to zero after the assignment:

```
aNumber = 7;        // Assignment
if (aNumber != 0) { // Test against zero
    printf("Something happened\n");
}
```

It is *not* the same as the following condition, which tests whether a variable is equal to 7:

```
if (aNumber == 7)
```

This problem was a nasty one in the early days of C when compiler technology was not what it is today. You'd make a mistake by accidentally writing something like the following code, only much more complicated:

```
aNumber = 5;
if (aNumber = 7) {  // Notice the missing '=' character.
    printf("Something happened\n");
}
```

The code within the if statement would be executed, as the variable would be reassigned a value of 7, which as a nonzero value would immediately make the condition true, even though you intended aNumber to be 5, not 7. With the modern GCC compiler, assignment in a condition generates a warning:

```
equal.c:14:5: warning: suggest parentheses around assignment used as truth value
[-Wparentheses]
 if (aNumber = 7) {
```

Here, GCC is telling you that if you want to suppress the warning because you really want to combine an assignment statement and an if statement, you should write the code as follows:

```
if ((aNumber = 7)) {    // Very very lousy programming
```

I've added the comment because I consider it poor programming practice to combine statements. Make one statement do one thing. For example, when you need to do an assignment and a test, do the assignment and then do the test.

The if/else Statement

We use the if/else statement when we want to make some statements execute if the condition is true and other statements execute when it is false. For example, consider the following:

```
if ((number % 2) == 0) {
    printf("Number is even\n");
} else {
    printf("Number is odd\n");
}
```

If the value of the number variable has a remainder of 0 when divided by 2, this code will print a message noting that the number is even; otherwise, it will print a message noting that the number is odd.

Now we come to another of C's darker little corners: you don't have to put curly brackets ({}) around a single statement after an if or an else. Consider the following code, deliberately indented incorrectly:

```
if (a == 1)
    if (b == 2)
        printf("Condition orange\n");
  else
    printf("Condition pink\n");
```

Which if does the else go with, the first if or the second if?

a. The first if: if (a == 1)

b. The second if: if (b == 2)

c. If you don't write code like this, you don't have to worry about such silly questions.

Let's use answer C and rewrite the code. Which if does the else go with in the following code?

```
if (a == 1) {
    if (b == 2) {
        printf("Condition orange\n");
    } else {
        printf("Condition pink\n");
    }
}
```

Here, you can tell it goes with the second if. That's the "official" answer to the previous question too, but by writing your code clearly, you can come up with the answer without having to go through the C language standard with a fine-tooth comb.

It should be noted that some style guides require that you always put the body of the if inside curly brackets; however, this is a decision best left up to the programmer.

Looping Statements

A *loop* is a programming feature that repeats some code as long as a condition is met. C has three looping statements: while, for, and do/while. We'll start with while, since it's the simplest, followed by for. We won't get into do/while because it's rarely used.

The while Loop

The general form of the while statement is as follows:

```
while (condition)
    statement;
```

Remember that *statement* can be a single C statement or a series of statements enclosed in {}. To see how a while loop can be useful, let's write a program that tests the numbers from 1 to 10 to see which ones are even and which ones are odd, as shown in Listing 5-1.

odd.c
```
/*
 * Test to see if the numbers 1 through 10 are even
 * or odd.
 *
#include <stdio.h>

int main()
{
    int aNumber;  // Number to test for oddness
    aNumber = 1;
    while (aNumber <= 10) {
        if ((aNumber % 2) == 1) {
            printf("%d is odd\n", aNumber);
        } else {
            printf("%d is even\n", aNumber);
        }
        ++aNumber;
    }
    return (0);
}
```

Listing 5-1: Testing for oddness

In the main function, we declare a variable, aNumber, to hold the value we'll test in our while loop. Then we set that variable to 1.

Next, we set the while loop to run as long as aNumber is less than or equal to 10. Inside the loop (that is, inside the brackets) we use the if/else statement introduced in the previous section of this chapter to check the remainder of dividing aNumber by 2. This lets us know whether it's even or odd.

Before we finish the loop, we add 1 to aNumber with ++aNumber;. Thus, the next time the loop runs, aNumber will have a value of 2, and so on. Eventually, when aNumber's value reaches 11, the loop ends and the program exits with the return value 0.

When this program runs, the output looks like this:

```
1 is odd
2 is even
3 is odd
4 is even
5 is odd
6 is even
7 is odd
8 is even
9 is odd
10 is even
```

The for Loop

Our while loop had three main components: an initialization statement (aNumber = 1), a test statement (checking whether aNumber is greater or equal to 10), and a statement to increment the variable after the loop was executed (++aNumber).

This design pattern (initialization, condition, and increment) is so common it has its own statement: the for statement. We write this statement as follows:

```
for (initialization; condition; increment)
```

To see how it works, let's convert our while loop into a for loop. The following code shows the same odd-or-even program using a for statement:

```
/*
 * Test to see if the numbers 1 through 10 are even
 * or odd.
 */
#include <stdio.h>

int main()
{
    int aNumber;  // Number to test for oddness
    for (aNumber = 1; aNumber <= 10; ++aNumber) {
        if ((aNumber % 2) == 1) {
            printf("%d is odd\n", aNumber);
        } else {
            printf("%d is even\n", aNumber);
        }
    }
    return (0);
}
```

Notice that the for clause includes our three statements, separated by semicolons.

Any one of the statements may be left out of the for loop. For example, we could have written our program by initializing aNumber before entering the loop:

```
aNumber = 1;
for (; aNumber <= 10; ++aNumber) {
```

Alternatively, we could increment the variable's value within the loop's body, rather than in the for clause:

```
for (aNumber = 1; aNumber <= 10;) {
    // Oddness test
    ++aNumber;
```

If the condition is left out, however, the loop will never terminate. This is why the following statement loops forever:

```
for (;;)
```

We use this "for-ever" loop in our embedded programs, because the programs should never exit.

Using the Button

Now that we know how to make decisions, we'll write a program that makes a decision based on the one input source our development board has by default: a blue button. Our program will make use of the one output we know how to control: the LED. Let's turn our development board into a tiny computerized lamp.

Start System Workbench for STM32 and begin a new embedded project. The *main.c* file should look like this:

```
/**
  ***********************************************************
  * @file     main.c
  * @author   Steve Oualline
  * @version  V1.0
  * @date     11-April-2018
  * @brief    Push the button -- flash the LED
  ***********************************************************
*/

#include "stm32f0xx.h"
#include "stm32f0xx_nucleo.h"

int main(void)
{
❶ GPIO_InitTypeDef GPIO_LedInit; // Init. for the LED
   GPIO_InitTypeDef GPIO_ButtonInit;  // Init. for push button
   GPIO_PinState result; // The result of reading the pin

   HAL_Init();

   // LED clock initialization
❷ LED2_GPIO_CLK_ENABLE();

   // Initialize LED.
❸ GPIO_LedInit.Pin = LED2_PIN;
   GPIO_LedInit.Mode = GPIO_MODE_OUTPUT_PP;
   GPIO_LedInit.Pull = GPIO_PULLUP;
   GPIO_LedInit.Speed = GPIO_SPEED_FREQ_HIGH;
   HAL_GPIO_Init(LED2_GPIO_PORT, &GPIO_LedInit);

   // Push button clock initialization
   USER_BUTTON_GPIO_CLK_ENABLE();
```

```
  /* Configure GPIO pin : For button */
  GPIO_ButtonInit.Pin = USER_BUTTON_PIN;
  GPIO_ButtonInit.Mode = GPIO_MODE_INPUT;
❹ GPIO_ButtonInit.Pull = GPIO_PULLDOWN;
  GPIO_ButtonInit.Speed = GPIO_SPEED_FREQ_HIGH;
  HAL_GPIO_Init(USER_BUTTON_GPIO_PORT, &GPIO_ButtonInit);

  for(;;) {
      // Get the current state of the push button
      result = HAL_GPIO_ReadPin(USER_BUTTON_GPIO_PORT,
                                USER_BUTTON_PIN);
      if (result == GPIO_PIN_SET)
          HAL_GPIO_WritePin(LED2_GPIO_PORT,
                            LED2_PIN, GPIO_PIN_SET);
      else
          HAL_GPIO_WritePin(LED2_GPIO_PORT,
                            LED2_PIN,GPIO_PIN_RESET);
  }
}
```

Let's go over this code in detail.

Initialization

To begin our program, we'll make use of a lot of code that is defined by the hardware abstraction layer (HAL). In the next few chapters, you'll learn about every one of these pieces.

First, we define a new variable named GPIO_LedInit of type GPIO_InitTypeDef ❶. The GPIO_InitTypeDef type is not a standard C type: it's defined by the HAL include files brought in at the top of the program. At this point, the details of this type don't matter. We need the variable to define how the LED pin is going to be configured. (You'll learn about defining variable types in later chapters.)

Similarly, we define another variable, GPIO_ButtonInit, to define how the button GPIO pin is going to be configured, and a variable to hold the state of the button pin (GPIO_PinState).

Inside the main procedure, the first thing we do is call HAL_Init to set up the hardware, as we did in the blink program from Chapter 3. You need to call HAL_Init at the top of every STM32 program.

Next, we turn on the clock for LED2 (the user LED) ❷. The *clock* controls how the data we write to the GPIO pin gets to the actual pin. Without this line, writing to the LED doesn't work. Although it looks like a procedure call to a function named LED2_GPIO_CLK_ENABLE, it's actually a preprocessor macro, which we will study later.

Now we come to the part where we assign values to the GPIO_LedInit variable ❸, which is a structure type that has a bunch of pieces we need to assign individually. Later, you will learn the details of what's going on here.

Similar code initializes the pin used for the button, except that the pin mode is set to GPIO_MODE_INPUT because we'll be reading the pin to get the state of the button, not writing it.

Choosing a Pulldown Circuit

Notice that we set the `Pull` field to `GPIO_PULLDOWN` ❹, not `GPIO_PULLUP`.

The `Pull` field tells the CPU what type of pullup/pulldown circuity to use. An input pin can have one of three states: floating, pullup, and pulldown. Figure 5-1 shows the circuit for a *floating* input.

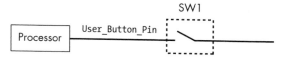

Figure 5-1: A floating circuit

When the switch SW1 is open, no voltage is applied to the `User_Button_Pin`. As such, it could be high (about 3 volts or more) or low (less than about 3 volts) or somewhere in between. It could be set by whatever stray electrical noise is floating around near it. The key here is that there is no way to know the value of this signal unless it's actually shorted to ground or power.

Now let's take a look at an input with a *pullup* circuit (see Figure 5-2).

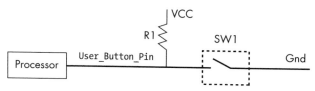

Figure 5-2: A pullup circuit

When SW1 is open, voltage flows though the resistor R1, raising (or *pulling up*) the `User_Button_Pin` to VCC, or a positive level. When SW1 is closed, the pin is shorted to ground (Gnd). R1 is a very big resistor, so the current flowing through it is negligible and the voltage on the pin goes to zero.

A *pulldown* circuit is similar, except R1 is connected to ground, and SW1 to VCC, so the `User_Button_Pin` goes to ground (that is, it's pulled down to zero) if SW1 is open (see Figure 5-3).

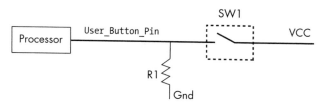

Figure 5-3: A pulldown circuit

On the STM32 chip, circuits are cheap and pins are expensive. Therefore, the chip's creators wanted to get as much out of each pin as possible. For every GPIO pin, there is a pullup resistor, a pulldown resistor, and the transistors to connect these resistors, depending on how the pin may be configured. This makes things easy, as we don't have to put these resistors on the board ourselves. It also makes things difficult, however, because we have to program them. Figure 5-4 shows the internal wiring of a single GPIO pin on the STM32. (Even this is a simplified version.) The key thing to note is that there are pullup (R_{PU}) and pulldown (R_{PD}) internal resistors that can be turned on and off.

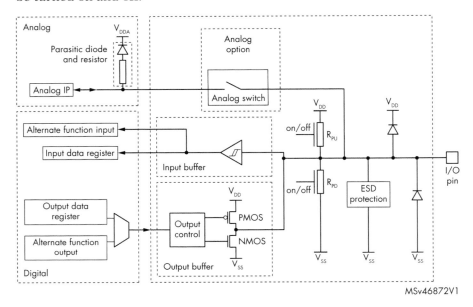

MSv46872V1

Figure 5-4: STM32 internal wiring for a GPIO pin

We chose to use a pulldown circuit because the other side of the button is connected to +5 V, so when the button is not pressed and the switch is open, our pulldown resistor kicks in and the GPIO pin has a value of 0. When the button is pressed, the 5 V coming from the button cause the GPIO pin to have a value of 1. (A little current will also flow through the resistor, but that amount of current is negligible.)

Getting the State of the Button

Next, we reach our main loop. The for statement loops forever, or until we reset the machine. Inside the loop, the first statement initializes a variable called result of type GPIO_PinState (a nonstandard type defined by the HAL include files) with the result of a call to the function HAL_GPIO_ReadPin. HAL_GPIO_ReadPin reads the GPIO pin connected to the button. More specifically, it reads the 32-bit GPIO port USER_BUTTON_GPIO_PORT and then tests the value of the USER_BUTTON_PIN. (A lot of the bit manipulation we covered in the previous chapter goes on inside the HAL_GPIO_ReadPin function.)

Now we test to see if the pin is set by comparing result to the symbol GPIO_PIN_SET (a constant defined by the HAL code), and then we turn on the LED pin if the button pin is set. Otherwise, we turn off the LED pin. (The code to do this was covered in Chapter 3.)

Running the Program

When we run the program, the LED turns on. Press the user button and the LED turns off. Release the button and the LED will come back on, and so on. Although a simple operation, it took a lot of learning to get us here.

Unfortunately, we've made a very complex flashlight with a button that turns the light off instead of on. The good news is that it's computer-controlled, so we can fix it in software. I'm going to leave that for you to figure out.

Loop Control

Our programming example made basic use of looping statements, but C gives you several ways of adding extra control to your loops. The two major statements that modify the loop control are break and continue.

The break Statement

The break statement allows you to exit a loop early (that is, break out of the loop). For example, consider the following short program, which looks through an array for a key number. If the number is there, the program prints it:

```
/*
 * Find the key number in an array.
 */
#include <stdio.h>
#include <stdbool.h>

#define ARRAY_SIZE  7    // Size of the array to search

int main()
{
    // Array to search
    int array[ARRAY_SIZE] = {4, 5, 23, 56, 79, 0, -5};
    static const int KEY = 56; // Key to search for

    for (unsigned int index = 0; index < ARRAY_SIZE; ++index) {
        if (array[index] == KEY) {
            printf("Key (%d) found at index %d\n",
                KEY, index);
          ❶ break;
        }
    }
    return (0);
}
```

This program searches an array for a key value. Once we find the key value, we're done. We don't want to go through the entire rest of the loop, so to exit, we use the break statement ❶.

The continue Statement

The other loop control statement, continue, starts execution at the top of the loop. The following program prints a list of commands, skipping those that start with a dot. When we encounter one of these, we jump to the top of the loop with the continue command:

```
/*
 * Find the key number in an array.
 */
#include <stdio.h>

#define COMMAND_COUNT 5 // Number of commands

// Commands, ones beginning with . are secret
static const char commands[COMMAND_COUNT][4] = {
    "help",
    "exec",
    ".adm",
    "quit"
};
int main()
{
    // Print the help text
    for (unsigned int index = 0;
         index < COMMAND_COUNT;
         ++index) {
    ❶ if (commands[index][0] == '.') {
            // Hidden command
          ❷ continue;
        }
        printf("%s\n", commands[index]);
    }
    return (0);
}
```

The key to this program is the test to see if we have a dot command ❶ and then continue ❷ to start over (thus skipping the rest of the loop and the printf).

Anti-patterns

While you're learning how to use loops, you should also learn how *not* to use loops. Several programming patterns have crept into the programming industry that do more to confuse things than promote good programming, which is why they're called *anti-patterns*. I'm going to warn you about two.

The Empty while Loop

The first anti-pattern is the empty while loop. Consider the following code:

```
while (GPIO_PIN_SET == HAL_GPIO_ReadPin(USER_BUTTON_GPIO_PORT, USER_BUTTON_PIN));
{
    // ... do something
}
```

You probably gather that this code repeats some action as long as the user button is pressed. But it doesn't. The reason it doesn't is that the while loop affects a single statement only. You might assume that the statement within the while loop is the one enclosed in curly brackets, but there is a statement before the brackets too. It's a very short statement and very easy to miss, because it's an empty statement. We can tell it's there because there is a semicolon after the statement:

```
while (GPIO_PIN_SET == HAL_GPIO_ReadPin(USER_BUTTON_GPIO_PORT, USER_BUTTON_PIN));
{
    // ... do something
}
```

The semicolon is easy to overlook. That's why I had to set it in boldface. It's also why this type of coding is considered bad. Very bad.

The continue statement comes to our rescue. We can rewrite this while loop as follows:

```
while (GPIO_PIN_SET == HAL_GPIO_ReadPin(BTN_PORT, BTN_PIN))
    continue;
{
    // ... do something
}
```

Now we can see that the while loop controls the continue statement and nothing else. The indentation and the big obvious statement tell us that.

Assignment in while

The second anti-pattern is assignment in the while loop:

```
while ((result = ReadPin(BTN_PORT, BTN_PIN)) == GPIO_PIN_SET) {
    // ... statements
}
```

This statement does two things at once. First, it calls ReadPin and assigns the result to result. Second, it tests result to see if it is set.

Programs are much easier to understand and maintain if they do small, simple things one at a time. This shortcut saves typing a couple of newlines at the cost of program clarity. It could just as easily have been written like this:

```
while (1) {
    result = ReadPin(BTN_PORT, BUTTON_PIN);
    if (result != GPIO_PIN_SET)
        break;
    // ... statements
}
```

Our goal should be to make our programs as simple and easy to read as possible, not as compact and clever as possible.

Summary

We now have two key aspects of computing under our belt: numbers and how to make decisions based on those numbers. Single decisions can be made with the if statement, while the while and for statements let us make repeating decisions. The break and continue keywords give us more control over those decisions.

Decision statements gave us the ability to write a small program that flashes the LED at the touch of a button. Although the program is simple, we took input, processed it, and produced output, which is the basis for a huge number of embedded programs. In the next few chapters, you'll learn how to deal with more complex data and more complex ways of processing it, all of which builds on the basics you learned here.

Programming Problems

1. Write a program to produce a multiplication table for the numbers from 0×0 to 9×9.

2. Write a program to count the number of bits that are set in a uint32_t integer. For example, the number 0x0000A0 has two bits set in it.

3. Write a program that flashes a pattern on the LED. Use one array of integers to control the delay for LED on and LED off. Repeat the pattern.

4. Write a program that blinks the letter "H" in Morse code using the LED. When the button is pressed, it blinks "E." If you keep pressing the button, you'll get all of "HELLO WORLD" in Morse code.

5. Write a program to compute the first 10 primes.

6. Write a program to find the largest and smallest elements in a set.

7. Create a program that goes through a string and prints only the vowels.

6

ARRAYS, POINTERS, AND STRINGS

So far, we've used very simple integers to represent data. But let's face it, not everything in the world can be described as a single integer. In this chapter you'll learn some of the basics of organizing your data.

First, you'll learn about *arrays*, which are data structures that hold multiple items you can select using an integer index. I'll also go a little beyond simple arrays to show you how the compiler implements arrays and how arrays implement strings of characters like "Hello World!\n". Along the way, you'll learn to work with C's char type.

You'll learn how to use memory *pointers*, which hold the address of a memory location, and then see how arrays and pointers are both similar and different.

You'll also learn how to use the const modifier to create a variable that cannot be modified, better known as a *constant*. Constants help you organize your data by preventing unintentional changes to it.

Arrays

You've already seen how to declare a basic variable, like this:

```
int aNumber;        // A number
```

This variable can hold only one value at a time. Yet we can also declare a variable that holds a set of values using an *array declaration*, which places the number of items to include in the array in brackets:

```
int anArray[5];     // An array of numbers
```

This code declares an array of five integers numbered 0, 1, 2, 3, and 4. The element numbers are called *indices*, and the first index is 0, not 1. To access individual elements of the array, we use square brackets containing an index. For example, the following line assigns a value of 99 to the fourth item in the array (the one at index 3):

```
anArray[3] = 99;    // Store an element in the array.

if (anArray[3] == 98) {
```

There is nothing in the C language that prevents you from indexing a nonexistent array element, but although it is possible to use an illegal index, the results are not defined (meaning something bad will probably happen). For example, the last element of anArray is 4, so the following declaration is legal:

```
anArray[4] = 0;     // Legal
```

However, this one isn't:

```
anArray[5] = 9;     // Illegal, 5 is too big
```

This statement tries to access an element that isn't in the array.

Let's see how arrays work in action. Take a look at Listing 6-1, which is a program that sums the elements of an array and outputs the total.

```
/*
 * Sum up a series of numbers.
 */
#include <stdio.h>

int main()
{
    const int NUMBER_ELEMENTS = 5;      // Number of elements
    int numbers[NUMBER_ELEMENTS];       // The numbers
    int sum;                            // The sum so far
    int current;                        // The current number we are adding

    numbers[0] = 5;
    numbers[1] = 8;
```

```
    numbers[2] = 9;
    numbers[3] = -5;
    numbers[4] = 22;

    sum = 0;
    // Loop over each element and add them up.
    for (current = 0; current < NUMBER_ELEMENTS; ++current)
    {
        sum += numbers[current];
    }
    printf("Total is %d\n", sum);
    return (0);
}
```

Listing 6-1: Basic array usage

We start by defining a variable, NUMBER_ELEMENTS, to hold the number of elements we have in the array. The keyword const tells C that this variable is not to be changed (more on this later).

We use this constant two places. The first declares the array. The second loops through each element of the array. While we could have instead used the value 5 in both of these places, doing so would have introduced a *magic number* into our code. A *magic number* is a number that appears in the program in multiple places but whose connection to the code is unclear. Using a magic number is risky; in this case, if we changed the 5 in the array declaration, we would have to remember to also change the 5 in the loop. By using the constant declaration, we define the size of the array in only one place. If we change the constant to 14, we take care of every place it is used automatically.

Back to the code. We need to put some numbers in our array, so we do so by assigning a value to each of its indices. Next, we use a for loop to access each element of the array. The for loop statement illustrates a common C programming phrase for looping through an array. The loop starts at zero and continues as long as the index is *less than* (<) the size of the array. The index must be less than 5, because number[5] is a nonexistent element.

Arrays can be initialized at the time of declaration, just like simple variables, by listing all of the elements inside curly brackets:

```
// Define some numbers to sum.
int numbers[5] = {5 8, 9, -5, 22};
```

In this case, the number of elements must match the size of the array or you'll get a warning message.

C is a smart language. It can deduce the size of the array from the number of elements, so this declaration also works:

```
// Define some numbers to sum.
int numbers[] = {5 8, 9, -5, 22};
```

Under the Hood: Pointers

My father, C. M. Oualline, famously taught me, "There are things and there are pointers to things." See Figure 6-1 for a detailed diagram of what this means. Although it looks simple, understanding this diagram is extremely important.

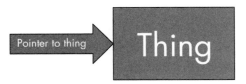

Figure 6-1: Things and pointers to things

An integer is a thing. In fact, it is a thing that has an integer in it. A pointer is an address of a thing.

Things come in different sizes. A uint64_t integer is a relatively big thing, while a uint8_t is a small thing. The key here is that things come in different sizes. A pointer is a fixed size. The thing it points to can be big or small, but the pointer is always the same size.

Pointers are useful for quickly accessing data structures and linking data structures together. In embedded programming, pointers are used to point to memory-mapped I/O devices, which gives the program control of the devices.

The big advantage of pointers is that they can point to anything. The biggest disadvantage is that they can point to things they shouldn't. When that happens, programs start to do strange and unexpected things, so use pointers very carefully.

To declare a pointer, use an asterisk (*) in the declaration to indicate that the variable is a pointer and not a thing:

```
uint8_t* thingPtr;      // A pointer to an integer
```

The *address of* (&) operator changes a thing into a pointer to a thing:

```
uint8_t thing = 5;      // A thing
thingPtr = &thing;      // thingPtr points to 5.
```

Now thingPtr points to thing. The *dereference* (*) operator turns a pointer back into a thing:

```
otherThing = *thingPtr; // Get what's pointed to by thingPtr.
```

This assigns otherThing to the value *pointed to* by thingPtr.

The following program shows how these operations work. In this program, we introduce a new printf conversion, %p, which prints pointers:

```
/*
 * Demonstrate pointers.
 */
#include <stdio.h>
#include <stdint.h>

int main()
{
    uint8_t smallThing = 5;     // Something small
    uint8_t smallThing2 = 6;    // Something else small
    uint64_t largeThing = 987654321; // Something large

    uint8_t* smallPtr;          // Pointer to small thing
    uint64_t* largePtr;         // Pointer to large thing

❶ printf("smallThing %d\n", smallThing);
    printf("sizeof(smallThing) %lu\n", sizeof(smallThing));
    printf("largeThing %ld\n", largeThing);
    printf("sizeof(largeThing) %lu\n", sizeof(largeThing));

    // smallPtr points to smallThing.
    smallPtr = &smallThing;

❷ printf("smallPtr %p\n", smallPtr);
    printf("sizeof(smallPtr) %lu\n", sizeof(smallPtr));
    printf("*smallPtr %d\n", *smallPtr);

    // smallPtr points to smallThing2.
    smallPtr = &smallThing2;
    printf("*smallPtr %d\n", *smallPtr);

    largePtr = &largeThing;
    printf("largePtr %p\n", largePtr);
    printf("sizeof(largePtr) %lu\n", sizeof(largePtr));
    printf("*largePtr %ld\n", *largePtr);

    return (0);
}
```

Let's go through this in detail. We start by declaring three things and two pointers. We use the suffix Ptr when naming all pointers to make them very obvious. At this point, smallPtr does not point to any particular thing.

Before we use the pointer, let's use our smallThing. Using two calls to printf, we print the value and the size of smallThing ❶. This will output the following:

```
smallThing 5
sizeof(smallThing) 1
```

Now let's take a look at the pointer ❷. First, we print the value of the pointer, which is a memory address. We are on an x86-type machine with 64-bit pointers, so the value of the pointer is a 64-bit number. The actual number value comes from the way that memory is laid out, which we will discuss in detail in Chapter 11. When we print sizeof(smallPtr), we see that it is indeed 8 bytes or 64 bits long, and the value *pointed to* by smallPtr is 5. All in all, these three calls to printf will print the following:

```
smallPtr 0x7fffc3935dee
sizeof(smallPtr) 8
*smallPtr 5
```

We do something similar with largePtr. Notice that while the size of the thing being pointed to is different, the size of the pointer remains the same. The size of the pointer depends on the processor type, not the type of data being pointed to. On our STM32 processor, we have 32-bit addresses, so the pointer will be a 32-bit value. On an x64 machine with 64-bit addresses, the size of a pointer is 4 bytes:

```
largeThing 987654321
sizeof(largeThing) 8

largePtr 0x7fffc3935df0
sizeof(largePtr) 8
*largePtr 987654321
```

To see what the pointers are actually pointing to, enter this program into the STM32 Workbench and run it using the debugger. Put a breakpoint just after everything has been assigned and run the program up to the breakpoint.

Opening the Variables panel shows us all the variables and their values (see Figure 6-2).

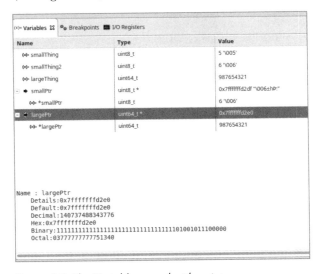

Figure 6-2: The Variables panel with pointers

Usually, the value of the pointer is not that interesting. What's more interesting is what it points to. Clicking the + icon expands the smallPtr entry, and we can see that smallPtr points to 6 (also known as the character '\006'). Similarly, we can see that largePtr points to 987654321.

Array and Pointer Arithmetic

C treats array variables and pointers very much alike. Consider the following code:

```
int array[5] = {1,2,3,4,5};
int* arrayPtr = array;
```

We've assigned arrayPtr the value of array, not &array, because C will automatically turn an array into a pointer when it's used like a pointer. In fact, arrays and pointers are almost interchangeable, except that they are declared differently.

Now let's access an element of the array:

```
int i = array[1];
```

This syntax is the same as the following, which says to take the value of arrayPtr, add 1 to it (scaled by the size of the data being pointed to), and return the data pointed to by the result of this expression:

```
int i = *(arrayPtr+1);
```

The following program demonstrates the relationship between arrays and pointers in more detail:

```
/*
 * Demonstrate the relationship between arrays and pointers.
 */
#include <stdio.h>
int main()
{
    int array[] = {1,2,3,4,-1}; // Array
    int* arrayPtr = array;       // Pointer to array

    // Print array using array.
    for (int index = 0; array[index] >= 0; ++index) {
        printf("Address %p Value %d\n",
                &array[index], array[index]);
    }
    printf("--------------\n");
    // Same thing with a pointer
    for (int index = 0; *(arrayPtr +index) >= 0; ++index) {
        printf("Address %p Value %d\n",
                arrayPtr + index, *(arrayPtr + index));
    }
    printf("--------------\n");
    // Same thing using an incrementing pointer
    for (int* current = array; *current >= 0; ++current) {
```

```
        printf("Address %p Value %d\n", current, *current);
    }

}
```

The first thing this program does is print the address and contents of each array element in the conventional manner: by using a for loop to access each index in turn.

In the next loop, we print using pointer arithmetic. Now, we need to understand exactly what we are dealing with. The variable array is an array. The expression array[index] is an integer, and the & (address of) operator changes an integer into a pointer, so &array[index] is a pointer. As a result, this code prints the following memory addresses for each element in the array:

```
Address 0x7fffa22e0610 Value 1
Address 0x7fffa22e0614 Value 2
Address 0x7fffa22e0618 Value 3
Address 0x7fffa22e061c Value 4
```

The pointer value increases by 4, the size of an integer, each time, so array[0] is at address 0x7fffa22e0610, and array[1] is at a memory location 4 bytes larger, at 0x7fffa22e0614.

This method uses pointer arithmetic. (We actually used pointer arithmetic in the first method too, but C hid it all behind our back.) With this loop, you can see that arrayPtr + 1 is 0x7fffa22e0614, which is exactly the same as &array[1]. Again, notice that with pointer arithmetic, things are automatically scaled by the size of the item being pointed to. In this case, the type of the data being pointed to is int, so the expression arrayPtr + 1 is actually arrayPtr + 1 * sizeof(int), and thus 0x7fffa22e0610 + 1 is really 0x7fffa22e0610 + 1 * sizeof(int), which is 0x7fffa22e0614.

Finally, we do the same thing a third way using an incrementing pointer.

Using pointers to access arrays is common, because many people think doing so is more efficient than using an array index. After all, computing array[index] involves an address calculation, but compiler technology has improved over the years. Today's compilers are very good at generating more efficient code, so using pointers for array indexing is not actually more efficient.

Using address logic is, however, more confusing. It's not clear what's being pointed to and what the limits of the array are, so the second two methods should be avoided. I've included them in the example because there's a lot of legacy code out there that uses pointer arithmetic to access arrays, and to show you what not to do.

Array Overflow

C does not do *bounds checking*, meaning it does not check whether you're trying to access elements outside the bounds of an array. The legal elements of a five-element array (int a[5]) are a[0], a[1], a[2], a[3], a[4], but there's nothing to prevent you from using illegal values such as a[5], a[6], a[7], or even a[932343]. The trouble with the illegal values is that they are the locations of some other variables or data in memory. The program in Listing 6-2 demonstrates what happens when you go beyond the end of array (called *array overflow*).

array.bad.c

```
/*
 * Demonstrate what happens
 * when you overflow an array.
 */
#include <stdio.h>

int main()
{
    int numbers1[5] = {11,12,13,14,15};    // Some numbers
    int numbers2[5] = {21,22,23,24,25};    // Variable to be overwritten

  ❶ printf("numbers2[0] %d\n", numbers2[0]);

  ❷ numbers1[8] = 99;    // <------------ Illegal

    // Illegal -- loops past the end
    for (int i = 0; i < 9; ++i)
        printf("numbers1[%d] %p\n", i, &numbers1[i]);

    printf("numbers2[%d] %p\n", 0, &numbers2[0]);
  ❸ printf("numbers2[0] %d\n", numbers2[0]);
    return (0);
}
```

Listing 6-2: Array overflow

The key item to watch is numbers2[0], which we set to 21 when we initialize it. When we print it the first time, at ❶, its value is, in fact, 21. However, when we print it later, at ❸, it is 99. What happened?

Let's look at the output of this program:

```
numbers2[0] 21
numbers1[0] 0x7ffc5e94ff00
numbers1[1] 0x7ffc5e94ff04
numbers1[2] 0x7ffc5e94ff08
numbers1[3] 0x7ffc5e94ff0c
numbers1[4] 0x7ffc5e94ff10
numbers1[5] 0x7ffc5e94ff14
numbers1[6] 0x7ffc5e94ff18
numbers1[7] 0x7ffc5e94ff1c
numbers1[8] 0x7ffc5e94ff20
numbers2[0] 0x7ffc5e94ff20
numbers2[0] 99
```

From this, we see that `numbers1` is allocated the memory from `0x7ffc5e94ff00` to `0x7ffc5e94ff13`. The variable `numbers2` is allocated `0x7ffc5e94ff20` to `0x7ffc5e94ff33`. This memory layout is visually expressed in Table 6-1.

Table 6-1: Memory Layout

Variable	Address	Contents
numbers1	0x7ffc5e94ff00	11
	0x7ffc5e94ff04	12
	0x7ffc5e94ff08	13
	0x7ffc5e94ff0c	14
	0x7ffc5e94ff10	15
numbers2	0x7ffc5e94ff20	21
	0x7ffc5e94ff24	22
	0x7ffc5e94ff28	23
	0x7ffc5e94ff2c	24
	0x7ffc5e94ff30	25

The statement at ❷ in Listing 6-2 uses an illegal index, since `numbers1` has only five elements. So, what memory does this overwrite? From the output of our program, we see that the address of this value is `0x7ffc5e94ff20`. By a strange coincidence, this is also the address of `numbers2[0]`. Our sample program makes the memory corruption immediately apparent when it prints the content of `numbers2[0]` the second time.

This program is a simple illustration of what can go wrong when an array overflows. In real life, identifying such problems is much harder. Usually, these errors show up as weird program behavior that occurs long after the index error, so debugging them is complicated. Avoid making this type of mistake.

The most common error novice C programmers make is to forget that C arrays start at 0 and go to *size*-1. For example, you might write the following:

```
int array[5];
// Wrong
for (int i = 1; i <= 5; ++i)
    array[i] = 0;
```

If you program on Linux machines, tools such as Valgrind and the GCC address sanitizer will do a runtime check for array overflows. In the embedded world, we have no such tools, so we just have to be careful.

Characters and Strings

We've discussed working with numbers, but you might sometimes want to include other kinds of data, like text, in your programs. For this, we turn to a new variable type, char, which holds a single character enclosed in single quotes ('). For example, the following creates a char variable called stop to hold the character 'S':

```
char stop = 'S'; // Character to indicate stop
```

A *string* is an array of characters that ends with an end-of-string (\0) character. The character \0 is known as the NUL character (with one *L*) as well. That's because, during original serial communications, it signified nothing.

To practice using strings, let's now take a look at the following program, which prints the string "Hello World":

```
/*
 * Hello World using string variable
 */
#include <stdio.h>

// The characters to print
const char hello[] = {'H', 'e', 'l', 'l', 'o', ' ',
                      'W', 'o', 'r', 'l', 'd', '\0'};

int main()
{
    puts(hello); // Write string and newline
    return (0);
}
```

We first define a string called hello with the value "Hello World". This initialization explicitly defines every element of the string. You hardly ever see initializations like this in real life because C provides a shortcut that makes things a lot easier. (We'll see that shortly.) This version makes everything obvious, which is good for learning but not for brevity.

Later, we print the string using the standard C function puts. The puts function prints a single string and is simple, whereas printf can do formatting and is a large, complex function. The puts function also adds a newline, so we didn't put one in our original string.

C has a shorthand for initializing strings, allowing us to write the same declaration like this:

```
const char hello[] = "Hello World";    // The characters to print
```

Both statements create an array of 12 characters and initialize it. ("Hello World" contains 11 characters, and the 12th is the end-of-string character '\0', which is automatically supplied when you use the shorthand.)

Because arrays and pointers are very similar, you can also declare the string as a pointer:

```
const char* const hello = "Hello World";    // The characters to print
```

You'll notice that we now have two const keywords. Things are getting a little tricky here. The first const affects the pointer; the second affects the data being pointed to. The following program illustrates how these work:

```
/**
 * @brief Program to demonstrate the use of const
 * with pointers
 */

char theData[5] = "1234";              // Some data to play with

      char*       allChange;           // Pointer and value can change
const char*       dataConst = "abc"    // Char const, pointer not
      char* const ptrConst = theData;  // Char var, ptr not
const char* const allConst = "abc";    // Nobody change nothing

int main()
{
    char otherData[5] = "abcd";    // Some other data

    allChange = otherData;         // Change pointer
    *allChange = 'x';              // Change data

    dataConst = otherData;         // Change pointer
    // *dataConst = 'x';           // Illegal to change data

    // ptrConst = otherData;       // Illegal to change pointer
    *ptrConst = 'x';              // Change data

    // allConst = otherData;       // Illegal to change pointer
    // *allConst = 'x';            // Illegal to change data
    return (0);
}
```

This program shows every possible way const can be used to define a character pointer. We then try to modify the pointer and the data being pointed to. Depending on where we put const modifiers, some of these statements will fail and some will work.

Summary

We started this book by dealing with variables that could hold single values. Arrays let us deal with a set of data. This gives us much more power when it comes to organization.

Strings are a special type of array. They hold characters and have an end-of-string marker to signal their end.

Pointers and arrays are similar in that both can be used to access a section of memory. Arrays are restricted by their size (although they can overflow), while pointers are not. C does not restrict the use of pointers, and that gives the language a lot of power. This power can be used for good, such as when dealing with memory-mapped I/O, or bad, such as when accidentally destroying random memory.

As we are seeing, C gives programmers the power to fully use their machines. But this power comes at a cost. C does not prevent you from doing something stupid. C gives you tools like arrays and pointers to organize your data. It's up to you to do it wisely.

Programming Problems

1. Write a program to find the lowest and highest numbered elements in an array of integers.

2. Write a program to scan an array for duplicate numbers. The duplicated numbers will be in consecutive elements.

3. Write a program to scan an array for duplicate numbers that may occur anywhere in the array.

4. Create a program that prints only the odd numbers of an array.

5. Write a program that goes through a string and makes the first letter of each word uppercase. You'll need to look up the standard C functions `isalpha` and `toupper`.

7

LOCAL VARIABLES AND PROCEDURES

So far, we've been using a design pattern called "one big mess." All code is dumped into main, and all variables are defined at the beginning of the program. This method works fine when your program is 100 or fewer lines long, but when you're dealing with a 500,000-line program, you're going to need some organization. This chapter discusses ways of limiting the scope of variables and instructions so you can make long, unmanageable blocks of code easier to understand, manage, and maintain.

For example, you can use a *global variable* anywhere in a program. To know where and how it's used in a 500,000-line program, however, you have to scan all 500,000 lines. A *local variable* has limited scope. To understand where and how a local variable is used, all you need to do is examine the, say, 50 to 200 lines of code where it is valid.

As your programs get longer and longer, you'll learn how to divide the code into easily understood sections called *procedures*. Global variables will be available to every procedure, but you can define local variables that are available only to a single procedure. You'll also learn how local variables are organized internally into stack frames. Given the limited amount of memory on our STM microcontroller, it's very important to understand how much stack memory we are using.

Finally, you'll learn about *recursion*, which is where a procedure refers to itself. Recursion is complex in what it can do but simple if you understand the rules and follow them.

NOTE *Nothing in C's syntax prevents evil programmers from writing 30,000-line procedures or creating local variables whose scope is just as large. However, I'm assuming you're sane and want to code in a manner that decreases confusion instead of increasing it.*

Local Variables

Up to this point, we've been using only global variables that are available everywhere in the program, from the line they are declared to the end of the program. Local variables are available to a much smaller, or local, area of a program. This area where a variable is valid is called its *scope*. Listing 7-1 demonstrates the declaration of local variables.

```
local.c    /*
            * Useless program to demonstrate local variables
            */
           #include <stdio.h>

           int global = 5;     // A global variable

           int main()
           {
               int localToProcedure = 3;
               // ... do something
               {
                 ❶ int local = 6; // A local variable

                   {
                       int veryLocal = 7;  // An even more local variable
                       // ... do something
                 ❷ }
                   // veryLocal is no longer valid.
               ❸ }
               // local is no longer valid.
               return (0);
           }
```

Listing 7-1: Local variables

The scope of a local variable starts where it is declared and goes to the end of the enclosing curly brackets ({}). The variable localToProcedure is valid for the entire main function.

Now let's look at smaller scopes, starting with the declaration of the local variable ❶. The scope of this variable doesn't end at the very next closing curly bracket ❷, which is for a different block (section of code enclosed in curly brackets). Instead, it goes to the end bracket ❸ for the block that started right before local was declared. The veryLocal variable has an even smaller scope. It starts with the declaration int veryLocal = 7; and ends when the block ends ❷.

When a variable's scope ends, the program can't use the variable anymore. For example, trying to return the value of veryLocal at the end of main using the return(veryLocal); statement wouldn't work.

Hidden Variables

In the previous example, all the local variables had different names in addition to having different scope. However, variables can also have the same name in different scopes. If multiple variables have the same name, C will use the value of the one in the current scope and hide the others. (Please don't do this because it makes code confusing. It's mentioned here so you know what to avoid.)

Let's take a look at Listing 7-2, which demonstrates a very badly written program.

hidden.c
```
/*
 * Useless program to demonstrate hidden variables
 */
#include <stdio.h>

❶ int var = 7;              // A variable

int main()
{
    // ... do something
    {
      ❷ int var = 13;    // Hides var = 7

        {
          ❸ int var = 16;      // Hides var = 7, var = 13

            // ... do something
        }
        // ... do something
    }
    // ... do something
    return (0);
}
```

Listing 7-2: Hidden variables

In this program, we define three variables, all named var. When the second one is defined ❷, it hides the first one ❶. Similarly, the int var = 16; declaration hides the second variable var ❷, which hides the first one ❶.

Suppose we were to add the following statement after the third declaration:

```
var = 42;
```

Which var are we assigning? The one declared at ❶, ❷, or ❸? The fact that we have to ask this question is a good indicator that this code is confusing. I'm not going to leave it as an exercise for the reader to find the answer because the proper solution is to never do this in the first place.

Procedures

A *procedure* is a way to define code so it can be used again. Let's look at Listing 7-3, which provides a simple example.

hello3.c
```
/**
 * Print hello, hello, hello, world.
 */
#include <stdio.h>

/**
 * Tell the world hello.
 */
❶ void sayHello(void)
{
  ❷ puts("Hello");
}

int main()
{
  ❸ sayHello();
    sayHello();
    sayHello();
    puts("World!");
    return (0);
}
```

Listing 7-3: A procedure demonstration

This program prints Hello three times, then World!. The procedure starts with a comment block, which isn't strictly necessary, but if you're going to write quality code, you should put one in before each procedure. The beginning (/**) of the comment block indicates that the Doxygen documentation tool should process it. To be compatible with the format of the STM libraries, we are using the same commenting convention.

The statement void sayHello(void) ❶ tells C that our procedure's name is sayHello. It returns nothing (first void) and takes no parameters (second void). The {} block that follows this statement defines the body of the procedure and contains all the instructions executed by the procedure ❷. The three sayHello(); lines ❸ are calls to the sayHello procedure. They tell the processor to save the location of the next statement (either another call to sayHello or the call to puts) and then start execution with the first line of sayHello. When the procedure finishes (or hits a return statement), execution continues at the point saved during the call.

Stack Frames

Procedures have their own local variables. The compiler's job is to organize memory so it can hold those variables. For global variables (not in a procedure), the compiler says something like, "I need 4 bytes to hold the integer named Total." The linker then sees that and assigns the variable a physical location in memory (for example, 0xffffec04). Global variables are allocated statically at compile time, meaning the compiler allocates space for the variables and that's it. The variables are never destroyed, and their memory is not reallocated.

Variables that are local to a procedure are more complex. They have to be allocated dynamically at runtime. When a procedure starts, all the local variables for that procedure are allocated. (Note: there is a static local variable that's allocated at compile time, but we haven't covered that yet.) When the procedure ends, they are deallocated. The compiler accomplishes this by creating a *stack frame* when the procedure starts and destroying it when the procedure ends. The stack frame holds all the temporary information the procedure needs.

Let's look at Listing 7-4, which shows a sample program.

```
proc.c   /**
          * @brief Program to demonstrate procedures and local variables
          */

         /**
          * Function that is called from another function
          */
         void inner(void) {
             int i = 5;      // A variable
             int k = 3;      // Another variable
       ❶    i = i + k;       // Do something with variables
         }
         /**
          * Outer-level function
          */
         void outer(void) {
             int i = 6;      // A variable
             int j = 2;      // Another variable
             i = j + i;      // Use variables
             inner();
```

```
}

int main()
{
    outer();
    return(0);
}
```

Listing 7-4: A stack frame demonstration

Let's create a project for this program and start debugging it. Run the program in the debugger, then step through it using the command **Run ▸ Step Into** (F5) until you reach ❶. Your screen should look like Figure 7-1.

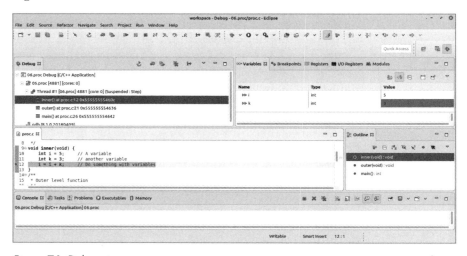

Figure 7-1: Debugging proc.c

When a program is loaded, all the statically allocated variables get their own memory locations. In the STM32 chip, they are assigned to the lower portion of the random access memory (RAM). The leftover memory is reserved for dynamic allocation. Specifically, two memory areas are used dynamically: the *stack*, which holds local variables, and the *heap*. We won't worry about the heap for now; our microprocessor doesn't have enough memory to use it. (We'll discuss the heap in Chapter 13, when we talk about programming for larger systems.)

The name *stack* comes from the fact that data is stacked on top of each other in memory. When your program starts, the main function allocates a stack frame for its local variables and temporary values. When outer is called, it allocates another stack frame on top of the one for main. The call to inner adds a third stack frame to the stack.

To see where the stack is in each procedure, click the **Registers** tab in the upper-right panel and scroll down until you see the rsp register. Figure 7-2 shows that it contains 0x7fffffffd0e0.

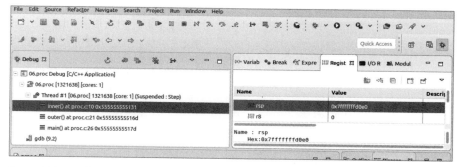

Figure 7-2: Displaying the registers

Depending on the machine, the stack may either start at a low memory address and grow up or at a high memory address and grow down. On this machine (the x86), it starts high and goes down.

The stack from the outer frame is at 0x7fffffffd0f0. Because our stack grows down, this number is lower than the stack frame for main. The inner frame is at 0x7fffffffd110 (see Table 7-1).

Table 7-1: Stack Usage

Address	Procedure	Contents	Comments
0x7fffffffd110	main	\<overhead>	Bottom of stack
0x7fffffffd0f0	outer	\<overhead> i j	
0x7fffffffd0e0	inner	\<overhead> i k	Top of stack

One key concept to understand is that stack frames are allocated in last in, first out (LIFO) order. When we are done with inner, its stack frame will be destroyed and then the outer frame will be destroyed.

The Variables panel (shown in Figure 7-1, upper right) displays the i and k variables. The debugger is displaying the variables in the stack frame for inner, indicated by the fact that the stack frame for inner is highlighted in the Debug panel (upper left). Click the outer stack frame in the Debug panel, and you'll see the Variables panel change and show the variables for outer, as in Figure 7-3.

Figure 7-3: The outer stack frame

Let's continue debugging the program by stepping past the last instruction of inner. When we exit inner, the stack frame for that function disappears, because we are no longer executing inner and have no need for a place to store its variables.

Figure 7-4 shows the stack after we exit the inner stack frame.

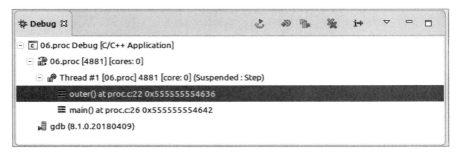

Figure 7-4: The stack after exiting the inner stack frame

Notice there are now only two stack frames on the stack.

Recursion

So far, we've been dealing with basic procedure calls; each procedure was given a different name, and the calling process was simple. Now we're going to focus on *recursion*, which is when a function calls itself. Recursion can be a powerful tool, but it's tricky to use if you don't understand the rules.

The classic recursive problem is computing a factorial. The factorial function is defined as follows:

$f(n) = 1$, when n is 1

otherwise, $f(n) = n \times f(n-1)$

Turning this into code gives us Listing 7-5.

factor.c
```
/**
 * Compute factorial recursively
 * (the basic recursive example)
 */

#include <stdio.h>

/**
 * Compute factorial
 *
 * @param x The number to compute the factorial of
 * @returns the factorial
 */
int factor(const int x) {
    if (x == 1)
        return (1);
    return (x * factor(x-1));
```

```
}

int main()
{
    int result = factor(5);
    printf("5! is %d\n", result);
    return (0);
}
```

Listing 7-5: A program to compute factorials

First, we call factor(5) to get the factorial of 5. For that, we need factor(4), so we suspend factor(5) while we call factor(4). But factor(4) needs factor(3), so we suspend work and call factor(3). Now factor(3) needs factor(2), and, again, factor(2) needs factor(1). Finally, factor(1) doesn't need anything, so it returns 1 to its caller, factor(2). The function factor(2) is running, so it computes 2 × 1 and returns 2 to its caller, factor(3). Next, factor(3) takes the return value (2), computes 2 × 3, and returns 6 to its caller, factor(4). Nearing the end, factor(4) computes 6 × 4 and returns 24. Finally, factor(5) computes 24 × 5 and returns 120.

When you execute this program in the debugger, you should see the stack grow and shrink as the program computes the factorial. You also should see a stack with five stack frames allocated for the factor procedure, one for each instance: factor(1), factor(2), factor(3), factor(4), and factor(5).

Two rules determine when you can use recursion:

1. Each call to the procedure must make the problem simpler.

2. There must be an end point.

Let's see how those rules work with our factorial program. In order to compute factor(5), we need to compute factor(4). The first rule is satisfied because factor(4) is simpler than factor(5). Sooner or later, we reach factor(1), and that's the end point, which satisfies the second rule.

Let's violate the rules to see what happens; we'll modify the program and try to compute factor(-1).

Does this satisfy the two rules? Well, factor(-1) needs factor(-2), which needs factor(-3), and so on, until we reach 1. But there is no way to go from −1 to 1 by subtraction, so we have no way of ending the program.

When I run this program on my little Linux box, I see the following:

```
$ ./06.factor-m1
Segmentation fault (core dumped)
```

The system ran out of stack memory, and the program aborted because it violated the constraints of the memory protection of the x86 processor. On other systems, the results may be different. For example, on ARM processors, the stack can run into the heap and trash it (more on the heap in Chapter 13), or something else can get clobbered. In any case, running out of stack is not a good thing to do.

Incidentally, the program got all the way to x=-262007 before it aborted.

Programming Style

In this book, we try to use good programming style whenever we can. For example, we've made sure to include a comment block at the top of every procedure, and we always include a comment after each variable declaration. Good programming style is designed the way it is for two reasons: to give the programmer who comes after you a clear idea of what you did and to make it difficult to make errors.

We violated one of those rules in the factorial example. This is the offending line:

```
int factor(const int x) {
```

What's wrong with it? The int type is signed, but you can compute the factorial only on positive numbers. We could have written our function as the following:

```
unsigned int factor(const unsigned int x) {
```

Writing it that way would make it impossible to pass in a negative number. Note that the compiler will helpfully change −1 to an unsigned number (4294967295) without warning, unless you include the compiler switch -Wconversion. GCC has hundreds of options, and finding out which to use is its own art form. The first version of that line did have two advantages, however; it's a good example of bad style, and it allowed us to demonstrate stack overflow with factor(-1).

Summary

You may have noticed something about this book. It's divided into chapters. Why? To make it easier to read, of course. A chapter provides the reader with an understandable unit of information that can be absorbed in one sitting.

Computer programs need to be divided into bite-size chunks as well. It's impossible to keep track of a 750,000-line program. It is possible to understand everything about a 300-line procedure. Local variables also help in this organization. If you have a variable that's local to a 300-line procedure, you know it will be used only in those 300 lines. On the other hand, a global variable can be used anywhere in a 750,000-line program.

The key to writing good code is to make it understandable and simple. Procedures help you divide your program into simple, understandable units, which helps you write code that's more reliable and easier to maintain.

Programming Problems

1. Write a function to compute the area of a triangle and a small main program to test it with three different sets of values.

2. Write a procedure called max that returns the maximum of two numbers.

3. Write a program that computes the fifth Fibonacci number. Bonus points for doing it recursively.

4. Create a function that adds up the digits in a number. For example, 123 results in 6 (in other words, 1 + 2 + 3). If the result is 10 or greater, the process should repeat until the result is a single digit. For example, 987 is 9 + 8 + 7 = 24. That's bigger than 10, so 24 is 2 + 4, which yields 6.

8

COMPLEX DATA TYPES

In this chapter, we'll move beyond arrays and simple types to create more complex data types. We'll start with a simple enum that defines a named list of items. Then we'll look at structures and unions, which hold values of different types, accessed by name (unlike arrays, which contain values of a single type accessed by number or index). To make a custom data type, we'll combine enums, structures, and unions. In addition, we'll explore how structures are used in embedded programming. Finally, we'll take a look at typedef, which allows us to define our own data type from existing types.

Enums

An *enumerated type*, or enum, is a data type that allows us to define a named list of items. For example, if we want to store a limited set of colors in a variable, we could enter the following:

```
const uint8_t COLOR_RED = 0;
const uint8_t COLOR_BLUE = 1;
const uint8_t COLOR_GREEN = 2;

#define colorType uint8_t;

colorType colorIWant = COLOR_RED
```

Although this will work, we would still need to keep track of the various colors. Fortunately, C will do that for us if we use an enum:

```
enum colorType {
    COLOR_RED,
    COLOR_BLUE,
    COLOR_GREEN
};

enum colorType colorIWant = COLOR_RED;
```

With enum, C does the bookkeeping for us. If we have only three colors, that's not much of a problem. However, the X Window System has more than 750 named colors. Keeping track of all those numbers is a nontrivial process.

C tends to be a bit loose when it comes to types. Internally, C assigns COLOR_RED, COLOR_BLUE, and COLOR_GREEN the integer values of 0, 1, and 2, respectively. We normally don't care about that, but sometimes this assignment surfaces. For example, this:

```
enum colorType fgColor = COLOR_GREEN;
printf("The foreground color is %d\n", fgColor);
```

will print the following:

```
The foreground color is 2
```

Also, C does not type-check enum assignments. For example, the following statement will not generate an error or warning:

```
colorIWant = 33;
```

Our enum defines three colors, so the legal numbers for colors are 0, 1, and 2—not 33. This can be a problem.

Suppose we write a function to print the color stored in colorIWant. What will users think when they see the following output?

```
Your box color is 33.
```

Printing an incorrect answer like this gives the user a good indication that your program is broken. You can give a better one if you use the enum value to index an array. Here's an example:

```
static const char* const colorNames = {"Red", "Blue", "Green"};
--snip--
printf("Your box color is %s\n", colorNames[colorIWant]);
```

Now if colorIWant is 33, the program will print:

```
Your box color is @ @@@�HH    pp�-�=�=px�-�=�=�888 XXXDDS�td888 P�td
```

Your results may vary, depending on what data there is in element 33 of a three-element array.

Preprocessor Tricks and Enums

In this section, you'll learn how to use some advanced preprocessor directives to make dealing with enums a little easier. First, I want to say that 999 times out of 1,000, using a clever trick will cause more trouble than it's worth. Simple and clear is almost always better than complex and clever. This situation is one of the few exceptions.

Let's take a look at some code that defines colors and the names of colors.

```
// WARNING: Do not change this without changing colorNames.
enum colorType {
    COLOR_RED,
    COLOR_BLUE,
    COLOR_GREEN
};

// WARNING: Do not change this without changing colorType.
static const char* const colorNames = {
    "COLOR_RED", "COLOR_BLUE", "COLOR_GREEN"};
```

This example has two items that depend on each other: colorType and colorNames. The programmer who wrote it was nice enough to put in a comment indicating that those two items are linked, and the two items are actually defined next to each other. (Sometimes two items that depend on each other can be in different files without comments indicating the linkage.)

As programmers, we want our code to be as simple as possible. Having two different items that must be updated simultaneously is not ideal. We can solve this problem through the clever use of the preprocessor:

```
// This is the beginning of a clever trick to define both the values and
// the names for the enum colorType. The list below will be used twice,
// once to generate the value and once to generate the names.

#define COLOR_LIST                                      \
```

```
        DEFINE_ITEM(COLOR_RED),         \
        DEFINE_ITEM(COLOR_BLUE),        \
        DEFINE_ITEM(COLOR_GREEN)

// Define DEFINE_ITEM so it generates the actual values for the enum.
#define DEFINE_ITEM(X) X
enum colorType {
    COLOR_LIST
};
#undef DEFINE_ITEM

// Define DEFINE_ITEM so it generates the names for the enum.
#define DEFINE_ITEM(X) #X
static const char* colorNames[] = {
    COLOR_LIST
};
#undef DEFINE_ITEM
```

Let's start with the first definition:

```
#define COLOR_LIST                      \
        DEFINE_ITEM(COLOR_RED),         \
        DEFINE_ITEM(COLOR_BLUE),        \
        DEFINE_ITEM(COLOR_GREEN)
```

The backslash (\) tells the C preprocessor that the line is continued. We've put them all in the same column, so it's obvious if we accidentally omit one.

Now everywhere we use COLOR_LIST, the C preprocessor will turn it into the following:

```
DEFINE_ITEM(COLOR_RED), DEFINE_ITEM(COLOR_BLUE), DEFINE_ITEM(COLOR_GREEN)
```

When we define the enum, we need our list to be the following:

```
COLOR_RED, COLOR_BLUE, COLOR_GREEN
```

We get this by defining DEFINE_ITEM to output only the item name:

```
#define DEFINE_ITEM(X) X
```

This means that the following code:

```
enum colorType {
    COLOR_LIST
};
```

gets turned into this:

```
enum colorType {
    COLOR_RED, COLOR_BLUE, COLOR_GREEN
};
```

Now we erase the definition of DEFINE_ITEM since we don't need it anymore for the enum definition:

```
#undef DEFINE_ITEM
```

Next, we define the colorNames list by redefining the DEFINE_ITEM macro:

```
#define DEFINE_ITEM(X) #X
```

The hash mark (#) tells the preprocessor to change the token that follows into a string, so now COLOR_LIST will expand into the following:

```
"COLOR_RED","COLOR_BLUE","COLOR_GREEN"
```

Here is the full definition for colorNames:

```
#define DEFINE_ITEM(X) #X
static const char* colorNames[] = {
    COLOR_LIST
};
#undef DEFINE_ITEM
```

The comments are a vital part of this definition. Any time you use a cute trick like this, document it well so that the poor person maintaining this code has some idea of what you did.

Structures

The C *structure* (struct) allows us to group together multiple items of different types. The items, called *fields*, are identified by name. It's different from an array that defines a data structure containing items of the same type, and the items, called *elements*, are indexed by number. For example, consider this structure that groups together information describing a house:

```
struct house {
    uint8_t stories;       // Number of stories in the house
    uint8_t bedrooms;      // Number of bedrooms
    uint32_t squareFeet;   // Size of the house
};
```

To access an element of a structure, use the format *variable.field*, with a dot in the middle. For example:

```
struct house myHouse;
--snip--
myHouse.stories = 2;
myHouse.bedrooms = 4;
myHouse.squareFeet = 5000;
```

The following program shows how to put this all together:

struct.c
```
/**
 * Demonstrate the use of a structure.
 */

#include <stdio.h>
#include <stdint.h>

struct house {
    uint8_t stories;        // Number of stories in the house
    uint8_t bedrooms;       // Number of bedrooms
    uint32_t squareFeet;    // Size of the house
};

int main() {
    struct house myHouse;   // The house for this demo

    myHouse.stories = 2;
    myHouse.bedrooms = 4;
    myHouse.squareFeet = 5000;
    printf("House -- Stories: %d Bedrooms %d Square Feet %d\n",
        myHouse.stories, myHouse.bedrooms, myHouse.squareFeet);
    printf("Size of the structure %ld\n", sizeof(myHouse));
    return (0);
}
```

Let's debug this program in the STM32 Workbench (see Figure 8-1).

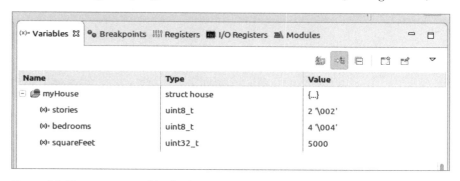

Figure 8-1: The struct variable display

Stopping on line 20, we can now see the structure in the variable list. Clicking the + icon expands the structure to show what's in it.

Structures in Memory

Let's take a look at how the C compiler will lay out this structure in memory. The compiler needs to allocate 1 byte for stories (uint8_t), 1 byte for bedrooms (uint8_t), and 4 bytes for squareFeet (uint32_t). Logically, the layout should look like Table 8-1.

Table 8-1: Structure Layout

Offset	Type	Field
0	uint8_t	stories
1	uint8_t	bedrooms
2	uint32_t	
3		
4		squareFeet
5		

From Table 8-1, we see that the structure takes up 6 bytes. However, when we run the program, we see the following output:

```
Size of the structure 8
```

Where did the other 2 bytes come from?

The problem is memory design. On the ARM chip (and many others), memory is organized as a series of 32-bit integers aligned on a 4-byte boundary, like so:

0x10000	32 bits
0x10004	32 bits
0x10008	32 bits
. . .	

Let's say we want an 8-bit byte at 0x10001. The machine fetches 32 bits from 0x10000 and then throws away 24 bits, which is wasteful because extra data is fetched, although there is no performance hit.

Now let's say we need a 32-bit integer starting at 0x10002. Attempting to fetch this data directly results in an alignment exception that will abort our program. The computer has to do the following:

1. Fetch 16 bits from 0x10000.
2. Fetch 16 bits from 0x10004.
3. Combine them.

The internal ARM circuitry does *not* complete these steps. Instead, the compiler must generate multiple instructions to do the work, which isn't good for performance. (We go into this in more detail later in the chapter.)

It would be much nicer if squareFeet aligned on a 4-byte boundary instead of a 2-byte boundary, so the compiler optimizes the layout of the structure by adding 2 bytes of padding. This makes the structure larger but much easier to deal with. Table 8-2 shows the structure's actual adjusted layout.

Table 8-2: Padded Structure Layout

Offset	Type	Field
0	uint8_t	stories
1	uint8_t	bedrooms
2	uint8_t	(padding)
3	uint8_t	(padding)
4	uint32_t	squareFeet
5		
6		
7		

This extra padding is sometimes a problem. For example, if you have a lot of houses and very limited memory, the padding in each house structure adds up to a lot of wasted space.

Another example is in embedded programming. I had an old, pre-iPod music device called the Rio that didn't come with Linux tools to load the music onto the device, so I wrote some tools myself. Every data block had a header that looked something like this:

```
struct dataBlockHeader {
    uint32_t nextBlock;      // Number of the next block in this song
    uint16_t timeStamp;      // Time in seconds of this section of the song
    uint32_t previousBlock;  // Number of the previous block in the song
};
```

When I first loaded songs on my Rio, they would play fine. But when I pressed Rewind to back up a few seconds, the device would go crazy and start the song all over again. The problem was that GCC was adding padding to the structure:

```
struct dataBlockHeader {
    uint32_t nextBlock;      // Number of the next block in this song
    uint16_t timeStamp;      // Time in seconds of this section of the song
    uint16_t padding;        // Automatically added
    uint32_t previousBlock;  // Number of the previous block in the song
};
```

As a result, what the Rio thought was the previous block was instead some padding and half the value of the previous block. No wonder the device became confused.

The solution was to tell the compiler not to add padding with the packed attribute:

```
struct dataBlockHeader {
    uint32_t nextBlock;      // Number of the next block in this song
    uint16_t timeStamp;      // Time in seconds of this section of the song
```

```
    uint32_t previousBlock;   // Number of the previous block in the song
} __attribute__((packed));
```

In this example, __attribute__((packed)) is a GNU extension to the
C language, and it may not work on other compilers.

Accessing Unaligned Data

By default, the compiler will "adjust" the alignment of elements of a structure for efficient memory access. As we've seen, hardware designers sometimes have different ideas, and in order to get the structure to match the
hardware, we have to include the __attribute__((packed)) directive.

To see why the compiler makes such adjustments, let's write a program
that does both aligned and unaligned 32-bit accesses. The packed structure
is more compact, but it requires more code to access the 32-bit value. The
unpacked structure is efficient to access, but it takes up more memory.

NOTE   *Every time I've had to use the __attribute__((packed)) directive, it was to make a
structure compatible with the hardware I was given—hardware designed by other
engineers who didn't know about the alignment issues they were causing.*

The following program shows how both the packed and unpacked
structures are accessed:

```
/*
 * A demonstration of packed and unpacked.
 * This program does nothing useful except
 * generate an assembly listing showing
 * how hard it is to access squareFeet
 * in a packed structure.
 *
 * To run -- don't. Compile and look at the
 * assembly listing instead.
 */

#include "stm32f0xx.h"
#include "stm32f0xx_nucleo.h"

// An example of an unpacked structure
struct unpackedHouse {
    uint8_t stories;      // Number of stories in the house
    uint8_t bedrooms;     // Number of bedrooms
    uint32_t squareFeet;  // Size of the house
    uint8_t doors;        // Number of doors
    uint8_t windows;      // Number of windows
};

// An example of a packed structure
struct packedHouse {
    uint8_t stories;      // Number of stories in the house
    uint8_t bedrooms;     // Number of bedrooms
    uint32_t squareFeet;  // Size of the house
```

```
    uint8_t doors;        // Number of doors
    uint8_t windows;      // Number of windows
} __attribute__((packed));

// A place to dump squareFeet for unpackedHouse
volatile uint32_t unpackedFeet;
volatile uint32_t packedFeet;    // A place to dump squareFeet for packedHouse

// An example unpackedHouse -- values chosen to make demonstration easier
struct unpackedHouse theUnpackedHouse = {0x01, 0x02, 0x11223344, 0x03, 0x04};

// An example packedHouse -- values chosen to make demonstration easier
struct   packedHouse thePackedHouse = {0x01, 0x02, 0x11223344, 0x03, 0x04};

int main(void)
{
  ❶ unpackedFeet = theUnpackedHouse.squareFeet;
  ❷ packedFeet = thePackedHouse.squareFeet;

    for(;;);
}
```

First, let's look at the code generated to fetch an aligned uint32_t ❶ (comments added):

```
;unpackedFeet = theUnpackedHouse.squareFeet;
    ldr     r3, .L3        ; Get address of theUnpackedHouse.
    ldr     r2, [r3, #4]   ; Get data at offset 4
                           ; (theUnpackedHouse.squareFeet).
--snip--
L3: theUnpackedHouse
```

It uses one instruction to get the address of the structure and one to get the value.

Now let's look at the unaligned fetch ❷:

```
;  packedFeet = thePackedHouse.squareFeet;
    ldr     r3, .L3+8      ; Get address of thePackedHouse.
    ldrh    r2, [r3, #2]   ; Get uint16_t at offset 2 (0x3344).
                           ; (Byte order puts the low-order bytes first.)

    ldrh    r3, [r3, #4]   ; Get uint16_t at offset 4 (0x1122).
                           ; (High bytes come after low.)

    lsls    r3, r3, #16    ; r3 contains the top 1/2 of squareFeet
                           ; in the bottom 16 bits of r3.
                           ; Shift it left into the top half.

    orrs    r3, r2         ; Combine the two halves.

.L3: theUnpackedHouse
     thePackedHouse
```

The unaligned fetch requires four instructions instead of the one required by an aligned fetch. The program must use two load instructions to get the two halves of the number: one shift to get the top half to the top of the register, and a logical OR to combine the two numbers.

Code like this must be used every time an unaligned uint32_t is loaded or stored. You can see why the compiler might want to avoid doing that and adds padding.

Structure Initialization

We can initialize structures by putting the initializer list inside curly brackets ({}). For example, the following statement declares and initializes myHouse with one statement:

```
struct house {
    uint8_t stories;        // Number of stories in the house
    uint8_t bedrooms;       // Number of bedrooms
    uint32_t squareFeet;    // Size of the house
};

// 2 stories
// 5 bedrooms
// 2500 square feet
struct house myHouse = {2, 5, 2500};
```

In early versions of the language, that was the only way to initialize structures. Later, when C99 (the C specification finalized in 1999) came along, a new feature called *designated initializers* was added to let you initialize fields by name. Here's an example:

```
struct house myHouse = {
  stories: 2,
  bedrooms: 5,
  squareFeet: 2500
};
```

The fields must be in the same order as they are declared in the structure. The GCC compiler has an extension that lets you use designated initializers using a different method:

```
struct house myHouse = {
    .stories: 2,
    .squareFeet: 2500,
    .bedrooms: 5
};
```

In this case, the order does not have to match the order in which the fields were declared.

Structure Assignment

C does not allow you to assign one array to another, but it does allow you to assign one structure to another. Here's an example:

```
int array1[5];          // An array
int array2[5];          // Another array

array1 = array2;        // Illegal

struct example {
    int array[5];       // Array inside a structure
};
struct example struct1; // A structure
struct example struct2; // Another structure

// Initialize structure 2

struct1 = struct2;      // Structure assignment allowed
```

If these were arrays, assignment would be illegal, but since they are structures, it works.

Structure Pointers

C's parameter-passing mechanism uses *call by value*, meaning that if we pass a parameter to a procedure, it copies the value of the parameter onto the stack. This practice is not a problem when we have something small like a 2-byte integer, but most structures are not very small and actually can be quite large. When a structure is passed as a parameter, *the entire structure is copied onto the stack*, making it an expensive operation. Here's an example:

```
// A rectangle
struct rectangle {
    unsigned int width;  // Width of the rectangle
    unsigned int height; // Height of a rectangle
};

// Inefficient parameter passing
unsigned int area(const struct rectangle aRectangle)
{
    return (aRectangle.width * aRectangle.height);
}
```

What's going on here is that in order to perform the "call by value" parameter passing, the compiler must generate code to copy aRectangle in its entirety onto the stack. For larger structures, that can use a lot of stack space and take up a lot of time copying the data.

It's more efficient to pass a structure as a pointer:

```
// Efficient parameter passing
unsigned int area(const struct rectangle* const aRectangle)
```

```
{
    return ((*aRectangle).rectangle * (*aRectangle).height);
}
```

In this case, only the pointer (a small item) is passed as a parameter. In the case of the ARM compiler, this is done by putting it in a register: quick, easy, and no stack space used.

One of the advantages of call by value is any changes to the parameter are not passed back to the caller. But we didn't make any changes, so that's not an issue.

When we passed parameters as pointers, we used const to indicate that no changes to the parameters were allowed.

It's a little awkward to access a member of a structure pointer using the (*rectangle).height syntax. Because of this, C has added some syntactic sugar that allows us to use a shortcut—the -> operator:

```
// Efficient parameter passing
unsigned int area(const struct rectangle* const aRectangle)
{
    return (aRectangle->rectangle * aRectangle->height);
}
```

C feels free to treat an array as a pointer and a pointer as an array. When an array is passed in as a parameter, the array is automatically turned into a pointer. When an array is specified as a procedure parameter, it is automatically turned into a pointer behind your back.

Saying C is "call by value" is not strictly true. It's more precise to say, "C is called by value, except for arrays, which are called by pointer value."

Structure Naming

Like many things in C, the naming of structures is not all that simple. That's because in a single C structure declaration, we can define a structure name (or not) and a variable (or not). Here's the general syntax for a structure definition:

```
struct [struct-name] {
    field1;
    field2;
--snip--
} [var-name(s)];
```

Let's consider the example when we don't have a structure name:

```
// A box to put our stuff into
struct {
    uint32_t width;     // Width of the box
    uint32_t height;    // Height of the box
} aBox;
```

This defines the aBox variable, but what type is aBox? It is a structure with no name, or an *anonymous structure*. Anonymous structures can be used to define a variable only when the structure is defined. They do not specify a structure name that can be used in later declarations.

Now let's consider the case where we leave off the variable name:

```
struct box {
    uint32_t width;      // Width of the box
    uint32_t height;     // Height of the box
};
```

This defines a structure type but no variables. It can be used later to define a variable:

```
struct box aBox; // Box to put stuff into
```

We can put in both a structure name and a variable name in the same declaration:

```
struct box {
    uint32_t width;      // Width of the box
    uint32_t height;     // Height of the box
} aBox;
```

This defines both a box structure and a variable aBox.

C has one more trick up its sleeve—we can have a structure definition with no structure name and no variable name:

```
// Silly definition
struct {
    uint32_t width;      // Width of the box
    uint32_t height;     // Height of the box
};
```

Because there is no structure name, we can use this only to access the variable defined here. But no variable is defined here, so we can't access anything, which means that although it's perfectly legal, it's also perfectly useless.

Unions

A union is like a struct except that instead of each field being assigned a different location, all the fields are stored in the same location. Here's an example:

```
union value {
    uint32_t anInteger;
    float aFloat;
};
```

The compiler allocates 4 bytes for the uint32_t and *the same 4 bytes* for the float. Let's take a look at this in action:

```
union value theValue;    // Define the value.

theValue.anInteger = 5; // anInteger is 5.
theValue.aFloat = 1.0;   // Assign the field aFloat/wipe out anInteger.
```

The second assignment actually changes anInteger to 1065353216 (0x3f800000). It's a very strange integer, but as a floating point, it's 1.0.

Good programming practice is to use the same field name for storing and retrieving a value from an union. For example:

```
theValue.aFloat = 1.2;
float someFloat = theValue.aFloat;    // Assigns someFloat 1.2
```

When you use different fields, the results will be different on different machines.

```
theValue.aFloat = 1.2;
int someInt = theValue.anInteger;    // Results machine-dependent
```

In this case the value of someInt will depend on the size of an integer, the size of a float, the floating-point format, and the byte order, all of which are processor-dependent.

Now let's talk about the byte order problem. Let's say you have four cards in your hand, numbered 1, 2, 3, and 4. You want to put them into a row of four boxes in front of you. So, you take the top card and put it in the leftmost box, you put the next card in the box to the right of that, and so on. Your boxes now contain the following:

| 1 | 2 | 3 | 4 |

When you pick up the cards, you start at the right and put each card on top of the pile. The result is that you get 1, 2, 3, and 4 in order back in your hand.

Now another person comes along and puts the cards in the boxes starting on the right side and going left. Their boxes look like this:

| 4 | 3 | 2 | 1 |

They pick up the cards starting at the left and work right. Again, this person will wind up with 1, 2, 3, and 4 in their hand, in exactly that order.

What I've just described is how two different CPU architectures will store numbers in memory. In some cases it will be 1, 2, 3, and 4 and in others 4, 3, 2, and 1. As long as you are storing and retrieving the same size number, byte order makes no difference.

Now let's say you want to store four cards in the boxes but retrieve only two, which means your boxes look like this:

When you pick up your cards, you get only 1 and 2.
However, the other person's storage looks like this:

The leftmost *n* boxes are always used when retrieving cards, so this person will start at the left and grab 3 and 4, meaning they'll get a different result.

This difference is caused by the two of you using a different order when storing and retrieving cards. The same thing happens in computers. Different computers store things in different orders. As a result, you are going to get different answers on different machines if you try and store one type of data and retrieve another.

Therefore, if you put something in theValue.anInteger, the only way you're guaranteed to get consistent results is to take it out using only the theValue.anInteger field.

Creating a Custom Type

We're now going to take all three of our new data types—struct, union, and enum—and combine them into one large data type in order to draw a shape on the screen. The shape can be a square, rectangle, circle, or triangle. Each of those shapes can be described differently.

All we need to describe a square is a single side:

```
struct square {
    unsigned int side; // Size of the square
};
```

To describe a rectangle, we need a width and height:

```
struct rectangle {
    unsigned int width;   // Width of the rectangle
    unsigned int height;  // Height of the rectangle
};
```

We can draw a circle with only its radius:

```
struct circle {
    unsigned int radius;  // Radius of the circle
};
```

Finally, to draw a triangle, we describe the base and height:

```
struct triangle {
```

```
    unsigned int base;      // Base of the triangle
    unsigned int height;    // How high is it?
};
```

A generic shape type should hold any one of these, which indicates that we need a union. But in order to draw a shape, we need to know not only its description but also what type of shape it is. The enum data type was designed for a limited list of simple values:

```
enum shapeType {
    SHAPE_SQUARE, SHAPE_RECTANGLE, SHAPE_CIRCLE, SHAPE_TRIANGLE
};
```

Now we get to define our data structure:

```
struct shape {
    enum shapeType type;    // The type of the shape
    union {
        struct square theSquare;
        struct rectangle theRectangle;
        struct circle theCircle;
        struct triangle theTriangle;
    } dimensions;
};
```

The first field is type, which contains the type of shape contained in the structure. The second field contains the dimensions of the shape. It's a union because different shapes have different dimensions.

The code to draw the shapes looks something like the following:

```
void drawShape(const shape* const theShape) {
    switch (theShape->type) {
        case SHAPE_SQUARE:
            drawSquare(theShape->dimensions.theSquare.side);
            break;
        case SHAPE_RECTANGLE:
            drawSquare(theShape->dimensions.theRectangle.width,
                        theShape->dimensions.theRectangle.height);
        // ... other shapes
```

This design pattern is fairly common in C programming: a union that can hold many different types of data and an enum that tells which type we actually have.

Structures and Embedded Programming

In this section, we take a hardware specification and turn it into a C structure, using what we've learned so far about structures and alignment.

The small computer system interface (SCSI) was designed to provide a standard way of transferring data to and from devices. It started in 1986 and since has been expanded and enhanced a great deal. It works by sending a structure called a command block to the device and getting back data and status messages in return.

When first written, the SCSI standard defined the READ (6) command, which limited the block address to 16 bits, allowing for a disk of up to 16MB, which was large for the time. Of course, disk makers quickly created bigger disks, so the SCSI people had to create a new command to allow for a bigger drive. This was the READ (10) command, which was followed by the READ (12), READ (16), and READ (32) commands. The READ (32) command uses a 64-bit block address. Hopefully, it will take the disk manufacturers a little time to catch up and create an 8-zebibyte disk.

Figure 8-2 shows the command block for the READ (10) command. If we want to read data from the disk, we'll need a C structure to contain this information and send it to the device.

Bit Byte	7	6	5	4	3	2	1	0
0	OPERATION CODE (28h)							
1	RDPROTECT			DPO	FUA	RARC	Obsolete	Obsolete
2	(MSB)							
...	LOGICAL BLOCK ADDRESS							
5								(LSB)
6	Reserved			GROUP NUMBER				
7	(MSB)							
8	TRANSFER LENGTH							(LSB)
9	CONTROL							

Figure 8-2: The READ (10) command block

At first, it seems like a simple translation:

```
struct read10 {
    uint8_t opCode;     // Op code for read
    uint8_t flags;      // Flag bits
    uint32_t lba;       // Logical block address
    uint8_t group;      // Command group
    uint16_t transferLength;  // Length of the data to read
    uint8_t control;    // Control bits, the NACA being the only one defined
};
#include <assert.h>

int main() {
    assert(sizeof(struct read10) == 10);
```

Now, because we're paranoid and careful, the first thing we did in the program was to put in an assert statement to make sure our definition matches the hardware. An assert statement aborts the program if the condition is not true. If we expect the `read10` control block to contain 10 bytes and it doesn't, our program has a big problem. And we do too, because the assert fails.

So what happened? Inspecting the structure, we see that the `lba` field (a `uint32`) is aligned on a 2-byte boundary. The compiler wants to put it on a 4-byte boundary, so it added 2 bytes of padding. We need to pack the structure:

```
struct read10 {
    uint8_t opCode;      // Op code for read
    uint8_t flags;       // Flag bits
    uint32_t lba;        // Logical block address
    uint8_t group;       // Command group
    uint16_t transferLength; // Length of the data to read
    uint8_t control;     // Control bits, the NACA being the only one defined
} __attribute__((packed));
```

The packed attribute tells GCC to not add any padding. As a result, our structure is inefficient, but it matches the hardware. Also, our assert doesn't fail, so we've done it right.

typedef

We can define our own types using the `typedef` statement. For example, the following statement defines a new `dimension` type:

```
typedef unsigned int dimension;  // Dimension for use in the plans
```

This type is equivalent to an unsigned `int` and can be used like any other type:

```
dimension width;   // Width of the thing in furlongs
```

The syntax of a `typedef` is similar to that of a variable declaration. It contains the `typedef` keyword and the name of the initial type, as well as the name of the defined type:

```
typedef initialtype newtypename;  // A type definition
```

One example of `typedef` can be found in the *stdint.h* file, which is included in many of our programs:

```
// These typedefs are system-dependent.
typedef signed char        int8_t;
typedef unsigned char      uint8_t;
typedef signed short int   int16_t;
typedef unsigned short int uint16_t;
typedef signed int         int32_t;
typedef unsigned int       uint32_t;
```

In the early days of C, an int could be 16 or 32 bits, depending on the processor. In the early days of programming, if users wanted to use a 16-bit integer (which the old C standard didn't support), they had to put something like this in their code:

```
#ifdef ON_16_BIT_CPU
typedef signed int    int16_t;
#else // ON_32_BIT_CPU
typedef signed short int    int16_t;
#endif
```

After years of having to define our own precise data types, the C standards committee created the *stdint.h* header file and made it a part of the language.

Function Pointers and typedef

C allows pointers to functions, which are useful when doing callbacks. For example, we might tell a graphics system to call a given function when a button is pressed. The code for that might look like the following:

```
registerButtonPressHandler(functionToHandleButtonPress);
```

The functionToHandleButtonPress parameter is a pointer to a function that returns an integer and takes a constant event pointer as its single argument. That sentence is a mess, and it doesn't get any easier when we translate it to C:

```
int (*ButtonCallback)(const struct event* const theEvent);
```

The first set of parentheses is required because without it we define a function that returns an integer pointer:

```
// Define function that returns int*
int* getPointer(...)
```

Rather than remember these convoluted syntax rules, let's simplify the syntax using typedef:

```
// Function type for callback function
typedef int ButtonCallbackType(const struct event* const theEvent);

// Pointer to callback function
typedef ButtonCallbackType* ButtonCallbackPointer;
```

This changes the definition of registerButtonPressHandler from:

```
void registerButtonPressHandler(int (*callbackPointer)
    (const struct event* const theEvent));
```

to this:

```
void registerButtonPressHandler(ButtonCallbackPointer callbackPointer);
```

The typedef provides a way of organizing types to simplify our code, as well as make things clearer.

typedef and struct

We've already seen how we can use struct to define a structured data type.

```
struct rectangle {
    uint32_t width;  // Width of the rectangle
    uint32_t height; // Height of the rectangle
};
```

To use this structure, we must use the struct keyword:

```
struct rectangle bigRectangle;   // A big rectangle
```

The typedef statement allows us to avoid using the struct keyword:

```
typedef struct{
    uint32_t width;      // Width of the rectangle
    uint32_t height;     // Height of the rectangle
} rectangle;

rectangle bigRectangle;   // A big rectangle
```

The typedef in this case tells C that we want to define a new rectangle type.

Some people believe that using typedef to define a new structure type makes the code simpler and cleaner. Others prefer to use struct because it makes it obvious that a variable is a struct. The syntax is optional, so use whatever works best for you.

Summary

This chapter is all about organizing data. The enum type allows you to organize simple name lists without having to worry about which field gets what value. Structures provide a powerful tool for organizing data of different types. For embedded programmers, they are also useful for communicating with actual hardware devices. However, keep in mind that a hardware designer's idea of how a structure is laid out can be different from what C thinks it should be.

While structures can hold only a fixed set of data, unions can hold multiple sets (just not at the same time). Between the two of them, we have a great deal of control over how we store data.

Another tool for organizing data is the typedef directive, which allows us to define our own types. It lets us represent data using familiar types instead of being forced to use the basic C types.

Many complex data types exist, and C provides a good set of tools for managing them.

Programming Problems

1. Create a structure to hold a fraction. Then create procedures that add, subtract, multiply, and divide fractions. The fractions should be stored in normalized form. In other words, 2/4 should be stored as 1/2.

2. Create a structure called car that holds attributes common to both electric and gas-powered cars. Add to it a union with two fields, electric and gas, that are structures that hold attributes specific to that type of car. For example, numberOfPassengers is common to all cars. The field chargingTime would be electric-only.

3. Write a structure to describe a student (single class). The data should contain not only the student's name and ID number but also an array containing the student's grades.

4. Write a structure to handle the data shown in Figure 8-3.

Offsets	Octet	0								1								2								3							
Octet	Bit	1	2	3	4	5	6	7	8	9	10	11	12	13	14	15	16	17	18	19	20	21	22	23	24	25	26	27	28	29	30	31
0	0	Version				IHL				DSCP						ECN		Total Length															
4	32	Identification																Flags			Fragment Offset												
8	64	Time to Live								Protocol								Header Checksum															
12	96	Source IP Address																															
16	128	Destination IP Address																															
20	160	Options (if IHL > 5)																															
24	192																																
28	224																																
32	256																																

Figure 8-3: IPv4 header format

NOTE *The IP structure uses* network byte order, *or big-endian format.*

5. The Southern California Railroad has the only Acme Traffic Signal (the one with arms and lights) actually at an intersection. To change the signal from STOP to GO, the controller must do the following:

   a. Turn off the STOP light.

   b. Turn on the GO light.

   c. Turn on the DIRECTION relay.

   d. Energize the ARM relay.

   e. Wait 3 seconds.

f.   Turn off the ARM relay.

g.   Turn off the DIRECTION relay.

We have the following commands available: (1) change state of light x to y, where x is STOP or GO, and y is ON or OFF; (2) set DIRECTION relay power to x, where x is ON or OFF; and (3) sleep for n seconds. Write a structure for each command. Then write a union that holds an enum to identify the command and the structure for the given command.

9

SERIAL OUTPUT ON THE STM

We're now back to "Hello World," only this time we'll use our Nucleo board, which presents several challenges. The first is where to write the message. There is no display. Fortunately, the chip has a serial port that's nicely connected to a USB/serial port on the top half of the board.

The next challenge is the writing itself. We need to initialize the device and create a procedure to actually write a character. The device is designed to accept one character at a time, and we must keep that limitation in mind when writing our program.

We'll simulate the process before working with the device. C has a great deal of standard functions, such as puts, that make outputting data easy. The Nucleo board doesn't have such nice features, so we must write our own output functions. In order to transition into the low-level coding we need for the Nucleo, we'll write out "Hello World" one character at a time.

Writing a String One Character at a Time

When a C program calls the standard puts function, it starts a long programming process that involves kernel calls, internal buffering, interrupt scheduling, and device drivers (more on those in the next chapter). Ultimately, it reaches the point where it sends one character at a time to the device. To simulate this, we'll send one character at a time to the operating system. In other words, we'll limit ourselves to using only the standard putchar function to write the output.

Listing 9-1 contains a program that writes out "Hello World\n" the hard way. Again, we're doing this the hard way because later, with the Nucleo board, we're going to have to do it the *really* hard way.

putchar.c
```
/*
 * Print a string one character at a time.
 */
#include <stdio.h>

char hello[] = "Hello World\n"; // The characters to print
int curChar;     // Character number we are printing

int main()
{
❶ for (curChar = 0; hello[curChar] != '\0'; ++curChar)
       putchar(hello[curChar]);
    return (0);
}
```

Listing 9-1: Writing a string one character at a time

The only interesting piece in this program is the for loop ❶, which does not stop after a certain number of characters. Instead, it stops when the program reaches the end-of-string ('\0') character. That way, the program can output any length of string.

Defining Our Own putchar

To improve this program, first we'll make curChar a local variable. Then we'll define a function called myPutchar that sends the character to standard out (see Listing 9-2).

my_putchar.c
```
/**
 * Print a string one character at a time
 * using our own function.
 */
#include <stdio.h>

char hello[] = "Hello World\n"; // The characters to print

❶ /**
  * Reimplementation of putchar
  *
  * @param ch The character to send
```

```
 *
 * @note Not as apparently useless as it seems
 */
❷ void myPutchar(const char ch)
 {
   ❸ putchar(ch);
 }

 int main()
 {
     int curChar;        // Index of the current character we
                         // are printing
     for (curChar = 0; hello[curChar] != '\0'; ++curChar)
       ❹ myPutchar(hello[curChar]);
     return (0);
 }
```

Listing 9-2: One character at a time using our own output function

At the beginning of myPutchar, we've added some additional elements ❶ to the comment block. The keyword @param indicates a parameter, and the @note keyword defines a note. You can use lots of other keywords in Doxygen-style comments, but for now we'll use the basics to be compatible with the existing STM code.

The actual function starts with the void myPutchar(const char ch) declaration ❷, which indicates that the myPutchar procedure returns nothing and takes one parameter of type char. The const modifier indicates that we don't change it inside the procedure. (In fact, we can't change it, because if we try, the compiler will generate an error.)

When the procedure is executed ❹, the program performs the following steps:

1. It computes the value of hello[curChar].
2. It places this value in a location where myPutchar can find it.
3. It records the address of the next instruction (the end of the for loop).
4. It starts executing myPutchar. (The ch variable will have been initialized by step 2.)

A similar set of steps is executed when we call putchar ❸. The only difference is that we had to write myPutchar, and the people who wrote the standard C library supplied putchar.

Creating a function (myPutchar) that does nothing but call another (putchar) is not very useful. The Nucleo board doesn't have a putchar function, so we'll write our own later in the chapter. But before we do that, let's look at the details of the serial device.

Serial Output

Serial output is one of the easiest ways to get data out of an embedded system. The electrical interface consists of a send line (TX), a receive line

(RX), and ground (GND). Most embedded systems have them hidden away, available only to developers willing to crack open the case and connect to the serial port.

Our chip has a serial device we can write to. All we need to do is connect TX, RX, and GND between our microcontroller (the bottom half of the development board) and the USB/serial device on the top half of the board.

The following table shows the connections we need:

Microcontroller		USB/serial and other support devices	
RX	CN9-1	TX	CN3-1
TX	CN9-2	RX	CN3-2
GND	CN6-5	GND	CN4-3

We would have to make these connections if we had a Raspberry Pi or other embedded system without a built-in serial controller. Figure 9-1 shows the layout of these components and the internal wiring supplied by STM.

STM has already made the connections for us. No jumpers needed.

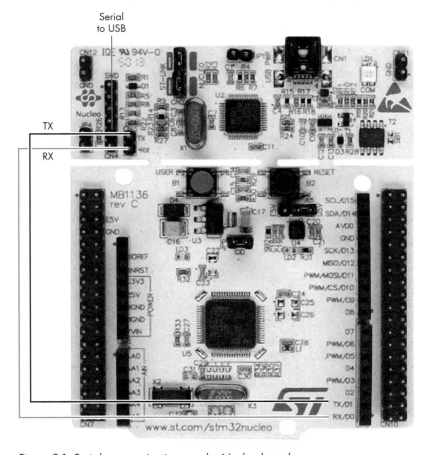

Figure 9-1: Serial communications on the Nucleo board

A Brief History of Serial Communications

Serial communications go back a long way, back to the BC years (as in, *before computers*). The telegraph was the internet of its day, allowing for the transmission of long-distance messages over wires. The sender consisted of a telegraph key that, when pressed, would cause the receiver to "click." The clicks were encoded using a system called *Morse code* (still in use today). This invention revolutionized communications. You could send a message to the next city and get a response the same day. Take that, Pony Express.

There was just one problem, however; you needed skilled operators at both ends of the telegraph who knew Morse code. Unskilled people could not send or receive messages, and training operators was expensive. One solution was to use two clocks: one for the transmitter and one for the receiver. On the clock dial were the letters, from *A* to *Z*. To send an *S*, for example, the sender would wait until the single hand on the clock pointed to the *S* and press the telegraph key. The receiver would see that the hand pointed to *S* and record the letter.

Keeping the clocks in sync was next to impossible, though, so a very smart inventor decided that each clock would stop its hands at the top position. When the sender wanted to send a letter, they would press the telegraph key as a *start signal*. The clocks would keep good enough time to make it around the dial once correctly. The sender would then press the letter signal. When the hand reached the top, a short pause called the *stop time* would give the slower clock a chance to catch up. The sequence of events went like this: start signal, letter signal, stop time.

Now let's fast-forward to the invention of the teletype machine, which could send text over the equivalent of telegraph lines. Instead of a single letter pulse, the teletype encoded the characters into a series of eight pulses (seven for data and one for primitive error checking). It used a keyboard encoder built out of levers to turn a key press into an 8-bit code that was fed to a mechanical shift register that looked like a distributor cap. This device sent the pulses down the wire, where another teletype would turn them into a single printed letter.

The teletype sequence went like this: The sender would press a key, and the mechanical sender would send out a 10-bit signal (1 start bit, 8 data bits, and 1 stop bit). When the receiver got the start bit, it turned on its shift register (another motor with a distributor cap) and used the incoming pulses to turn a print head so the right letter printed. After the 8 data bits were sent, both machines paused at least 1 bit time (the stop bit) to remain synchronized.

Most teletypes could transmit characters at 110 baud (bits/second), or 10 characters a second. That doesn't sound like much in the day of megabit internet connections, but it was a revolutionary improvement in communications.

Computers today still use the serial communication that the teletype used. The speeds have improved, but the basic protocol remains the same.

Line Endings

In fact, we're still dealing with one other teletype legacy: line endings. After typing 80 characters, you could send the machine a character called a *carriage return* to make it return to position 1. The problem was that it took two-tenths of a second to move the printhead. If you sent a character immediately after the carriage return, you'd get a blurred blob printed in the middle of the line as the printhead tried to print while moving.

The teletype people solved this issue by making the end of a line two characters. The first, the carriage return, moved the print head to position 1. The second, the line feed, moved the paper up one line. Since the line feed didn't print anything on the paper, the fact that it was done while the printhead was flying to the left didn't matter.

However, when computers came out, storage cost a lot of money (hundreds of dollars *per byte*), so storing two characters for an end of line was costly. The people who created Unix, the inspiration for Linux, decided to use the line feed (\n) character only. Apple decided to use the carriage return (\r) only, and Microsoft decided to use both the carriage return and the line feed (\r\n) for its line ending.

C automatically handles the different types of newlines in the system library, but only when you use the system library. If you are doing it yourself, like we are about to do, you must write out the full end-of-line sequence (\r\n).

Serial Communications Today

Today, almost every embedded processor has a serial interface on it. Serial devices are simple and cheap to make. The only difference between the interface of today and that of the 1800s is that speed has gone up (from 110 bits/second up to 115,200 bits/second), and the voltages have changed. In the 1800s they used −15 to −3 as a zero bit and +3 to +15 as a one bit. That's still the "standard," but most computers use voltages of 0 (for zero) and 3 (for one).

The device that handles the serial I/O is called a *universal asynchronous receiver-transmitter (UART)*. There are two major types of serial communication: *asynchronous* and *synchronous*. With synchronous communications, the sender's and receiver's clocks must be synchronized by having the sender continually send out characters. The receiver then looks at the incoming characters and deduces the clock timing from them. The sender must always send characters, even if it's just an "idle" character (indicating no data). With asynchronous communications, there is no shared clock. The start bit triggers the receiver to start its clock and look for a character. Asynchronous communications assume that the sender and receiver can keep their clocks close enough together for one character time. Because there is no need for continuous transmissions to keep the clocks synchronized, there is no idle character. When idle, the transmitter just doesn't send anything.

The STM chip has one port that allows for both synchronous and asynchronous communications, so in the STM documentation, you'll see it referred to as a *universal synchronous/asynchronous receiver-transmitter (USART)*. This program uses the term *UART* to be compatible with the STM HAL library.

Serial Hello World!

Let's create a new project for *main.c*, which is a somewhat long "Hello World," but it has to do all the things that the operating system hides from us. First, we include the header files that define the information about the UART (and lots of other devices as well):

```
#include "stm32f0xx.h"
#include "stm32f0xx_nucleo.h"
```

For the code, we'll start with the main function:

```
int main(void)
{
❶ HAL_Init(); // Initialize hardware.
   led2_Init();
   uart2_Init();

   // Keep sending the message for a long time.
❷ for (;;) {
       // Send character by character.
       for(current = 0; hello[current] != '\0'; ++current) {
       ❸ myPutchar(hello[current]);
       }
     ❹ HAL_Delay(500);
   }
}
```

The main function looks pretty much like the one in Listings 9-1 and 9-2. One addition is that it must initialize all the devices we're going to use ❶, including the hardware library (HAL_Init), the red LED (led2_Init), and the UART (uart2_Init). Our embedded program can't stop, so we have an infinite loop ❷ that sends out the string ❸ and then sleeps for half a second ❹.

One of the first things to do next is create an ErrorHandler function, which the HAL library calls if something goes wrong. We can't print an error message, because our printing code just went south, so we resort to blinking the red light. True, it's a very limited error indication, but so is the check engine light in your car. In both cases, the designers are doing the best they can. We won't go through the Error_Handler function here; it's "blink" from Chapter 3 with a new name.

UART Initialization

A serial device should be simple to program. The engineers at STMicro-electronics, however, have decided to improve the simple UART by providing additional features. As a result, our simple serial device now takes 45 pages worth of reference manual to describe. We just want to use the thing to send characters. It doesn't even need to receive them.

Fortunately, the HAL library provides a function called HAL_UART_Init that hides many of the messy details from us. Unfortunately, it doesn't hide the messy details of calling HAL_UART_Init, but you can't have everything. In the uart2_Init function, we have to set up an initialization structure and then call HAL_UART_Init:

```
void uart2_Init(void)
{
    // UART initialization
    // UART2 -- one connected to ST-LINK USB
 ❶ uartHandle.Instance = USART2;
 ❷ uartHandle.Init.BaudRate = 9600;                            // Speed 9600
 ❸ uartHandle.Init.WordLength = UART_WORDLENGTH_8B;            // 8 bits/character
 ❹ uartHandle.Init.StopBits = UART_STOPBITS_1;                // 1 stop bit
 ❺ uartHandle.Init.Parity = UART_PARITY_NONE;                 // No parity
 ❻ uartHandle.Init.Mode = UART_MODE_TX_RX;                    // Transmit & receive
 ❼ uartHandle.Init.HwFlowCtl = UART_HWCONTROL_NONE;           // No hw control

    // Oversample the incoming stream.
    uartHandle.Init.OverSampling = UART_OVERSAMPLING_16;

    // Do not use one-bit sampling.
 ❽ uartHandle.Init.OneBitSampling = UART_ONE_BIT_SAMPLE_DISABLE;

    // Nothing advanced
 ❾ uartHandle.AdvancedInit.AdvFeatureInit = UART_ADVFEATURE_NO_INIT;
    /*
     * For those of you connecting a terminal emulator, the above parameters
     * translate to 9600,8,N,1.
     */

    if (HAL_UART_Init(&uartHandle) != HAL_OK)
    {
        Error_Handler();
    }
}
```

We first tell the system which UART to use ❶. Our chip has more than one, and the second one is connected to the USB serial interface. Next, we set the speed to 9,600 baud (bits/second) ❷, or 960 characters a second. Why the 10 to 1 ratio? We have 1 bit for the start bit, 8 data bits, and 1 stop bit. The number of bits per character is 8, because C stores characters in 8-bit units. It is possible to have systems with 5, 6, 7, or 9 bits per character, but almost everyone uses 8, except for a TDD deaf communication device, which uses 5. We need to tell the system that we're using 8 bits ❸.

The next line configures the number of stop bits ❹, which is the amount of time (in bits) that occurs between characters. Most people use 1 stop bit. (If the sender uses 2 and the receiver uses 1, it still works. The extra bit will be interpreted as between-character idle time.)

Early serial devices used a 7-bit character and 1 parity bit. The parity bit provided a simple, primitive method of error checking. We do not use this feature, so we turn parity off ❺. We then enable the transmitter and receiver ❻.

The original serial interface (RS-232 standard) has a number of hardware flow control lines. On our board, they are not wired up, and we don't use them ❼.

One of this UART's advanced features is *oversampling*, which allows the receiver to check the state of an incoming bit multiple times before deciding whether it is a one or a zero. This feature is sometimes useful when you have a noisy electrical environment and are running serial cables over long distances. Our serial "cable" consists of two traces that run from the bottom of the board to the top, a distance of about 3 inches. We don't need oversampling, but we do have to turn it off ❽. Finally, we are not using any advanced features.

Next, we call `HAL_UART_Init` to initialize the UART ❾, which needs help to do its job. The general-purpose input/output (GPIO) pins on our processor can do a lot of different things, including act as GPIO pins. Most of them have "alternate functions," meaning that you can program them to act as different devices (GPIO pin, USART device, SPI bus, I2C bus, PWM pin, and so on). Note that not all pins support all devices. Finally, `HAL_UART_Init` calls `HAL_UART_MspInit`, which sets up pins for the UART:

```
HAL_StatusTypeDef HAL_UART_Init(UART_HandleTypeDef *huart)
{
  /* Check the UART handle allocation. */
  if(huart == NULL)
  {
    return HAL_ERROR;
  }
  // ...
  if(huart->gState == HAL_UART_STATE_RESET)
  {
    /* Allocate lock resource and initialize it. */
    huart->Lock = HAL_UNLOCKED;

    /* Initialize the low-level hardware: GPIO, CLOCK. */
    HAL_UART_MspInit(huart);
  }
```

We need to supply `HAL_UART_MspInit`. Keep in mind that pins are expensive and transistors to drive them are cheap. By default, the two pins that drive our serial device, named PA2 and PA3, are GPIO pins. We need to tell the system to use the pins' alternate function and turn them into serial device pins.

Our `HAL_UART_MspInit` function looks a lot like the initialization code for the GPIO pin we used for "blink," but with some slight differences:

```
void HAL_UART_MspInit(UART_HandleTypeDef* uart)
{
  GPIO_InitTypeDef GPIO_InitStruct;
❶ if(uart->Instance == USART2)
  {
    /* Peripheral clock enable */
❷    __HAL_RCC_USART2_CLK_ENABLE();
```

```
        /*
         * USART2 GPIO Configuration
         * PA2      ------> USART2_TX
         * PA3      ------> USART2_RX
         */
        GPIO_InitStruct.Pin = GPIO_PIN_2|GPIO_PIN_3;
        GPIO_InitStruct.Mode = GPIO_MODE_AF_PP;
        GPIO_InitStruct.Pull = GPIO_NOPULL;
        GPIO_InitStruct.Speed = GPIO_SPEED_FREQ_LOW;
        // Alternate function -- that of UART
    ❸ GPIO_InitStruct.Alternate = GPIO_AF1_USART2;
        HAL_GPIO_Init(GPIOA, &GPIO_InitStruct);
    }
}
```

This function starts by checking which USART we are using. We only set up USART2 in this code ❶. Then we enable the clock for the device ❷. Next, we configure the GPIO pins ❸ (we've done this before in our blink program), which tells the chip that PA2/PA3 are not GPIO pins but instead should be connected to USART2.

Transmitting a Character

We'll use the myPutchar function to transmit characters over the serial device. The USART is a memory-mapped I/O device. To send a character, we have to assign (write) it to the magic memory location (a *register*), and then it goes out the wire:

```
uartHandle.Instance->TDR = ch;     // Send character to the UART.
```

We also need to time the character just right, and that requires some extra code:

```
void myPutchar(const char ch)
{
    // This line gets and saves the value of UART_FLAG_TXE at call
    // time. This value changes so if you stop the program on the "if"
    // line below, the value will be set to zero because it goes away
    // faster than you can look at it.
    int result __attribute__((unused)) =
        (uartHandle.Instance->ISR & UART_FLAG_TXE);

    // Block until the transmit empty (TXE) flag is set.
    while ((uartHandle.Instance->ISR & UART_FLAG_TXE) == 0)
        continue;

    uartHandle.Instance->TDR = ch;     // Send character to the UART.
}
```

The register we are writing is called the *transmit data register (TDR)*. If we write this register while a character is being transmitted, the new character overwrites the old one, causing errors and confusion. To send a, b, c, we'd write code like this:

```
uartHandle.Instance->TDR = 'a';
sleep_1_960_second();
uartHandle.Instance->TDR = 'b';
sleep_1_960_second();
uartHandle.Instance->TDR = 'c';
sleep_1_960_second();
```

This sort of timing is tricky, especially if we want to execute code between characters. The STM32 chip has a bit for everything, including "TDR empty, you can write another character now."

This bit is in a register called the *interrupt and status register (ISR)* that has a number of bits in it indicating the status of the device. Figure 9-2 shows a diagram of this register from the STM32F030R8 reference manual ("RM0360 Reference manual/STM32F030x4/x6/x8/xC and STM32F070x6/xB").

22.7.7 Interrupt and status register (12C_ISR)

Address offset: 0x18
Reset value: 0x0000 0001
Access: No wait states

31	30	29	28	27	26	25	24	23	22	21	20	19	18	17	16
Res.	Res.	Res.	Res.	Res.	Res.	Res.	Res.	ADDCODE [6:0]							DIR
											r				r

15	14	13	12	11	10	9	8	7	6	5	4	3	2	1	0
BUSY	Res.	ALERT	TIME OUT	PEC ERR	OVR	ARLO	BERR	TCR	TC	STOPF	NACKF	ADDR	RXNE	TXIS	TXE
r		r	r	r	r	r	r	r	r	r	r	r	r	rs	rs

Figure 9-2: Interrupt and status register contents

We are interested in the bit named TXE (bit 0 in the diagram). The HAL defines the TXE bit using the name UART_FLAG_TXE. We must wait for the TXE bit to clear (become zero) before we can send data to the TDR without clobbering a character being transmitted. Nothing in the code changes uartHandle.Instance->ISR.

However, uartHandle.Instance->ISR is a magic memory location electrically connected to the device. The state of the device changes when something like a character transmission completes, and when that happens, the contents of uartHandle.Instance->ISR change as well.

The ISR field is declared volatile *to tell C that it can change magically at any time in ways that are not under the control of the compiler.*

Now if you try to examine uartHandle.Instance->ISR using the debugger, the UART_FLAG_TXE flag will appear always to be set. That's because it's cleared when a character is transmitted (in 1/960th of a second), which is a long time in terms of computers, but a very short time in terms of humans typing commands.

To help show what's going on, we've added a useless statement:

```
int result __attribute__((unused)) =
    (uartHandle.Instance->ISR & UART_FLAG_TXE);
```

This statement tests the value of UART_FLAG_TXE and stores it in result. Now the value of (uartHandle.Instance->ISR & UART_FLAG_TXE) might magically change, but the value result will remain the same for the lifetime of the procedure.

You can look at result in the debugger and see what the value of the bit was at the beginning of the loop. You'll notice a strange phrase in the code:

```
__attribute__((unused))
```

This is a GCC extension to the C language. It tells the compiler that we know this variable is not used, so it doesn't generate a warning. (In fact, it's not used by the program, but it may be used by the debugger. The compiler doesn't see anything outside the program itself.)

The string we send for "Hello World" ends with \r\n (carriage return, line feed). In our original "Hello World" program from Chapter 1, the operating system edited the output stream and changed \n into \r\n for us. We have no operating system, so we must do it all ourselves.

Listing 9-3 contains the full serial version of our "Hello World" program.

```
/**
 * @brief Write hello world on the serial port.
 */
#include <stdbool.h>
#include "stm32f0xx_nucleo.h"
#include "stm32f0xx.h"

const char hello[] = "Hello World!\r\n";   // The message to send
int current; // The character in the message we are sending

UART_HandleTypeDef uartHandle;       // UART initialization

/**
 * @brief This function is executed in case of error occurrence.
 *
 * All it does is blink the LED.
 */
void Error_Handler(void)
{
```

```
        /* Turn LED2 on. */
        HAL_GPIO_WritePin(LED2_GPIO_PORT, LED2_PIN, GPIO_PIN_SET);

        while (true)
        {
            // Toggle the state of LED2.
            HAL_GPIO_TogglePin(LED2_GPIO_PORT, LED2_PIN);
            HAL_Delay(1000);           // Wait one second.
        }
}
/**
 * Send character to the UART.
 *
 * @param ch The character to send
 */
void myPutchar(const char ch)
{
    // This line gets and saves the value of UART_FLAG_TXE at call
    // time. This value changes so if you stop the program on the "if"
    // line below, the value will be set to zero because it goes away
    // faster than you can look at it.
    int result __attribute__((unused)) =
        (uartHandle.Instance->ISR & UART_FLAG_TXE);

    // Block until the transmit empty (TXE) flag is set.
    while ((uartHandle.Instance->ISR & UART_FLAG_TXE) == 0)
        continue;

    uartHandle.Instance->TDR = ch;      // Send character to the UART.
}

/**
 * Initialize LED2 (so we can blink red for error).
 */
void led2_Init(void)
{
    // LED clock initialization
    LED2_GPIO_CLK_ENABLE();

    GPIO_InitTypeDef GPIO_LedInit;      // Initialization for the LED
    // Initialize LED.
    GPIO_LedInit.Pin = LED2_PIN;
    GPIO_LedInit.Mode = GPIO_MODE_OUTPUT_PP;
    GPIO_LedInit.Pull = GPIO_PULLUP;
    GPIO_LedInit.Speed = GPIO_SPEED_FREQ_HIGH;
    HAL_GPIO_Init(LED2_GPIO_PORT, &GPIO_LedInit);
}

/**
 * Initialize UART2 for output.
 */
void uart2_Init(void)
{
    // UART initialization
    // UART2 -- one connected to ST-LINK USB
```

```
    uartHandle.Instance = USART2;
    uartHandle.Init.BaudRate = 9600;                    // Speed 9600
    uartHandle.Init.WordLength = UART_WORDLENGTH_8B;     // 8 bits/character
    uartHandle.Init.StopBits = UART_STOPBITS_1;         // 1 stop bit
    uartHandle.Init.Parity = UART_PARITY_NONE;          // No parity
    uartHandle.Init.Mode = UART_MODE_TX_RX;             // Transmit & receive
    uartHandle.Init.HwFlowCtl = UART_HWCONTROL_NONE;    // No hw control

    // Oversample the incoming stream.
    uartHandle.Init.OverSampling = UART_OVERSAMPLING_16;

    // Do not use one-bit sampling.
    uartHandle.Init.OneBitSampling = UART_ONE_BIT_SAMPLE_DISABLE;

    // Nothing advanced
    uartHandle.AdvancedInit.AdvFeatureInit = UART_ADVFEATURE_NO_INIT;
    /*
     * For those of you connecting a terminal emulator, the above parameters
     * translate to 9600,8,N,1.
     */

    if (HAL_UART_Init(&uartHandle) != HAL_OK)
    {
        Error_Handler();
    }
}

int main(void)
{
    HAL_Init(); // Initialize hardware.
    led2_Init();
    uart2_Init();

    // Keep sending the message for a long time.
    for (;;) {
        // Send character by character.
        for(current = 0; hello[current] != '\0'; ++current) {
            myPutchar(hello[current]);
        }
        HAL_Delay(500);
    }
}

/**
 * Magic function that's called by the HAL layer to actually
 * initialize the UART. In this case we need to
 * put the UART pins in alternate mode so they act as
 * UART pins and not like GPIO pins.
 *
 * @note: Only works for UART2, the one connected to the USB serial
 * converter
 *
 * @param uart The UART information
```

```
 */
void HAL_UART_MspInit(UART_HandleTypeDef* uart)
{
    GPIO_InitTypeDef GPIO_InitStruct;
    if(uart->Instance == USART2)
    {
        /* Peripheral clock enable */
        __HAL_RCC_USART2_CLK_ENABLE();

        /*
         * USART2 GPIO Configuration
         * PA2       ------> USART2_TX
         * PA3       ------> USART2_RX
         */
        GPIO_InitStruct.Pin = GPIO_PIN_2|GPIO_PIN_3;
        GPIO_InitStruct.Mode = GPIO_MODE_AF_PP;
        GPIO_InitStruct.Pull = GPIO_NOPULL;
        GPIO_InitStruct.Speed = GPIO_SPEED_FREQ_LOW;
        // Alternate function -- that of UART
        GPIO_InitStruct.Alternate = GPIO_AF1_USART2;
        HAL_GPIO_Init(GPIOA, &GPIO_InitStruct);
    }

}

/**
 * Magic function called by HAL layer to de-initialize the
 * UART hardware. It's something we never do, but we put it
 * in here for the sake of completeness.
 *
 * @note: Only works for UART2, the one connected to the USB serial
 * converter
 *
 * @param uart The UART information
 */
void HAL_UART_MspDeInit(UART_HandleTypeDef* uart)
{
    if(uart->Instance == USART2)
    {
        /* Peripheral clock disable */
        __HAL_RCC_USART2_CLK_DISABLE();

        /*
         * USART2 GPIO Configuration
         * PA2       ------> USART2_TX
         * PA3       ------> USART2_RX
         */
        HAL_GPIO_DeInit(GPIOA, GPIO_PIN_2|GPIO_PIN_3);
    }
}
```

Listing 9-3: Program 08.serial

Communicating with the Device

We now have a program that sends out the "Hello World" message on the serial line. The serial line is connected to the USB/serial device on the board, which is plugged in to your computer. To view the message, you need to run a terminal emulator on your computer. Figure 9-3 shows the setup.

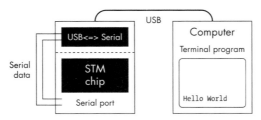

Figure 9-3: Serial communications

Each operating system has a different terminal emulator program, and in some cases, more than one. The ones mentioned here are common, free, and easy to use.

Windows

On Windows, we'll use the PuTTY program (*https://putty.org*). Download and install it on your system, selecting the defaults for all options, and then follow these steps:

1. Make sure the Nucleo board is *not* connected to your computer. Open the Control Panel and go to the Device Manager screen (see Figure 9-4). There is no serial device and, therefore, no Ports section in the list.

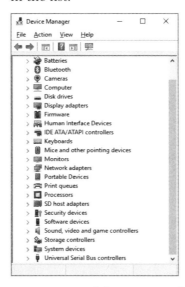

Figure 9-4: Serial device not installed

2. Plug in the Nucleo board. The device list will change as shown in Figure 9-5.

Figure 9-5: New USB serial device

You should see a new USB serial device named COM3. (Windows has a system for assigning COM parts to serial devices, but no one knows what that is. You may see a different COM port on your machine.)

3. Start PuTTY. In the main window, shown in Figure 9-6, select the **Serial** radio button. Under **Serial Line**, select the new COM port you just found in the Device Manager. The speed should default to 9600.

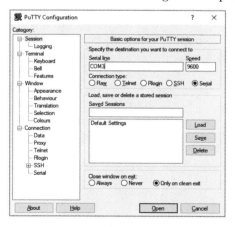

Figure 9-6: Starting PuTTY

4. Click **Open**. A terminal window should appear, and the device should start greeting you.

Linux and macOS

On Unix-based systems like Linux and macOS, the screen program works well. (The minicom program also does the job.) To use screen, you need to know the serial device's name, which is different on different operating systems. On Linux, the device is most likely */dev/ttyACM0*, although if you have other serial devices plugged in, it might be */dev/ttyACM1*, */dev/ttyACM2*, or similar. On macOS, the name is likely */dev/tty.usbmodem001*, but it could be */dev/tty.usbmodem002*, */dev/tty.usbmodem003*, or something similar.

To find the name, make sure the Nucleo board is *not* connected to your computer, then execute one of the following commands in the terminal:

```
$ ls /dev/ttyACM*        (Linux)
$ ls /dev/tty.usbmodem*  (macOS)
```

Plug in the device and execute the same command again. You should see one more device in the list. Use that one. Now execute the following command:

```
$ screen /dev/ttyACM0 9600
```

You should see "Hello World" appear. To exit the program, press CTRL-A-\.

Summary

This programming book covers "Hello World" in Chapter 9. Why? Because we had to do everything ourselves. Writing a simple program to send out our message, character by character, involved initializing the UART (a nontrivial process), telling the GPIO pin that it was now a serial pin, and using a hardware register (those mysterious memory locations that magically change depending on the state of the device) to see when the UART was ready to transmit a character.

We've made a tremendous leap forward. First, we've programmed a moderately complex device and in the process learned a lot about direct low-level I/O. Second, the serial port is the main diagnostic and maintenance device hidden in many embedded devices. Despite all the advances in computer technology in the last 60 years, the most commonly used debugging technique is still printf to the serial port. The serial port is a very simple robust device that's cheap to make and easy to connect to, and now we know how to use it to debug our embedded systems.

Programming Problems

1. For the student: After you get the program working, see what happens if you remove the \r. Then try it with the \r back in, but the \n removed.

2. Moderately difficult mystery: Try changing the configuration so that you send 7 data bits and even parity (instead of 8 data bits, no parity). Do not change your terminal emulator's configuration. Some of the characters will be changed. Examine the bit pattern of the characters and figure out which ones changed and why.

3. Advanced: As written, our program has no flow control. You're going to get a "Hello World" whether you like it or not. Change the initialization code to use soft flow control. This means when you type the XOFF character (CTRL-S), the output should stop. When you type XON (CTRL-Q), it should resume.

4. Advanced: Write a function for the Nucleo board that reads a character. It will look much like the myPutchar function, only it will check a different bit and read the I/O port instead of writing to it. You'll need to read the microcontroller's documentation to see what the RDR bit does.

10

INTERRUPTS

The two main methods for handling I/O are *polling*, which repeatedly asks the device whether it has any data ready, and *interrupts*, which are when the device interrupts normal workflow to tell you it's ready. This chapter describes the difference between polling and interrupts as well as explains how interrupts work so you can use them to write a string to the serial port more efficiently (yes, "Hello World" again).

Polling vs. Interrupts

Let's consider how polling and interrupts would work in the case of the telephone. With polling, the ringer is turned off, and you must check the phone every 10 seconds to see whether a call is coming in. You must sit by the phone and not get bored easily. This method is what we used in our previous serial program in Chapter 9, which basically went like the following dialogue:

"Are you busy?" "Yes."

"Are you busy?" "Yes."

"Are you busy?" "Yes."

"Are you busy?" "No." "Here's the next character."

The computer is stuck in a polling loop, waiting for the UART status register to indicate that the UART is ready for the next character. At this point, the computer has nothing else to do and doesn't get bored. The main advantages of polling are that it's easy to understand and implement.

Let's go back to the telephone again, but this time we'll use the interrupt method. You don't sit by the phone continually checking whether a call is coming in. Instead, you go about your normal business until the phone rings (an interrupt occurs). Then you drop everything, race to the phone, and pick up it—only to discover that it's another telemarketing call for something you wouldn't buy in a million years.

The key sequence of events in the interrupt scenario is as follows:

1. We go about our normal work.

2. We get an interrupt (the phone rings).

3. We pick up the phone (service the interrupt), shout "No, I don't want to buy a combination shaving brush and fountain pen," and hang up.

4. We resume our normal work where we left off.

Interrupts for Serial I/O

We can send characters to the UART only when the transmit data register (TDR) is empty. Figure 10-1 shows a block diagram of a portion of the UART to illustrate how the TDR works.

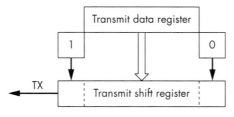

Figure 10-1: UART transmission hardware

When we want to send a character, we dump it in the TDR, which holds 8 bits. The character is then dumped into the *transmit shift register (TSR)*, which holds 10 bits. The 2 extra bits are the start bit at the beginning of the character and the stop bit at the end of the character. The TSR then sends the data out the *transmit serial line (TX)* one bit at a time.

When the data is moved from the TDR to the TSR, the TDR becomes empty and is ready to receive another character.

The polling loop we've been using looks like the following:

```
// Block until the transmit empty (TXE) flag is set.
while ((uartHandle.Instance->ISR & UART_FLAG_TXE) == 0)
    continue;
```

In English, this says, "Are you empty yet? Are you empty yet? Are you empty yet?" And it's just as annoying in C code as it is in English. Again, polling's main advantage is its simplicity.

The other way to transmit characters is to tell the system we want an interrupt when the UART is ready to receive another character. An interrupt function is called automatically when something occurs. In our case, we want an interrupt when the TDR is empty.

With interrupts, we tell the processor, "I'm going to go off and do useful work. When the TDR is empty, I want you to interrupt the normal flow and call an *interrupt routine* function, so I can give you the next character."

Interrupt Routines

When an interrupt occurs, the CPU calls an interrupt routine function, located at a fixed address determined by the CPU's design. Early CPUs had *one* address for all interrupts, so the code had to go through a number of checks to see what had interrupted:

```
if (diskInterrupt)     { handleDiskInterrupt(); return;}
if (serialInterrupt)   { handleSerialInterrupt(); return;}
if (keyboardInterrupt) { handleKeyboardInterrupt(); return;}
if (mouseInterrupt)    { handleMouseInterrupt(); return;}
logUnknownInterrupt();
```

Nowadays, even a simple chip can have many different devices. Checking all of them to see which one interrupted is a time-consuming process. As a result, chips (including our ARM chip), now use *vectored interrupts*, which means each peripheral gets its own interrupt address. Interrupts from UART1 will call an interrupt routine at one address, while interrupts from UART2 will go to another (specifically USART2_IRQHandler), and so on for other peripheral devices.

The interrupt vector is defined in the *startup/startup_stm32f030x8.S* file:

```
g_pfnVectors:
  .word   _estack
  .word   Reset_Handler
  .word   NMI_Handler
  .word   HardFault_Handler
# Many more handlers
  .word   USART1_IRQHandler          /* USART1 */
  .word   USART2_IRQHandler          /* USART2 */
```

Later, the code defines the USART2_IRQHandler symbol:

```
.weak       USART2_IRQHandler
.thumb_set  USART2_IRQHandler,Default_Handler
```

The second directive (.thumb_set) defines the procedure USART2_IRQHandler to be the same as Default_Handler.

The first .weak directive defines it as a *weak symbol*. If it were a regular symbol and we tried to define our own USART2_IRQHandler, the linker would abort with a Duplicate symbol error message. However, because the symbol is weak, the linker will throw away the weak definition and use the one that we provide.

NOTE *The STM documentation sometimes labels our serial I/O port as both a UART (asynchronous I/O) and a USART (synchronous I/O) port. The port can do either one depending on configuration. Thus, we have one serial I/O port that has two names: USART and UART. It'd just be too easy if they picked one name and stuck to it.*

The *startup/startup_stm32f030x8.S* file defines Default_Handler later:

```
    .section .text.Default_Handler,"ax",%progbits
Default_Handler:
Infinite_Loop:
  b Infinite_Loop
```

The default response to an interrupt is to loop forever, making the machine almost totally useless (I say "almost totally useless" because the machine will still respond to the debugger and a reset).

We'll write our own USART2_IRQHandler to respond when the TDR is empty and thereby replace the default handler with something more useful.

Writing a String with Interrupts

Now let's change our serial I/O program from Chapter 9 so that it uses interrupts instead of polling to write a string. All that's communicated between the upper layer (the main program) and the lower layer (interrupt routine) is a single global variable:

```
const char* volatile usart2String = NULL;      // The string we are sending
```

The const qualifier tells C that the character data is constant and we'll never attempt to change it. The volatile qualifier tells C that this variable may be changed at any time by something outside the flow of a normal C program, such as an interrupt function.

To clarify, because C's syntax is a little complex at this point, the const appears before the char declaration and means that the character data is constant. It does not appear after the pointer operator (*), so the pointer is not constant. The `volatile` modifier appears after the pointer operator, indicating the pointer may be changed. The lack of the `const` modifier after the pointer operator means that the program can change this value.

It is possible to have a `const` `volatile` variable, which would tell C that the program cannot change the value of the variable, but something outside the scope of the program can. For example, the UART receive register can be `const` `volatile`. We can't change it, but every time a character comes in, it changes.

We need to be careful with any variables used by both layers. Fortunately, for this example, that's just one variable, `usart2String`. The following lists show the workflow for that variable:

Upper Layer (Main Program)

1. Wait for `usart2String` to become `NULL`.
2. Point it to the string we want to send to the output.
3. Send the first character.
4. Increment the pointer.
5. Enable the UART interrupt.

Lower Layer (Interrupt)

1. If we've reached the end of the string, set `usart2String` to `NULL`.
2. Acknowledge that the UART received the interrupt.
3. Send the character pointed to by the string.
4. Increment the pointer.

Both the upper and lower layers increment the pointer. We need to be very careful when it comes to enabling the interrupt to make sure both layers don't try to use the pointer at the same time. The upper layer won't do anything until `usart2String == NULL`, and the lower layer sets `usart2String` to `NULL` only when it has run out of data and disables the UART2 interrupt. The upper layer protects itself by not enabling interrupts until after it performs the increment. Thus, the interrupt routine cannot monkey with the code.

This analysis is extremely important. When it's not done or not done properly, the program will fail, and the failures will occur at random times with random results. These results pose an extremely difficult, debug-resistant problem.

I actually spent about three years finding one of these bugs. The problem occurred only for one customer and only about once every two months. We were completely unable to reproduce it in the lab. Fortunately, the customer was very mellow and willing to work with us on the solution. Later in this chapter, we'll explore what happens when this analysis is not done and consider some techniques for diagnosing interrupt-related bugs.

Listing 10-1 contains the interrupt-driven serial I/O program.

```
/**
 * @brief   Write Hello World to the serial I/O.
 * Use interrupts instead of polling.
 */

#include <stdbool.h>
#include "stm32f0xx_nucleo.h"
#include "stm32f0xx.h"

const char hello[] = "Hello World!\r\n";   // The message to send
int current; // The character in the message we are sending

UART_HandleTypeDef uartHandle;       // UART initialization

... Error_Handler same as Listing 9-3 ...

const char* volatile usart2String = NULL;       // The string we are sending
/**
 * Handle the USART2 interrupt.
 *
 * Magically called by the chip's interrupt system.
 * Name is fixed because of the startup code that
 * populates the interrupt vector.
 */
void USART2_IRQHandler(void)
{
    if ((uartHandle.Instance->ISR & USART_ISR_TXE) != 0) {
        // This should never happen, but we don't want to crash if it does.
        if (usart2String == NULL) {
            // Turn off interrupt.
            uartHandle.Instance->CR1 &= ~(USART_CR1_TXEIE);
            return;
        }
        if (*usart2String == '\0') {
            usart2String = NULL;        // We're done with the string.
            // Turn off interrupt.
            uartHandle.Instance->CR1 &= ~(USART_CR1_TXEIE);
            return;
        }
        uartHandle.Instance->TDR = *usart2String; // Send character to the
UART.
        ++usart2String;                 // Point to next character.
        return;
    }
    // Since the only interrupt we enabled was TXE, we should never
    // get here. When we do enable other interrupts, we need to put
    // code to handle them here.
}
/**
 * Our version of puts
 *
 * Outputs the exact string given to the output
 *
 * @param str String to send
 *
```

```
 * @note Assumes that str is not null and not
 * pointing to the empty string
 */
void myPuts(const char* str)
{
    // If someone is sending a string, wait for it.
    while (usart2String != NULL)
        continue;

    // Tell the interrupt route what string to use.
    usart2String = str;

    uartHandle.Instance->TDR = *usart2String;   // Send character to the UART.
    ++usart2String;                // Point to next character.
    // Enable the interrupt.
    uartHandle.Instance->CR1 |= USART_CR1_TXEIE;
}

... led2_Init and uart2_Init, same as Listing 9-3 ...

int main(void)
{
    HAL_Init(); // Initialize hardware.
    led2_Init();
    uart2_Init();
    // Tell the chip that we want the interrupt vector
    // for USART2 to be enabled.
    NVIC_EnableIRQ(USART2_IRQn);

    // Keep sending the message for a long time.
    for (;;) {
        myPuts(hello);
        HAL_Delay(500);
    }
}

... HAL_UART_MspInit and HAL_UART_MspDeInit, same as Listing 9-3 ...
```

Listing 10-1: 10.serial.int/main.c

Program Details

Listing 10-1 looks a lot like the serial I/O program from Chapter 9, because setting up the I/O system is the same, with a lot of extra little details. But in this case, we added something new:

```
int main(void)
{
    HAL_Init(); // Initialize hardware
    led2_Init();
    uart2_Init();
    // Tell the chip that we want the interrupt vector
    // for USART2 to be enabled.
    NVIC_EnableIRQ(USART2_IRQn);
```

The NVIC_EnableIRQ function initializes the *nested vectored interrupt controller (NVIC)*, which is a bit of hardware that decides what the processor does when it receives an interrupt and enables the USART2 interrupt. When the processor is reset, it turns off all interrupts, so we need to tell it that we want USART2 to interrupt it.

Now let's look at the myPuts function, which sends a string (instead of a single character, like myPutchar from Chapter 9) to the serial device:

```
void myPuts(const char* str)
{
    // If someone is sending a string, wait for it.
  ❶ while (usart2String != NULL)
        continue;

    // Tell the interrupt route what string to use.
  ❷ usart2String = str;

  ❸ uartHandle.Instance->TDR = *usart2String;  // Send character to the UART.
    ++usart2String;               // Point to next character.
    // Enable the interrupt.
  ❹ uartHandle.Instance->CR1 |= USART_CR1_TXEIE;
}
```

The first thing we do is wait for the previous string to finish ❶. We know that if usart2String is not NULL, the interrupt routine is active and we should wait until the previous string is transmitted. When it becomes NULL, the interrupt routine is inactive and we can start our transmission.

When we do get our turn, we tell the interrupt function what string we are transmitting ❷, and then we transmit the first character ❸. As a final step, we enable the transmit data buffer empty interrupt ❹.

Several symbols control what interrupts are enabled. The USART_CR1_TXNEIE bit tells the UART to interrupt when the transmit data buffer is empty. Here are some other symbols to note:

USART_CR1_IDLEIE   IDLE interrupt enable

USART_CR1_RXNEIE   Receive interrupt enable

USART_CR1_TCIE   Transmission complete interrupt enable (interrupt when the character has gone out, not when we first load a character into the transmission register)

USART_CR1_PEIE   Parity error interrupt enable

Once we send the first character, the TDR is filled. When it is transferred to the TSR, the TDR will be empty and we'll get an interrupt. From here on, the interrupt routine does the work.

The actual interrupt routine is as follows:

```
❶ void USART2_IRQHandler(void)
{
  ❷ if ((uartHandle.Instance->ISR & USART_ISR_TXE) != 0) {
        // This should never happen, but we don't want to crash if it does.
      ❸ if (usart2String == NULL) {
```

```
                    // Turn off interrupt.
                    uartHandle.Instance->CR1 &= ~(USART_CR1_TXEIE);
                    return;
            }
   ❹ if (*usart2String == '\0') {
                    usart2String = NULL;        // We're done with the string.
                    // Turn off interrupt.
                    uartHandle.Instance->CR1 &= ~(USART_CR1_TXEIE);
                    return;
            }
   ❺ uartHandle.Instance->TDR = *usart2String; // Send character to the
UART.
   ❻ ++usart2String;              // Point to next character.
           return;
   }
   // Since the only interrupt we enabled was TXE, we should never
   // get here. When we do enable other interrupts, we need to put
   // code to handle them here.
}
```

The function declaration uses a magic name that identifies it as the interrupt routine ❶.

If the function gets called, we know we have an interrupt from USART2, but we don't know what type of interrupt it is because the USART has multiple types of interrupts:

USART_ISR_TXE   TDR empty

USART_ISR_CTSIF   CTS interrupt

USART_ISR_TC   Transmission complete

USART_ISR_RXNE   Receive data register not empty (data ready to be read)

USART_ISR_ORE   Overrun error detected

USART_ISR_IDLE   Idle line detected

USART_ISR_FE   Framing error

USART_ISR_PE   Parity error

USART_ISR_NE   Noise flag

USART_ISR_CMF   Character match

USART_ISR_TXE   Receiver timeout

All of these interrupts will result in a call to USART2_IRQHandler.

First, we need to check whether we have a transmit buffer empty interrupt ❷. Our interrupt function should never be called with usart2String set to NULL, but "should" and "reality" are vastly different, so we put in a little bit of paranoia to make sure we don't crash if something goes wrong ❸. The variable usart2String should never be NULL at this point, but if it is, we don't want to cause trouble.

Without that check, we might try to deference a NULL pointer ❹. Dereferencing a NULL pointer is illegal, and the STM32 is nice enough to have hardware to check for this condition. When it occurs, the STM32 generates a *memory fault interrupt*. In other words, the interrupt handler is being interrupted, and control transfers to the memory fault interrupt handler. However, we haven't written one, so the default handler is executed. As mentioned previously, the default handler locks up the system until you reset it. To protect ourselves against an improper usart2String, when we see it, we do the safest thing, which is to turn off the interrupt and do nothing else ❸.

Next, we check to see whether we've run out of string. If we have, we NULL out the string to signal to the top level that we're done and to turn off interrupts. Otherwise, we know we have data for the UART and that the TDR is empty, so we dump a character into it ❺. Once we've sent the character, we need to point to the next one for the next time we get interrupted, and then return to the main program ❻.

At this point, the TDR is full, and the UART is sending characters. The interrupt route has nothing more to do, so it will return and normal execution will resume. When the character is sent and the TDR is empty, we'll get another interrupt, which will continue until we run out of string and turn off the interrupt.

NOTE   *The ARM chip is nice in that an ordinary procedure can serve as an interrupt routine. The chip does the saving and restoring of all the state needed to execute the routine safely. Other chips are not so nice. For example, the PIC family of processors requires the use of a keyword interrupt (a PIC extension) before each interrupt routine:* interrupt PIC_GPIO_Interrupt(void).

The hardware engineers at STMicroelectronics have helpfully explained this process with a diagram (see Figure 10-2).

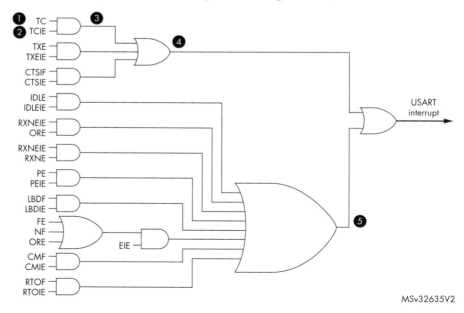

MSv32635V2

Figure 10-2: USART interrupt mapping

This diagram shows that if the TCIE (transmit character interrupt enable) bit is on ❶ and a character has been transmitted (TC) ❷, the output of the AND gate is true ❸. This result is combined with the output of three other interrupts, and if any one is true (OR gate), the result ❹ is true. Then that result is combined with the output of another OR gate ❺ for all the other signals, and the result of the last OR gate is the USART interrupt signal. Note that the diagram is meant to simplify this process. If you want to know what the alphabet soup of inputs mean, read the 800-page reference manual for this processor.

Interrupt Hell

Interrupts are extremely powerful tools when it comes to controlling hardware as well as dealing with events in real time. However, using interrupts can cause a number of unique and difficult problems to occur.

First, they can interrupt normal program flow at any time. For example, consider the following code:

```
i = 5;
if (i == 5) {
```

What's the value of i after this statement is executed? The answer is obviously 5, unless an interrupt routine just executed and modified it:

```
i = 5;
←----- interrupt triggers, i set to 6.
if (i == 5) { // No longer true
```

Second, interrupt routines execute asynchronously, which means they execute whenever they feel like it, so any bugs caused by poorly written interrupt routines can be difficult to reproduce. I've seen cases where a bug occurred only randomly after about two weeks of testing because the interrupt had to occur exactly when one of two instructions was executing—that's two out of the tens of thousands in the code. It took a lot of testing to stumble upon this problem.

Because of the inherent difficulties with interrupt routines, it pays to give them a lot of respect. The most important design rule when dealing with interrupt routines is to keep them small and simple, because the less the routine does, the less there is that can go wrong. It's better to leave the "thinking" to the higher-level code where debuggers work nicely and where reproducibility is not a problem.

Interrupt routines also need to execute quickly, because while an interrupt routine is executing, other interrupts are held off until the routine is finished. If you take a long time in an interrupt routine that's reading a character from UART1, another device, such as UART2, might lose data because its interrupt couldn't get serviced in time.

Using a Buffer to Increase Speed

The system we just used has some limits. It can transmit only one message at a time. Suppose we wanted to output multiple short messages. Each one would have to wait until the previous one finished. Here's an example:

```
myPuts("There are ");
if (messageCount == 0)
    myPuts(" no ");                // Blocks waiting on previous message
else
    myPuts(" some ");             // Blocks waiting on previous message
myPuts("messages waiting\r\n"); // Blocks waiting on previous message
```

One solution to this problem is to create a *buffer* to hold the character data until the interrupt routine can service it. Doing that adds complexity to the application, but it increases the speed at which your top-level program can send data.

Using serial I/O means considering the general trend of speed versus simplicity. The polling version was very simple and slow. The single string interrupt version was faster but more complex. The buffer system we are using now is much faster and much more complex. This trend is true for most programs.

For this problem, let's go back to the buffer. We'll use a *circular buffer* that has the following basic structure:

```
struct circularBuffer {
    uint32_t putIndex;      // Where we will put the next character
    uint32_t getIndex;      // Where to get the next character
    uint32_t nCharacters;   // Number of characters in the buffer
    char data[BUFFER_SIZE]; // The data in the buffer
}
```

It's called a circular buffer because the indices wrap. In other words, after a character is put in the last element of data, the putIndex will wrap from 7 (BUFFER_SIZE-1) to 0.

Graphically, this looks like Figure 10-3.

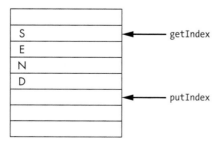

Figure 10-3: A circular buffer in action

Our implementation is going to contain a deliberate nasty mistake, so we can look at techniques and procedures for finding such mistakes in a small, controlled program. I'll show the symptoms of the bug, the diagnostic techniques used to locate it, and the fix as we go through the program.

The first time I encountered a problem like this was about 30 years ago. It wasn't in a 200-line demonstration program; it was in the BSD Unix kernel in a serial module with tens of thousands of lines. It occurred about once every three to seven days randomly and took three engineers two months to find it. To make matters worse, it was processor-dependent and didn't occur on the VAX processor that ran the original BSD.

The top-level program (the sender) puts data in the buffer. The lower-level interrupt routine (the receiver) removes data from the buffer.

In pseudocode, the sender's job is as follows:

```
If the buffer is full, wait.
Put a character in the buffer at putIndex.
Move putIndex up one, wrapping if needed.
Increment the number of characters in the buffer.
```

And the receiver's job is as follows:

```
Get a character from the buffer at getIndex.
Increment getIndex, wrapping as needed.
Decrement the number of characters in the buffer.
```

Sending Function

To use a circular buffer, we have to go back to sending one character at a time with another version of myPutchar. Let's look at the code doing the sending:

```
void myPutchar(const char ch)
{
    // Wait until there is room.
❶  while (buffer.nCharacters == BUFFER_SIZE)
        continue;
❷  buffer.data[buffer.putIndex] = ch;
❸  ++buffer.putIndex;
    if (buffer.putIndex == BUFFER_SIZE)
        buffer.putIndex = 0;

    // We've added another character.
❹  ++buffer.nCharacters;
    // Now we're done.

    // Enable the interrupt (or reenable it).
❺  uartHandle.Instance->CR1 |= USART_CR1_TXEIE;
}
```

In the beginning, we wait until there is room for at least one character in the buffer ❶. Then we dump the character in the buffer ❷. The putIndex advances by one and wraps back to 0 if necessary ❸.The number of characters in the buffer has increased, so we increment the nCharacters count in the buffer structure ❹. Finally, we enable the interrupt ❺. If we are transmitting, the interrupt may already be enabled. Enabling it again won't cause problems.

Interrupt Routine

The interrupt routine reads the data from the buffer and transmits it to the UART. If a character is in the buffer, the routine removes it and sends it to the UART. If nothing is in the buffer, the routine turns off the interrupt.

Here's the code for this procedure:

```
void USART2_IRQHandler(void)
{
❶ if ((uartHandle.Instance->ISR & USART_ISR_TXE) != 0) {
      if (buffer.nCharacters == 0) {
          // Turn off interrupt.
          uartHandle.Instance->CR1 &= ~(USART_CR1_TXEIE);
          return;
      }
  ❷ // Send to UART.
     uartHandle.Instance->TDR = buffer.data[buffer.getIndex];
  ❸ ++buffer.getIndex;
     if (buffer.getIndex == BUFFER_SIZE)
         buffer.getIndex = 0;

  ❹ --buffer.nCharacters;

  ❺ if (buffer.nCharacters == 0)
         uartHandle.Instance->CR1 &= ~(USART_CR1_TXEIE);
     return;
   }
   // Since the only interrupt we enabled was TXE, we should
   // never get here. When we do enable other interrupts,
   // we need to put the code to handle them here.
}
```

First, we check to see whether the device has run out of data. If it has, we shut down the interrupt until we get more data from the upper level ❶. Then we send the character ❷, move the getIndex up one, and wrap if needed ❸. Next, we let the upper layer know we have one less character ❹. Finally, we shut down the interrupt if this was the last character ❺.

Full Program

Listing 10-2 shows the complete program.

```
/**
 * @brief   Write Hello World to the serial I/O
 * using a circular buffer.
 *
 * @note Contains a race condition to demonstrate
 * how not do do this program
 */

#include <stdbool.h>
#include "stm32f0xx_nucleo.h"
#include "stm32f0xx.h"
```

```
const char hello[] = "Hello World!\r\n";    // The message to send
int current; // The character in the message we are sending

UART_HandleTypeDef uartHandle;        // UART initialization

#define BUFFER_SIZE 8   // The data buffer size

struct circularBuffer {
    uint32_t putIndex;      // Where we will put the next character
    uint32_t getIndex;      // Where to get the next character
    uint32_t nCharacters;   // Number of characters in the buffer
    char data[BUFFER_SIZE]; // The data in the buffer
};

// A simple, classic circular buffer for USART2
volatile struct circularBuffer buffer = {0,0,0, {'\0'}};

... Error_Handler from Listing 9-3 ...

/**
 * Handle the USART2 interrupt.
 *
 * Magically called by the chip's interrupt system.
 * Name is fixed because of the startup code that
 * populates the interrupt vector.
 */
void USART2_IRQHandler(void)
{
    if ((uartHandle.Instance->ISR & USART_ISR_TXE) != 0) {
        if (buffer.nCharacters == 0) {
            // Turn off interrupt.
            uartHandle.Instance->CR1 &= ~(USART_CR1_TXEIE);
            return;
        }
        // Send to UART.
        uartHandle.Instance->TDR = buffer.data[buffer.getIndex];
        ++buffer.getIndex;
        if (buffer.getIndex == BUFFER_SIZE)
            buffer.getIndex = 0;

        --buffer.nCharacters;

        if (buffer.nCharacters == 0)
            uartHandle.Instance->CR1 &= ~(USART_CR1_TXEIE);
        return;
    }
    // Since the only interrupt we enabled was TXE, we should never
    // get here. When we do enable other interrupts, we need to put
    // code to handle them here.
}

/**
 * Put a character in the serial buffer.
 *
 * @param ch The character to send
```

```c
 */
void myPutchar(const char ch)
{
    // Wait until there is room.
    while (buffer.nCharacters == BUFFER_SIZE)
        continue;
    buffer.data[buffer.putIndex] = ch;
    ++buffer.putIndex;
    if (buffer.putIndex == BUFFER_SIZE)
        buffer.putIndex = 0;

    // We've added another character.
    ++buffer.nCharacters;
    // Now we're done.

    // Enable the interrupt (or reenable it).
    uartHandle.Instance->CR1 |= USART_CR1_TXEIE;
}

/**
 * Our version of puts
 *
 * Outputs the exact string given to the output
 *
 * @param str String to send
 *
 * @note Assumes that str is not null
 */
void myPuts(const char* str)
{
    for (/* str set */; *str != '\0'; ++str)
        myPutchar(*str);
}

... led2_init and uart2_init same as Listing 9-3 ...

int main(void)
{
    HAL_Init(); // Initialize hardware.
    led2_Init();
    uart2_Init();
    // Tell the chip that we want the interrupt vector
    // for USART2 to be enabled.
    NVIC_EnableIRQ(USART2_IRQn);

    // Keep sending the message for a long time.
    for (;;) {
        myPuts(hello);
        HAL_Delay(500);
    }
}

... HAL_UART_MspInit and HAL_UART_MspDeInit same as Listing 9-3 ...
```

Listing 10-2: 10.serial.buffer.bad/src/main.c

The Problem

When we run the program, we expect to see the following:

```
Hello World!
Hello World!
Hello World!
```

Instead, we get this:

```
Hello World!
ello World!
Hello Wold!
Hello World!
```

There is no pattern to when this issue will occur, other than that the more data we send to the buffer, the more likely we are to have a problem.

With this tiny program, replicating that problem in the field is going to be difficult because it requires very precise timing. It's more likely that after implementing and testing this code, we would incorporate the module in another program that would make the timing more likely. Timing bugs are notoriously difficult to cause on demand, but there is one in this code.

We know that the busier the system is, the more likely it is that the problem will happen. Plus, we have another clue—we haven't been able to catch it in the act, but afterward we looked at the debugger and discovered the following:

```
nCharacters == 0
getIndex != putIndex
```

In a correctly working program, both of these conditions can never be true. There are two ways of attacking this problem. The first is to instrument the code and try to find out what is going on. The second is to perform very detailed analysis of any data shared between the upper and lower layers and the code that manipulates this data. Let's do both.

Instrumenting the Code

Instrumenting the code means putting in temporary debugging statements that will help find a problem. With most code, this means writing `printf` statements to output intermediate data that we can check as the program progresses. Sometimes data is printed to a logfile that can be analyzed after the problem occurs. Neither of these options is viable for our embedded program. We can't use `printf` because the output would go to the serial console, and that's the code with the bug. We can't write a logfile because we don't have a filesystem to write logging information to.

We need to use a log buffer that will store the last 100 events. When we encounter a problem, we can go back and look at the events to see what led up to the problem. The log records the relevant data (`getIndex`, `putIndex`, `nCharacters`) and the line number of the call to the event-logging code.

When the problem occurs and we get a chance to stop the program in the debugger, we can look through the log. If we are lucky, we should be able to find a few log entries where at line *X* the buffer information was consistent and at line *Y* it was screwed up, which reveals that the problem occurred between lines *X* and *Y*.

Listing 10-3 shows the code to record an event. Add this code after the other definitions and variable declarations.

```
#define N_EVENTS 100                      // Store 100 events.
uint32_t nextEvent = 0;                   // Where to put the next event
struct logEvent debugEvents[N_EVENTS]; // The log data

void debugEvent(const uint32_t line)
{
    debugEvents[nextEvent].line = line;
    debugEvents[nextEvent].putIndex = buffer.putIndex;
    debugEvents[nextEvent].getIndex = buffer.getIndex;
    debugEvents[nextEvent].nCharacters = buffer.nCharacters;
    ++nextEvent;
    if (nextEvent == N_NEVETS)
        nextEvent = 0;
}
```

Listing 10-3: The event recorder

This event recorder contains the same type of bug we're trying to find, but for now, we'll assume that it works well enough for us to locate the problem.

Now we need to put in a few calls to the debugEvent function to see whether we can spot the error. Since nCharacters is driving us nuts, we put a call to debugEvent before and after each operation we perform on nCharacters:

```
void USART2_IRQHandler(void)
--snip--
      debugEvent(__LINE__);
      --buffer.nCharacters;
      debugEvent(__LINE__);


void myPutchar(const char ch)
--snip--
      debugEvent(__LINE__);
      ++buffer.nCharacters;
      debugEvent(__LINE__);
```

We also put a consistency check at the beginning of myPutchar to make sure the buffer is sane. Specifically, if we see the condition where the buffer is inconsistent (nCharacters == 0 and getIndex != putIndex), we invoke the Error_Handler function to stop the program:

```
void myPutchar(const char ch)
{
    if ((buffer.nCharacters == 0) && (buffer.getIndex != buffer.putIndex))
        Error_Handler();
```

Let's start the program under the debugger with a breakpoint at Error
_Handler and see if we can catch the error. Eventually, we hit the breakpoint
and, using the debugger, examine the debugEvents. Looking back through
the traces using the debugger, we find the following:

Line 119: nCharacters == 3

Line 89: nCharacters == 3

Line 91: nCharacters == 2

Line 121: nCharacters == 4

Why did nCharacters jump by 2 between the last two events?
Here are the relevant lines:

```
77 void USART2_IRQHandler(void)
--snip--
89        debugEvent(__LINE__);
90        --buffer.nCharacters;
91        debugEvent(__LINE__);
```

and:

```
106 void myPutchar(const char ch)
--snip--
119        debugEvent(__LINE__);
120        ++buffer.nCharacters;
121        debugEvent(__LINE__);
```

Something is wrong with line 90 or 120, which also tells us something
important. After line 119 and before line 121, an interrupt occurred. We've
now pinpointed the error to a couple lines of code and an interrupt. Let's
shift gears and use code analysis to reach the same conclusion. We're
exploring both methods because sometimes one method works and the
other doesn't.

Analyzing the Code

The other way to figure out the problem is to analyze what is going on and
try to identify potential problem spots. The analysis starts by identifying
the shared data between the upper and lower layers—in other words, the
buffer:

```
struct circularBuffer {
    uint32_t putIndex;        // Where we will put the next character
    uint32_t getIndex;        // Where to get the next character
    uint32_t nCharacters;     // Number of characters in the buffer
    char data[BUFFER_SIZE];   // The data in the buffer
};
```

Neither putIndex nor getIndex should cause a problem, since they're used
by only one layer each (the upper and lower layer, respectively). The data
array is shared by both layers, but it's written by the upper layer and read by

the lower level, so each layer has a distinct job when it comes to that array. In addition, putIndex controls the portion of the array the upper layer uses, and getIndex controls the portion the lower layer uses. They point to different elements of the array, and nothing going into or out of data could affect the indices or character counter. The data array is not the problem.

All that's left is nCharacters, which the upper layer increments and the lower level decrements, so there are two potential problem lines. One is in the interrupt routine:

```
--buffer.nCharacters;
```

And the other is in myPutchar:

```
++buffer.nCharacters;
```

These are the same two lines our instrumented code indicated might be a problem.

Closely Examining the Code

Let's see exactly what happens when the following line is executed:

```
++buffer.nCharacters;
```

Here is the assembly code (comments added) for this line:

```
120:../src/main.c ***  ++buffer.nCharacters;
404              loc 2 118 0
405 005c 094B       ldr  r3, .L22    ; Load r3 with the address in .L22,
                                     ; which happens to be "buffer".
406 005e 9B68       ldr  r3, [r3, #8] ; Get the value of
                                     ; buffer.nCharacters.
407 0060 5A1C    ❶ adds r2, r3, #1  ; Add 1 to r3 and store the result in r2.
408 0062 084B       ldr  r3, .L22    ; Get the address again.
409 0064 9A60       str  r2, [r3, #8] ; Store buffer.nCharacters.
```

This code loads the value of nCharacters into register r3, increments it, and sticks it back in nCharacters. Interrupts can happen at any time, like right after the value is loaded into r3 ❶, which causes the following to happen (assuming nCharacters is 3):

1. At line 406, register r3 gets the value of nCharacters (r3 == 3).
2. Just before the instruction at line 407, an interrupt occurs.
3. The interrupt routine reads nCharacters (it's 3).
4. It decrements it, so the value of nCharacters is now 2.
5. The interrupt routine completes and returns control to line 407.
6. The instruction at line 407 adds 1 to register r3 and sticks the result in r2 (r3 contains 3, r2 contains 4).

7. Line 409 stores the value of r2 into nCharacters, which should be 3, but it's now 4.

8. At line 407, the program assumes that r3 has the correct value of nCharacters, but it doesn't.

The register r3 doesn't have the correct value of nCharacters because an interrupt occurred at just the right time and the variable was modified. We failed to protect the consistency of shared data. The upper layer was modifying nCharacters while the lower layer was modifying it *at the same time*.

If the interrupt occurs between some other instructions, the problem does not occur. This problem is random and happens infrequently, making it one of the more difficult problems to solve.

Fixing the Problem

The solution is to prevent the interrupt routine from modifying nCharacters while we are modifying it. To do that, we turn off interrupts before the increment and turn them on afterward:

```
119     __disable_irq();
120     ++buffer.nCharacters;
121     __enable_irq();
```

Keep the amount of time interrupts are turned off short. If interrupts are turned off for a long period of time, you might miss an interrupt and drop data.

In the interrupt routine, we decrement nCharacters, so don't we need to protect that with a __disable_irq and an __enable_irq? We don't, because when an interrupt occurs, the system automatically performs the following steps:

1. It disables interrupts for this level interrupt and lower. Higher-level interrupts can interrupt our interrupt routine, but lower ones cannot.

2. It saves the state of the machine, including all general-purpose registers and status registers.

3. It calls the interrupt function.

When the interrupt routine returns, the system then performs these steps:

1. It restores the state of the machine.
2. It turns the interrupts back on.
3. It returns control to the upper-level code.

A lot of bookkeeping needs to be done at the start and end of an interrupt routine. Fortunately, the designers of the ARM processor family decided to do it all in hardware. Other processors may not be so nice.

Summary

Interrupts allow you to respond to input and output requests in real time. They also allow you to screw up your program in strange and random ways. Be sure to keep interrupt routines and code that accesses shared data as simple and clear as possible. Spending extra time making sure that interrupt-related code is written properly will save you a tremendous amount of debugging time later.

Programming Problems

1. Create an interrupt routine that reads characters from the serial port.
2. Add an interrupt routine to service a button push and change the message when it occurs.
3. Browse the HAL library and find out how __disable_irq is implemented.

11

THE LINKER

This chapter explores in extreme detail how the linking process works. The linker's job is to take all the object files that make up a program and put them together. The linker must know exactly what the memory layout of your device is so it can fit the program into memory. It's also responsible for connecting external symbols in one file with their actual definitions in another. This process is called *linking symbols*.

It is the linker that knows exactly where things are. On big systems where we have gigabytes of memory, this doesn't matter that much, but on a microcontroller with 16KB of RAM, knowing what every byte is used for is important.

Let's take a look at a typical problem that shows how better understanding the linker can be helpful. Say you have a system in the field that's crashing. When it crashes, it prints a stack trace showing the call stack that details the faults leading up to the problem (see Listing 11-1).

```
#0  0x0000000000001136 in ?? ()
#1  0x0000000000001150 in ?? ()
#2  0x0000000000001165 in ?? ()
#3  0x000000000000117a in ?? ()
#4  0x00007ffff7de50b3 in __libc_main (main=0x555555555168) at ../csu/libc-start.c:308
#5  0x000000000000106e in ?? ()
```

Listing 11-1: A sample stack trace

This tells you that the fault was in the function whose address is 0x0000000000001136.

Since you didn't write your program using absolute addresses, the name of the function would be more useful to you. That's where the linker map comes in.

Listing 11-2 shows an excerpt from the map of this program.

```
.text       0x0000000000001129      0x58 /tmp/cctwz0VM.o
            0x0000000000001129           three
            0x000000000000113e           two
            0x0000000000001153           one
            0x0000000000001168           main
```

Listing 11-2: An excerpt from the map of the program in Listing 11-1

We aborted at 0x1136 in Listing 11-1. In Listing 11-2, function three starts at 0x1129 and goes on until the next function at 0x113e. In fact, we are 13 bytes into function three, so we are somewhere near the start of the function.

Listing 11-1 shows that function three was called by someone at address 0x1150. Listing 11-2 shows that function two goes from 0x113e to 0x1153, so it called three. Using a similar analysis, we can tell that two was called by one, and one was called by main.

The Linker's Job

The linker's job is to take the object files that make up the program and put them together to form a single program file. An object file contains code and data organized into named sections. (The actual names of the sections are compiler-dependent. Advanced programmers can even make up their own names.)

The sections in the object file have no fixed address. They are said to be *relocatable*, which means they can be put almost anywhere, but the linker puts them in a specific place in memory.

The ARM chip contains two types of memory: random access memory (RAM) and flash. RAM is where the variables go. One problem with this type of memory is that all the data is lost when the power goes off. Flash memory, for all practical purposes, is a type of read-only memory. (You can write to it if you're very clever with the I/O system.) The data in flash memory is not erased when the system loses power.

The linker takes the data from all the object files and packs it into the RAM. It then splits up the remaining RAM into the stack and the heap. The code and read-only data get put in the flash memory. This description is somewhat oversimplified, but we'll leave the details for later in this chapter.

The final thing the linker does is write out a map file telling you where it put everything. Why do we care where the linker puts things? After all, the principal thing is that the program gets put in the memory. When it comes to debugging in the field, however, we need to know where things are. Also, there are times when we may want to define specialized memory sections or attach additional memory chips to our system.

And then there's the big reason: the firmware upgrade. It has been said that the hardware people have to get the hardware right the first time. The only thing the software people have to get right is the firmware upgrade. But how do you use the running software to replace the running software? And more importantly, how do you do it without bricking your system? (*Bricking* refers to a failed upgrade process that turns your system into something about as useful as a brick.) That involves some tricky programming, which I'll explain near the end of this chapter.

Compilation and Linking Memory Models

A *memory model* describes how memory is specified in a system. Basically, memory is divided into named sections. The C standard, the object files, and the ARM chip all use different names to describe their memory. Worse, it is possible to define custom names through C language extensions. The linker must then be told what to do with those custom sections.

The Ideal C Model

Everything in a C program ideally will go into one of the standard sections: text, data, or bss.

Read-only instructions and read-only data go in the text section. Here, both the code for main and the text string (read-only) go in the text section:

```
int main() {
    doIt("this goes in text too");
    return();
}
```

Initialized data (initialized global variables) goes in the data section:

```
int anExample = 5;
```

Uninitialized data (uninitialized global variables) goes in the bss section:

```
int uninitialized;
```

Technically, bss is uninitialized according to the standard. However, in every implementation I've seen of a C programming system, the bss section is initialized to zero.

The data for these sections is allocated at compile time. The C compiler will spit out an object file that says, "I need this much text, and here are the contents. I need this much data, and here are the contents. I need this much bss, with no contents specified."

The size command shows how much space your program is using in each section.

```
$ size example.o
   text   data    bss    dec    hex   filename
    481      4      4    489    1e9   example.o
```

The object file uses 481 bytes of text, 4 bytes of data, and another 4 bytes of bss. The total number of bytes for all three is 489, or 1e9 in hexadecimal.

The ideal C model has two other memory sections. However, they are not allocated by the compiler; they are allocated by the linker. These are the *stack* and the *heap*. The stack is used for local variables and is dynamically allocated as procedures are called. The heap is a pool of memory that can be dynamically allocated and freed (more on the heap in Chapter 13).

The compiler takes our variable definitions and assigns them to memory sections. Those sections use a different namespace from the ideal C memory section names. In some cases the names are similar, and in some cases they are completely different. Different compilers and even different versions of the same compiler might use different names for the sections.

Listing 11-3 shows a program that contains every type of data we've discussed.

```
/**
 * A program to demonstrate various types of variable
 * storage, so we can see what the linker does with them
 */
int uninitializedGlobal;   // An uninitialized global (section bss)
int initializedGlobal = 1; // An initialized global (section data)
int initializedToZero = 0; // An initialized global (section bss)

// aString -- initialized variable (section bss)
// "A string." -- constant (section text)
const char* aString = "A string."; // String (pointing to ready-only data)
static int uninitializedModule;    // An uninitialized module-only symbol
                                   // (section bss)
static int initializedModule = 2;  // An initialized module-only symbol
                                   // (section data)

int main()
{
    int uninitializedLocal;        // A local variable (section stack)
    int initializedLocal = 1234;   // An initialized local (section stack)
```

```
static int uninitializedStatic;        // "Uninitialized" static (section bss)
static int initializedStatic = 5678; // Initialized static (section data)

while (1)
    continue; // Not much logic here
}
```

Listing 11-3: Examples of data types

Let's see what our GNU GCC compiler does with our sample program from Listing 11-3—specifically, how it really allocates memory for the various types of variables and data.

First, here's initializedGlobal from Listing 11-3:

```
int initializedGlobal = 1; // An initialized global (section data)

16                              .global initializedGlobal
17                              .data
18                              .align  2
21                  initializedGlobal:
22 0000 01000000                .word   1
```

The .global directive tells the assembler that this is a global symbol and can be referred to by other object files. The .data directive tells the assembler that what follows goes in the .data section. So far, we're following the ideal C memory model naming convention.

The .align directive tells the assembler that the following data should be aligned on a 4-byte boundary. (The last 2 bits of the address must be zero, thus the .align 2.) Finally, there is the initializedGlobal label and the .word 1 data.

When a variable is initialized to zero (initializedToZero in Listing 11-3), we see slightly different code:

```
int initializedToZero = 0; // An initialized global (section bss)

23                              .global initializedToZero
24                              .bss
25                              .align  2
28                  initializedToZero:
29 0000 00000000                .space  4
```

Here, the compiler uses the .bss directive to put the variable in the bss section. It also uses the .space directive instead of .word, which tells the assembler that this variable takes up 4 bytes of space and to initialize those bytes to zero.

Now let's deal with an uninitialized global variable (uninitializedGlobal from Listing 11-3):

```
int uninitializedGlobal; // An uninitialized global (section bss)

15                              .comm   uninitializedGlobal,4,4
```

The `.comm` section tells the assembler to define a symbol that is 4 bytes long and aligned on a 4-byte boundary. The symbol goes into a memory section called COMMON. In this case, the section name does not follow the ideal C memory model naming convention.

The statement that defines aString in Listing 11-3 also defines a string constant ("A string."). The string constant is read-only, while the pointer (aString) is read/write. Here's the generated code:

```
const char* aString = "A string."; // String (pointing to read-only data)

30                              .global aString
31                              .section        .rodata
32                              .align  2
33                  .LC0:
34 0000 41207374               .ascii  "A string.\000"
34      72696E67
34      2E00
35                              .data
36                              .align  2
39                  aString:
40 0004 00000000               .word   .LC0
```

First, the compiler must generate the constant for "A string.". It generates an internal name (.LC0) for this constant, and the contents of this constant are generated with the .ascii assembler directive. The .section .rodata directive puts the constant in a linker section called .rodata. (The ideal C memory model calls this text.)

Now we come to the definition of the variable itself, aString. The .data directive puts it in the data section. Since it's a pointer, it is initialized with the address of the string (namely, .LC0).

The last major section is the one that contains the code. The ideal C memory model calls this text. Here's the assembly listing for the start of main:

```
int main()

52                              .section        .text.main,"ax",%progbits
53                              .align  1
54                              .global main
60                  main:
67 0000 80B5                   push    {r7, lr}
```

The name for this section is text.main. In this case, the compiler decided to take the text prefix and add on the name of the module (main) to form the section name.

We've covered the major memory sections that the compiler knows about, so next let's look at the code generated by some other types of declarations. The static keyword used outside any procedure indicates a variable that can be used only within the current module.

Here's the code that creates the initializedModule variable from Listing 11-3:

```
static int initializedModule = 2; // An initialized module-only symbol
                                  // (section data)

46                                      .data
47                                      .align  2
50                          initializedModule:
51 0008 02000000                        .word   2
```

It looks pretty much the same as initializedGlobal, only the .global directive is missing.

Similarly, the uninitializedModule variable from Listing 11-3 looks much like uninitializedGlobal, only again, we are missing the .global directive:

```
static int uninitializedModule; // An uninitialized module-only symbol
                                // (section bss)

41                                      .bss
42                                      .align  2
43                          uninitializedModule:
44 0004 00000000                        .space  4
```

Now we come to the variables declared static inside a procedure. These variables are allocated at compile time in main memory, but their scope is local to the procedure where they are defined.

Let's start with the uninitializedStatic variable from Listing 11-3:

```
static int uninitializedStatic; // "Uninitialized" static (section bss)

94                                      .bss
95                                      .align  2
96                          uninitializedStatic.4108:
97 0008 00000000                        .space  4
```

It looks like any uninitialized local, except the compiler changed the name of the variable from uninitializedStatic to uninitializedStatic.4108. Why? Each block, or section of code enclosed in curly brackets ({}), can have its own uninitializedStatic variable. The scope of the C variable name is local to the block in which it is defined. The scope of the assembly language is the entire file, so the compiler makes the name unique by appending a unique random number to the end of the variable declaration.

Similarly, the initializedStatic variable looks pretty much like its global brother:

```
static int initializedStatic = 5678; // Initialized static (section data)

88                                      .data
89                                      .align  2
92                          initializedStatic.4109:
93 000c 2E160000                        .word   5678
```

In this case, the .global is missing and the name has been transformed by the addition of a suffix.

Nonstandard Sections

We've discussed the standard memory sections that the GNU toolchain generates. The STM32 chips use a custom section named .isr_vector, and it must be the first data programmed into the flash memory because the ARM hardware uses this section of memory to service interrupts and other hardware-related functions. Table 11-1, adapted from the STM32F030x4 manual, describes the interrupt vector.

Table 11-1: Interrupt Vector Documentation (Truncated)

Position	Priority	Type of priority	Acronym	Description	Address
—	—	—	—	Reserved	0x0000 0000
—	–3	Fixed	Reset	Reset	0x0000 0004
—	–2	Fixed	NMI	Non-maskable interrupt. The RCC Clock Security System (CSS) is linked to the NMI vector.	0x0000 0008
—	–1	Fixed	HardFault	All class of fault	0x0000 000C
—	3	Settable	SVCall	System service call via SWI instruction	0x0000 002C
—	5	Settable	PendSV	Pendable request for system service	0x0000 0038
—	6	Settable	SysTick	System tick timer	0x0000 003C
0	7	Settable	WWDG	Window watchdog interrupt	0x0000 0040
1				Reserved	0x0000 0044
2	9	Settable	RTC	RTC interrupts (combined EXTI lines 17, 19, and 20)	0x0000 0048

The STM firmware file *startup_stm32f030x8.s* (an assembly language file) contains the code that defines this table. Here's an excerpt:

```
131                     .section .isr_vector,"a",%progbits
134
135
136             g_pfnVectors:
137 0000 00000000        .word   _estack
138 0004 00000000        .word   Reset_Handler
139 0008 00000000        .word   NMI_Handler
140 000c 00000000        .word   HardFault_Handler
```

The first line tells the linker that the table goes in a section called .isr_vector. This section is highly hardware-specific, precisely defined, and must go in exactly the right place. Otherwise, nothing will work.

The code defines an array called g_pfnVectors that contains the following:

- The address of the initial stack
- The address reset handler
- The address of the non-maskable interrupt (NMI) handler
- Other interrupt vectors, as described in Table 11-1

We'll see how the linker handles this code in the next section.

The Linking Process

The compiler and assembler produced a set of object files that divide up the code and data into the following sections:

text. <name>   Read-only data and code

rodata   Read-only data

data   Initialized data

bss   Data initialized to zero (slightly different definition from the one the ideal C memory model uses)

COMMON   Uninitialized data

.isr_vector   Interrupt and reset handlers that must go in a specific place

The linker is controlled by a script named *LinkerScript.ld,* which is part of each STM32 Workbench project. The script tells the linker that the system's memory consists of two sections:

1. Flash, starting at 0x8000000, 64KB long
2. RAM, starting at 0x20000000, 8KB long

The linker's job is to take the data from the object files and pack it into memory via the following steps:

1. Put the .isr_vector section at the beginning of flash.
2. Put all the data from the .text.* sections into flash.
3. Put the .rodata section into flash.
4. Put the .data section into RAM, however the initializers for the .data section go into flash (we'll discuss this more later).
5. Put the .bss section into RAM.
6. Finally, load the COMMON section into RAM.

NOTE *There are some other steps in the linker script that are used when switching between thumb and ARM mode programming and for handling C++ constructors and destructors. We don't use these features here.*

The .data section is the tricky one. Consider the declaration:

```
int initializedGlobal = 1234;
```

The linker allocates space in RAM for initializedGlobal. The initializer (1234) goes into flash. At startup, the initializers are copied as a block into RAM to initialize the .data section.

Symbols Defined by the Linker

During the linking process, the linker defines some important symbols, including the following:

_sidata   Start of the initializers for the .data section in flash

_sdata   Start of the .data section in RAM

_edata   End of the .data section in RAM

_sbss   Start of the .bss and COMMON sections in RAM

_ebss   End of the .bss and COMMON sections in RAM

_estack   Last address of RAM

Upon reset, the code in *startup_stm32f030x8.S* executes and performs the following steps:

1. Load the stack register with _estack. The stack will grow down.
2. Fill the section of memory from _sdata to _edata with the initialization values stored starting at _sidata.
3. Zero the memory between _sbss and _ebss.
4. Call the function SystemInit to initialize the STM32 chip.
5. Call the function __libc_init_array to initialize the C library.
6. Call main.
7. Loop forever.

Relocation and Linking Object Files

There are two types of object files: *absolute* and *relocatable*. An absolute file defines everything in terms of a fixed (absolute) address. In other words, the symbol main is at 0x7B0, and it cannot be set to another address by the linker or any other tool.

A relocatable object file is designed to have the location of its data move around (relocate). For example, the *main.c* source file produces the *main.o* object file. If we look at the assembly listing, we see the symbol main is defined at 0000:

```
52                      .section    .text.main,"ax",%progbits
--snip--
60                      main:
61                      .LFB0:
--snip--
67 0000 80B5            push        {r7, lr}
```

This symbol is relative to the section where it resides (namely, text.main). Because the object file is relocatable, text.main can be located anywhere in memory. In this case, the linker decided to put it in flash memory at 0x00000000080007b0. (We found this value using the linker map, which is discussed in the next section.) Because main is at the beginning of this segment, it gets the value 0x00000000080007b0.

As part of the linker process, the linker takes the relocatable object files and assigns them a location in the memory. The result is a program file with absolute addresses for each object file.

The linker also links the object files together. For example, the *startup_stm32f030x8.S* file calls main. The problem is that this code doesn't know where main is. It's defined in another module (*main.o*), so at link time, the linker will see that *startup_stm32f030x8.S* needs to know where the main symbol is defined and will perform a link operation between the *startup_stm32f030x8.S* call to main and the absolute address of main (0x7B0).

A library is a collection of object (*.o*) files in an archive format (similar to *.zip*, but not as sophisticated). The linker script tells the linker to include the libraries *libc.a*, *libm.a*, and *libgcc.a*. For example, the *libm.a* library contains the following:

```
s_sin.o
s_tan.o
s_tanh.o
s_fpclassify.o
s_trunc.o
s_remquo.o
--snip--
```

When processing a library, the linker will load an object file only if it defines a symbol that your program needs. For example, if your program uses the sin function, it will link in the object *s_sin.o* file that defines this function. If you don't use the sin function, then the linker knows you don't need the code in *s_sin.o* and therefore will not link in the file.

The Linker Map

As the linker loads data into the program, it produces a map file (*Debug /output.map*) that contains information about where our code and data are.

This map file is very complete and contains a lot of useful information as well as a lot of stuff we don't care about. For example, it tells us what our memory configuration looks like, which shows the various types of memory and their locations for our processor:

```
Memory Configuration

Name            Origin              Length              Attributes
FLASH           0x0000000008000000 0x0000000000010000 xr
RAM             0x0000000020000000 0x0000000000002000 xrw
*default*       0x0000000000000000 0xffffffffffffffff
```

In this case, our chip has FLASH memory, which has the read (r) and execute (x) attributes set. It starts at 0x8000000 and goes on for 0x10000 bytes. The RAM section starts at 0x20000000 and goes on for only 0x2000 bytes. It is readable (r), writable (w), and executable (x).

As mentioned previously, the .isr_vector section is loaded first. The linker map tells us where this is located:

```
.isr_vector     0x0000000008000000          0xc0
```

The address 0x8000000 is the start of flash. The hardware expects the interrupt vector to be at this address, so that is a good thing. The other bit of information is that this section is 0xc0 bytes long.

The main symbol is defined in *src/main.o*. It is part of the .text.main segment and is located at 0x0000000008000138:

```
.text.main      0x0000000008000138          0x60 src/main.o
                0x0000000008000138                main
```

It also contains a bit of code (0x60 bytes, which is large considering Listing 11-3 is a nothing program).

We can also see where our global variables are located. For example, here's the location for uninitializedGlobal:

```
COMMON          0x0000000020000464          0x4 src/main.o
                0x0000000020000464                uninitializedGlobal
```

The linker map provides the absolute address of every variable and function in this program. Why is that useful? When we are debugging in the field (no JTAG debugger), frequently we have only absolute addresses, so if your program suffers a fatal error and you see:

```
FATAL ERROR: Address  0x0000000008000158
```

on the debug console, you'll know the error occurred 0x20 bytes into main.

We've been using an *external* debugger with our STM board. This system consists of a host computer running the debugger, a JTAG debugging pod, and a target machine. The debugger on the host computer has access to the source code and the symbol table (from the linker). When it detects an error at 0x8000158, it can look into the symbol table, see that the error occurred 0x20 bytes into the program, figure out on which line the error occurred, and display in the source file a big red arrow pointing to where the error occurred.

Some systems have an *internal* debugger, where the debugger and all the files it needs are on the target system. Some internal debuggers provide the ability to dump memory based on absolute addresses. Such debuggers are small and dumb, yet they can be surprisingly useful when it comes to debugging in the field.

Suppose you have such a debugger and need to know the value of uninitializedGlobal. A dumb debugger doesn't know anything about symbol names. It dumps memory based on address, and that's it.

On the other hand, you do know about symbol names. You've got the linker map, so you can tell the debugger to display a 4-byte value at location 0x20000464:

```
D> x/4 20000464
0x20000464:    1234    0x4D2
```

This sort of debugging is primitive and difficult, but sometimes with embedded systems, it's the only way to perform debugging.

Maybe you're wondering why we don't tell the debugger where uninitializedGlobal is, which would make things much easier. The problem is that a symbol table takes up a lot of space, and we are space-limited. Also, having the symbol table on the system itself is a security risk. (A hacker would just love to know the address of passwordCheckingFunction!)

Advanced Linker Usage

So far, we've used the linker only with the default settings. However, there will be times when you'll want to perform more advanced functions than what you get with the defaults.

Flash Memory for "Permanent" Storage

One of the problems with the default C memory model is that all your data is reset when the program starts. On the STM32, this means resetting the device causes it to lose all data. Suppose you want to keep some configuration data around between boots. The default setup won't let that happen. How do we do it?

Let's start with the serial "Hello World" program from Chapter 9. We're going to add a counter that tells how many times the system has booted and then write a message with the reset count to the serial device.

Our design is simple. We're going to take the top 4KB of flash and use it for configuration data. We'll give it the imaginative name of CONFIG, and we'll define a new memory section called .config in which we'll put our reset variable.

Here's the C code to do that:

```
static uint32_t resetCount __attribute__((section(.config))) = 0;
```

Now we need to modify the linker script to handle our new section. We start by dividing up the flash memory into two sections. The first will be the traditional flash memory we discussed earlier. The second, CONFIG, will hold our configuration data, which means we need to edit *LinkerScript.ld* and replace this:

```
MEMORY
{
    FLASH (rx)      : ORIGIN = 0x8000000, LENGTH = 64K
    RAM (xrw)       : ORIGIN = 0x20000000, LENGTH = 8K
}
```

with this:

```
MEMORY
{
    FLASH (rx)      : ORIGIN = 0x8000000,       LENGTH = 60K
    CONFIG (rw)     : ORIGIN = 0x8000000 + 60K, LENGTH = 4K
    RAM (xrw)       : ORIGIN = 0x20000000,      LENGTH = 8K
}
```

This reduces the size of FLASH by 4KB and then uses that 4KB for the memory section called CONFIG.

Flash is different from normal memory in that you can write it only once before you must erase it. Erasing must be done a page at a time. In the STM32's case, that means our CONFIG section must be at least 1KB long and must be a multiple of 1KB in size. We've chosen 4KB because we will probably want to store a lot more configuration data later on.

Now we need to tell the linker to put the .config section into the memory block called CONFIG. This is done by adding the following to the SECTIONS portion of the *LinkerScript.ld* file:

```
{
    . = ALIGN(4);
    *(.config*)
} >CONFIG
```

Changing this variable is not as simple as just writing the following:

```
++resetCount;
```

A whole sequence of steps is needed to program the chip. We've put all the steps in a function called updateCounter, shown in Listing 11-4.

```
/**
 * Update the resetCounter.
 *
 * In C this would be ++resetCount. Because we are dealing
 * with flash, this is a much more difficult operation.
 */
static HAL_StatusTypeDef updateCounter(void) {
  ❶ HAL_FLASH_Unlock(); // Allow flash to be modified.
```

```c
❷  uint32_t newResetCount = resetCount + 1;  // Next value for reset count

    uint32_t pageError = 0;       // Error indication from the erase operation

    // Tell the flash system to erase resetCounter (and the rest of the page).
❸  FLASH_EraseInitTypeDef eraseInfo = {
        .TypeErase = FLASH_TYPEERASE_PAGES,   // Going to erase one page
        .PageAddress = (uint32_t)&resetCount, // The start of the page
        .NbPages = 1                          // One page to erase
    };

    // Erase the page and get the result.
❹  HAL_StatusTypeDef result = HAL_FLASHEx_Erase(&eraseInfo, &pageError);
    if (result != HAL_OK) {
        HAL_FLASH_Lock();
        return (result);
    }

    // Program the new reset counter into flash.
    result = ❺ HAL_FLASH_Program(FLASH_TYPEPROGRAM_WORD,
            (uint32_t)&resetCount, newResetCount);

    HAL_FLASH_Lock();
    return (result);
}
```

Listing 11-4: The updateCounter procedure

The flash memory on the STM32 chip is protected, so we need to
unprotect it by calling HAL_FLASH_Unlock ❶. This function writes two pass-
word values to the flash protection system that enable the writing of flash.
However, we still can't write resetCount directly to flash, so instead we assign
resetCount (a flash value) to newResetCount (a regular variable) ❷, which we
can increment.

Before we can write to flash, we must erase it, and the smallest unit we
can erase is a page. We first need to initialize a structure ❸ to specify how
many pages to erase at what address, and then pass this as a parameter to
HAL_FLASHEx_Erase to erase the memory ❹.

Now that the memory holding resetCount has been erased, we can write
it. Unfortunately, we have a 32-bit value, and the flash memory writes only
16 bits at a time, so we use another HAL function, HAL_FLASH_Program ❺, to
do the job.

Listing 11-5 shows the whole program.

```c
/**
 * @brief Write the number of times the system reset to the serial device.
 */
#include <stdbool.h>
#include "stm32f0xx_nucleo.h"
#include "stm32f0xx.h"

const char message1[] = "This system has been reset ";  // Part 1 of message
const char message2[] = " times\r\n";                    // Part 2 of message
```

```
const char many[] = "many";          // The word many
// Number of times reset has been performed
uint32_t resetCount __attribute__((section(".config.keep"))) = 0;
int current; // The character in the message we are sending

UART_HandleTypeDef uartHandle;       // UART initialization

/**
  * @brief This function is executed in case of error occurrence.
  *
  * All it does is blink the LED.
  */
void Error_Handler(void)
{
    /* Turn ED3 on. */
    HAL_GPIO_WritePin(LED2_GPIO_PORT, LED2_PIN, GPIO_PIN_SET);

    while (true)
    {
    // Toggle the state of LED2.
        HAL_GPIO_TogglePin(LED2_GPIO_PORT, LED2_PIN);
        HAL_Delay(1000);          // Wait one second.
    }
}
/**
 * Send character to the UART.
 *
 * @param ch The character to send
 */
void myPutchar(const char ch)
{
    // This line gets and saves the value of UART_FLAG_TXE at call
    // time. This value changes, so if you stop the program on the "if"
    // line below, the value will be set to zero because it goes away
    // faster than you can look at it.
    int result __attribute__((unused)) =
        (uartHandle.Instance->ISR & UART_FLAG_TXE);

    // Block until the transmit empty (TXE) flag is set.
    while ((uartHandle.Instance->ISR & UART_FLAG_TXE) == 0)
        continue;

    uartHandle.Instance->TDR = ch;      // Send character to the UART.
}

/**
 * Send string to the UART.
 *
 * @param msg Message to send
 */
static void myPuts(const char* const msg)
{
    for (unsigned int i = 0; msg[i] != '\0'; ++i) {
        myPutchar(msg[i]);
    }
```

```
}

/**
 * Initialize LED2 (so we can blink red for error).
 */
void led2_Init(void)
{
    // LED clock initialization
    LED2_GPIO_CLK_ENABLE();

    GPIO_InitTypeDef GPIO_LedInit;        // Initialization for the LED
    // Initialize LED.
    GPIO_LedInit.Pin = LED2_PIN;
    GPIO_LedInit.Mode = GPIO_MODE_OUTPUT_PP;
    GPIO_LedInit.Pull = GPIO_PULLUP;
    GPIO_LedInit.Speed = GPIO_SPEED_FREQ_HIGH;
    HAL_GPIO_Init(LED2_GPIO_PORT, &GPIO_LedInit);
}

/**
 * Initialize UART2 for output.
 */
void uart2_Init(void)
{
    // UART initialization
    // UART2 -- one connected to ST-LINK USB
    uartHandle.Instance = USART2;
    uartHandle.Init.BaudRate = 9600;                        // Speed 9600
    uartHandle.Init.WordLength = UART_WORDLENGTH_8B;        // 8 bits/character
    uartHandle.Init.StopBits = UART_STOPBITS_1;            // One stop bit
    uartHandle.Init.Parity = UART_PARITY_NONE;            // No parity
    uartHandle.Init.Mode = UART_MODE_TX_RX;               // Transmit & receive
    uartHandle.Init.HwFlowCtl = UART_HWCONTROL_NONE;      // No hw control

    // Oversample the incoming stream.
    uartHandle.Init.OverSampling = UART_OVERSAMPLING_16;

    // Do not use one-bit sampling.
    uartHandle.Init.OneBitSampling = UART_ONE_BIT_SAMPLE_DISABLE;

    // Nothing advanced
    uartHandle.AdvancedInit.AdvFeatureInit = UART_ADVFEATURE_NO_INIT;
    /*
     * For those of you connecting a terminal emulator, the above parameters
     * translate to 9600,8,N,1.
     */

    if (HAL_UART_Init(&uartHandle) != HAL_OK)
    {
        Error_Handler();
    }
}
/**
 * Update the resetCounter.
 *
```

```
 * In C, this would be ++resetCounter. Because we are dealing
 * with flash, this is a much more difficult operation.
 */
static HAL_StatusTypeDef updateCounter(void) {
    HAL_FLASH_Unlock(); // Allow flash to be modified.
    uint32_t newResetCount = resetCount + 1;    // Next value for reset count

    uint32_t pageError = 0;     // Error indication from the erase operation
    // Tell the flash system to erase resetCounter (and the rest of the page).
    FLASH_EraseInitTypeDef eraseInfo = {
        .TypeErase = FLASH_TYPEERASE_PAGES,     // Going to erase 1 page
        .PageAddress = (uint32_t)&resetCount,   // The start of the page
        .NbPages = 1                            // One page to erase
    };

    // Erase the page and get the result.
    HAL_StatusTypeDef result = HAL_FLASHEx_Erase(&eraseInfo, &pageError);
    if (result != HAL_OK) {
        HAL_FLASH_Lock();
        return (result);
    }

    // Program the new reset counter into flash.
    result = HAL_FLASH_Program(FLASH_TYPEPROGRAM_WORD,
            (uint32_t)&resetCount, newResetCount);

    HAL_FLASH_Lock();
    return (result);
}

int main(void)
{
    HAL_Init(); // Initialize hardware.
    led2_Init();
    uart2_Init();

    myPuts(message1);

    HAL_StatusTypeDef status = updateCounter();

    switch (status) {
        case HAL_FLASH_ERROR_NONE:
            // Nothing, this is correct.
            break;
        case HAL_FLASH_ERROR_PROG:
            myPuts("HAL_FLASH_ERROR_PROG");
            break;
        case HAL_FLASH_ERROR_WRP:
            myPuts("HAL_FLASH_ERROR_WRP");
            break;
        default:
            myPuts("**unknown error code**");
            break;
    }
    // A copout to avoid writing an integer to an ASCII function
```

```
        if (resetCount < 10)
            myPutchar('0'+ resetCount);
        else
            myPuts("many");

        myPuts(message2);

        for (;;) {
            continue;        // Do nothing.
        }
}

/**
 * Magic function that's called by the HAL layer to actually
 * initialize the UART. In this case, we need to put the UART pins in
 * alternate mode so they act as UART pins and not like GPIO pins.
 *
 * @note: Only works for UART2, the one connected to the USB serial
 * converter
 *
 * @param uart The UART information
 */
void HAL_UART_MspInit(UART_HandleTypeDef* uart)
{
    GPIO_InitTypeDef GPIO_InitStruct;
    if(uart->Instance == USART2)
    {
        /* Peripheral clock enable */
        __HAL_RCC_USART2_CLK_ENABLE();

        /*
         * USART2 GPIO Configuration
         * PA2      ------> USART2_TX
         * PA3      ------> USART2_RX
         */
        GPIO_InitStruct.Pin = GPIO_PIN_2|GPIO_PIN_3;
        GPIO_InitStruct.Mode = GPIO_MODE_AF_PP;
        GPIO_InitStruct.Pull = GPIO_NOPULL;
        GPIO_InitStruct.Speed = GPIO_SPEED_FREQ_LOW;
        // Alternate function -- that of UART
        GPIO_InitStruct.Alternate = GPIO_AF1_USART2;
        HAL_GPIO_Init(GPIOA, &GPIO_InitStruct);
    }
}

/**
 * Magic function called by HAL layer to de-initialize the
 * UART hardware. Something we never do, but we put this
 * in here for the sake of completeness.
 *
 * @note: Only works for UART2, the one connected to the USB serial
 * converter
 *
 * @param uart The UART information
```

```
 */
void HAL_UART_MspDeInit(UART_HandleTypeDef* uart)
{
    if(uart->Instance == USART2)
    {
        /* Peripheral clock disable */
        __HAL_RCC_USART2_CLK_DISABLE();

        /*
         * USART2 GPIO Configuration
         * PA2      ------> USART2_TX
         * PA3      ------> USART2_RX
         */
        HAL_GPIO_DeInit(GPIOA, GPIO_PIN_2|GPIO_PIN_3);
    }
}
```

Listing 11-5: The reset counting program

Multiple Configuration Items

Suppose we want to keep more than one configuration variable in flash memory. The problem is that flash memory is not ordinary memory. After you store a value in a flash memory variable, you cannot change it until you erase the entire memory page containing the variable.

That works fine when you store one variable per page (a very wasteful way of doing things), but how do you store multiple configuration variables in memory and update one? It requires a little work. Here is the process:

1. Save all the configuration variables in RAM.
2. Update the value you need to change in RAM.
3. Erase all the configuration variables in flash. (Erase the flash page.)
4. Copy the RAM version back into flash.

Listing 11-6 shows an outline of the code to declare a configuration structure in the .config section and update a value in the struct.

```
struct config {
    char name[16];     // Name of the unit
    uint16_t sensors[10]; // The type of sensor connected to each input
    uint32_t reportTime;  // Seconds between reports
    // ... Lots of other stuff
};
struct config theConfig __attribute__((section ".config")); // The configuration

static void updateReportTime(const uint32_t newReportTime) {

    // <Prepare flash>

    struct config currentConfig = config;
    currentConfig.reportTime = newReportTime;
```

```
    // <Erase flash>
    writeFlash(&config, &currentConfig, sizeof(currentConfig));

    // <Lock flash>
}
```

Listing 11-6: Updating the configuration in flash

A number of problems are associated with flash memory. As mentioned previously, the first problem is that an entire page must be erased in order to write a single word. It takes time to write a page into flash, and it's possible for the system to be powered off or reset while you are writing. If that happens, the write will be incomplete and your configuration data will be corrupted.

A solution to this is to have two configuration sections, a primary and a backup, that each contain a checksum. The program first tries to read the primary configuration. If the checksum is bad, it reads the second. Because only one configuration is written at a time, you can be pretty sure that either the primary or the secondary is going to be correct.

Another problem with flash is that it suffers from *memory wear*. You can go through only so many program/erase cycles before the memory becomes corrupted. Depending on the type of flash being used, this can be between 100,000 and 1,000,000 cycles. So, using the flash memory to store a configuration that is expected to change at the rate of once per month will work. Using it for something that will change several times a second will quickly wear out the memory.

There are ways of programming around the limits of flash memory. You also can add external memory chips to your system that don't have the design limitations of flash.

Field Customization Example

Let's say we work for a company that makes alarms. These alarms go out to alarm service companies who install them at end-user sites. Now, Joe's Alarm Company and Bait Shop is not going to be happy if the alarm panel it installs shows an Acme Alarm Maker logo when it boots. Joe is into branding and wants his own logo to appear, which means we need to give customers a way of customizing the logos inside their boxes. We can reserve a section of memory for the logo:

```
MEMORY
{
    FLASH (rx)      : ORIGIN = 0x8000000,       LENGTH = 52K
    LOGO (r)        : ORIGIN = 0x8000000 + 52K, LENGTH = 8K
    CONFIG (rw)     : ORIGIN = 0x8000000 + 60K, LENGTH = 4K
    RAM (xrw)       : ORIGIN = 0x20000000,      LENGTH = 8K
}
```

Now the question is, how do we get the logo into the system? We could program it at the factory, but that would mean every time we shipped a unit, someone would have to open the box, plug in the device, program the logo, and put it back in the box, which is an expensive operation.

Instead, we could let the customers do it themselves. We'd give them a cable and some software and let them program the logo. We can sell that ability as a feature that allows customers to update units with a new logo if needed.

The programming can be accomplished using the same hardware and software we use to load our code into flash, or we can write an onboard program that takes data off the serial line and programs it into the LOGO memory.

Replacing a logo is a simple customization to perform. Also, if the replacement is botched, a bad logo won't stop the system. However, replacing the firmware is another matter.

Firmware Upgrade

Upgrading software while you are running that software is a bit tricky, but there are several ways to do it. One of the simplest is to divide up the flash memory into three sections:

1. The bootloader
2. Program section 1
3. Program section 2

The bootloader is a very small program that will never be upgraded. It has a rather simple job to do, so hopefully we'll get it right the first time. The program sections contain a complete version of the program. They also contain a program version number and a checksum.

The bootloader's job is to decide which program section should be used. It verifies the checksum for the two sections and then decides which one to use based on the following calculation:

```
if ((bad checksum1) and (good checksum2)) use section2
if ((good checksum1) and (bad checksum2)) use section1
if (both good) use the section with the highest version number
if (both bad) blink the emergency light; we're bricked
```

This is the general idea, but we've skipped some bookkeeping steps. For example, the interrupt table in the .isr_vector section needs to be changed so that all interrupts go to the proper place.

Summary

Memory is a limited resource, especially when you're doing embedded programming. You need to know exactly where your memory is located and how to get the most out of it.

The linker's job is to take the pieces of your program, link them together, and produce a program that you can load into memory. For simple programs, the default configuration works well. However, as you get into more advanced systems, you'll need to control more precisely exactly what's being done with your limited memory resources, so understanding the linker is vital to being an effective embedded programmer.

Programming Problems

1. Modify the config program (Listing 11-6) so that the CONFIG segment does not start on a page boundary. What happens?

2. Change the config program so that instead of printing a single-digit reset number, the program prints a complete number.

3. The linker script defines a number of symbols to indicate the start and end of a memory area. Examine the linker script or linker map to find the symbols that define the start and end of the text area. Using these symbols, print the size of the text area. Use the arm-none-eabi-size command to verify your result.

4. Use the same techniques to print the amount of stack space allocated.

5. Advanced: Print the stack space left. This will require reading the current value of the stack register into a variable using the asm keyword.

6. Figuring out what's in a binary file can be very useful, and the GNU toolchain has a number of programs to do so. Examine the documentation for the following commands:

    a. objdump, which dumps object file information

    b. nm, which lists the symbols in a file

    c. ar, which creates libraries or extracts information and files from them

    d. readelf, which displays information on elf (program) files

12

THE PREPROCESSOR

The basic C compiler has a number of powerful features, but there are some things it just can't do. To get around its limitations, a preprocessor was added to the language. The preprocessor is primarily a *macro processor*, a program that replaces text with other text, but it can also include and exclude text and perform other actions based on certain conditions. The idea is to have one program (the preprocessor) do a small, simple text editing job and then feed that into the compiler proper. Since those two steps (and a few others) are hidden behind the gcc command, you hardly think about them, but they are there.

For example, let's look at the following code:

```
#define SIZE 20    // Size of the array
int array[SIZE];   // The array
--snip--
    for (unsigned int i = 0; i < SIZE; ++i) {
```

When SIZE is defined to mean 20, the preprocessor essentially does a global search and replace of SIZE with 20.

The HAL library we're using with our STM microprocessor makes extensive use of the preprocessor in a couple of ways. First, the headers contain a #define for every gettable and settable bit in the processor, and there are quite a few of them. Second, STMicroelectronics doesn't make only one chip; it makes a wide variety. Rather than have 20 different header files with information on 20 chips, it uses a process called *conditional compilation* to compile only the parts of the header file that are needed.

Simple Macros

Let's start with the simple macros. A *macro* is basically a pattern (in this case, SIZE) that is replaced by something else (in this case, 20). The #define preprocessor directive is used to define the pattern and replacement:

size.c
```
#define SIZE 20
The size is SIZE
```

This is not a C program. The preprocessor works on anything, including just English text. Let's run it through the preprocessor using the -E flag, which tells gcc to run the program through the preprocessor only and stop:

```
$ gcc -E size.c
```

Here are the preprocessed results:

```
# 1 "size.c"
# 1 "<built-in>"
# 1 "<command-line>"
# 31 "<command-line>"
# 1 "/usr/include/stdc-predef.h" 1 3 4
# 32 "<command-line>" 2
❶ # 1 "size.c"

❷ The size is 20
```

The lines beginning with a hash mark (#) are called *line markers*. They consist of a hash mark, a line number, and the name of the file (and some other junk). Since the preprocessor may add or remove lines, it would be impossible for the compiler to know where it was in the original input file without them.

A lot happens before the first line is processed, but finally we get to the second occurrence of it ❶, and the output ❷ shows that SIZE has been replaced with the defined value.

The preprocessor takes things literally, which can get you into trouble, as shown here:

square.c

```
#include <stdio.h>

❶ #define SIDE 10 + 2    // Size + margin

int main()
{
❷  printf("Area %d\n", SIDE * SIDE);
   return (0);
}
```

This example finds the area of a square. It includes a little margin so the side of the square is defined ❶. To get the area, we multiply the sides together and print the result ❷. However, this program contains a bug: SIZE is not 12; it is 10 + 2. The preprocessor is a dumb text editor. It does not understand C syntax or arithmetic.

After passing the program through the preprocessor, we can see where we made our mistake:

square.i

```
# 5 "square.c"
int main()
{
    printf("Area %d\n", 10 + 2 * 10 + 2);
    return (0);
}
```

As mentioned previously, the preprocessor doesn't understand C. When we use the following statement, it defines SIZE as literally 10 + 2 rather than 12:

```
#define SIDE 10 + 2    // Size + margin
```

And as you can see, 12 * 12 is a different number from 10 + 2 * 10 + 2.

When using #define to define constants more complex than a simple number, we put parentheses around the entire expression, as shown here:

```
#define SIDE (10 + 2)    // Size + margin
```

Following this style rule prevents incorrect results from an unexpected order of operations after substitution.

To avoid the issue of incorrect macro evaluation entirely when the purpose of a #define is to set or calculate a value in one place and then use it throughout the program, use const, which is preferred over #define wherever possible. Here's an example:

```
const unsigned int SIDE = 10 + 2;        // This works.
```

The main reason for this rule is that the const modifier is part of the C language, and the compiler will evaluate the expression assigned to a const variable, so SIDE is actually 12.

When C was first designed, it had no const modifier, so everyone had to use the #define statement, which is why #define is so widely used, even though the more modern const has been available for some time.

Parameterized Macros

Parameterized macros allow us to give arguments to macros. Here's an example:

```
#define DOUBLE(x) (2 * (x))
--snip--
    printf("Twice %d is %d\n", 32, DOUBLE(32);
```

In this case, we don't need to put the parentheses around the argument in the expansion. We could write the macro as follows:

```
#define DOUBLE_BAD(x) (2 * x)
```

Why is this bad? Consider what happens when we use this macro with an expression:

```
value = DOUBLE_BAD(1 + 2)
```

The style rule is to include parentheses around the arguments to parameterized macros. Without the parentheses, DOUBLE(1+2) expands to the following:

```
DOUBLE(1+2) = (2 * 1 + 2) = 4   // Wrong
```

With the parentheses, we get this:

```
DOUBLE(1+2) = (2 * (1 + 2)) = 6
```

We already have a rule that states to not use ++ or -- except on lines by themselves. Let's see what happens when we break that rule using a parameterized macro:

```
#define CUBE(x) ((x) * (x) * (x))

    int x = 5;

    int y = CUBE(x++);
```

What's the value of x after this is executed? It's 8 instead of 6, as expected. Worse, the value of y can be anything, because C's order of execution rules are ambiguous when it comes to mixing multiply (*) and increment (++) operations.

If you're going to write code like this, consider `inline` functions, which replace the function call with the body of the function:

```
static inline int CUBE_INLINE(const int x) {
    return (x * x * x);
}
```

It works even if you use the following statement:

```
y = CUBE_INLINE(x++);
```

But again, you shouldn't write code like this. Instead, write code like this:

```
x++;
y = CUBE_INLINE(x);
```

Use `inline` functions instead of parameterized macros whenever possible. Because `inline` functions are part of the C language, the compiler can make sure they're being used correctly (unlike the preprocessor, which just replaces text blindly).

Code Macros

So far, we've been writing macros to define constants and simple expressions. We can use #define to define code. Here's an example:

```
#define FOR_EACH_VALUE for (unsigned int i = 0; i < VALUE_SIZE; ++i)
--snip--
    int sum = 0;
    FOR_EACH_VALUE
        sum += value[i]
```

However, this code has some problems. First, it's not obvious where the variable i comes from. We've also obscured what's incrementing it, which is why this sort of macro is rarely seen.

A more common macro is one that emulates a short function. Let's define a macro called DIE that writes out a message and then kills the program:

```
// Defined badly
#define DIE(why)                \
    printf("Die: %s\n", why); \
    exit(99);
```

We use the backslash (\) to extend the macro over multiple lines. We can use this macro as follows:

```
void functionYetToBeImplemented(void) {
    DIE("Function has not been written yet");
}
```

In this case, it works, which is due more to luck than design. The problem is that DIE looks like a function, so we can treat it as a function. Let's put it inside an if statement:

```
// Problem code
if (index < 0)
    DIE("Illegal index");
```

To understand why this is a problem, let's look at the expansion of this code:

```
if (index < 0)
    printf("Die %s\n", "Illegal index");
    exit(99);
```

Here it is properly indented:

```
if (index < 0)
        printf("Die %s\n", "Illegal index");
exit(99);
```

In other words, it will always exit, even if the index is good.

Let's see if we can fix this issue by putting curly brackets ({}) around our statements:

```
// Defined not as badly
#define DIE(why) {                  \
    printf("Die: %s\n", why); \
    exit(99);                 \
}
```

This now works in the following case:

```
// Problem code
if (index < 0)
    DIE("Illegal index");
```

However, it does not work in this case:

```
if (index < 0)
    DIE("Illegal index");
else
    printf("Did not die\n");
```

This code generates an error message: else without previous if. However, we have an if right there. Let's look at the expansion:

```
if (index < 0)
{
    printf("Die: %s\n", why); \
    exit(99);                 \
};                  // <=== Notice two characters here.
```

```
else
    print("Did not die\n");
```

The problem here is that before the else, C wants a statement ending with a semicolon (;) *or* a set of statements enclosed in curly brackets ({}). It doesn't know what to do with a set of statements enclosed in curly brackets that ends in a semicolon.

The solution to this problem is to use an obscure C statement called the do/while. It looks like this:

```
do {
    // Statements
}
while (condition);
```

The statements in the block after do always execute once, and then again as long the *condition* is true. Although it is part of the C language standard, I've seen it used only twice in the wild, and one of those times was as a punch line to a joke.

However, it is used for code macros:

```
#define DIE(why)
do {                      \
    printf("Die: %s\n", why); \
    exit(99);                 \
} while (0)
```

It works because we can put a semicolon after it:

```
if (index < 0)
    DIE("Illegal index");   // Note semicolon at the end of the statement.
else
    printf("Did not die\n");
```

This code expands to the following:

```
if (index < 0)
    do {
        printf("Die: %s\n", "Illegal index");
        exit(99);
    } while (0);
else
    printf("Did not die\n");
```

Syntactically, do/while is a single statement, and we can include a semicolon after it without trouble. The code within the curly brackets (printf and exit) is safely encapsulated inside the do/while. The code outside the curly brackets is one statement, and that's what we want. Now the compiler will accept the code macro.

Conditional Compilation

Conditional compilation allows us to change what's in our code at compile time. The classic use for this feature is to have a debug version and a production version of a program.

The #ifdef/#endif directive pair will compile the code between the two directives if a symbol is defined. Here's an example:

```
int main()
{
#ifdef DEBUG
    printf("Debug version\n");
#endif // DEBUG
```

Strictly speaking, the // DEBUG comment is not required, but be sure to include it because matching #ifdef/#endif pairs is hard enough.

If your program looks like:

```
#define DEBUG    // Debug version

int main()
{
#ifdef DEBUG
    printf("Debug version\n");
#endif // DEBUG
```

then the preprocessed result will be the following:

```
int main()
{
    printf("Debug version\n");
```

On the other hand, if your program looks like:

```
//#define DEBUG          // Release version

int main()
{
#ifdef DEBUG
    printf("Debug version\n");
#endif // DEBUG
```

then the preprocessed result will be the following:

```
int main()
{
    // Nothing
```

Because DEBUG is not defined, no code is generated.

One problem is that all the #ifdef statements tend to make the program look ugly. Consider the following:

```c
int main()
{
#ifdef DEBUG
    printf("Debug version\n");
#endif // DEBUG

#ifdef DEBUG
    printf("Starting main loop\n");
#endif // DEBUG

    while (1) {
#ifdef DEBUG
        printf("Before process file \n");
#endif // DEBUG
        processFile();
#ifdef DEBUG
        printf("After process file \n");
#endif // DEBUG
```

We can do the same thing with a lot less code:

```c
#ifdef DEBUG
#define debug(msg) printf(msg)
#else // DEBUG
#define debug(msg) /* nothing */
#endif // DEBUG

int main()
{
    debug("Debug version\n");
    debug("Starting main loop\n");

    while (1) {
        debug("Before process file \n");
        processFile();
        debug("After process file \n");
```

Notice that we used the #else directive to tell the preprocessor to reverse the sense of the #if. If DEBUG is defined, calls to debug will be replaced with calls to printf; otherwise, they'll be replaced by blank space. In this case, we don't need the do/while trick because the code macro contains a single function call (with no semicolon).

Another directive, #ifndef, is true if a symbol is not defined and otherwise is used the same way as the #ifdef directive.

Where Symbols Get Defined

We can define symbols in three ways:

1. Inside the program with a #define
2. From the command line
3. Predefined inside the preprocessor

We've already described symbols defined inside a program, so let's look at the other two options.

Command Line Symbols

To define a symbol on the command line, use the -D option:

```
$ gcc -Wall -Wextra -DDEBUG -o prog prog.c
```

The -DDEBUG argument defines the DEBUG symbol so the preprocessor can use it. In this example, it does a #define DEBUG 1 before the program starts. We used this symbol in the previous code to control whether debug statements were compiled in.

In addition to symbols, we add to the compilation command manually, and the STM32 Workbench generates a makefile to compile a program that defines a number of symbols on the command line. The most significant is defined by the -DSTM32F030x8 option. The *CMSIS/device/stm32f0xx.h* file uses the STM32F030x8 symbol to include board-specific files:

```
#if defined(STM32F030x6)
  #include "stm32f030x6.h"
#elif defined(STM32F030x8)
  #include "stm32f030x8.h"
#elif defined(STM32F031x6)
  #include "stm32f031x6.h"
#elif defined(STM32F038xx)
```

The STM firmware supports a number of boards, only one of which is the NUCLEO-F030R8. Each chip has a different set of I/O devices located at different places. You don't need to worry about where they are, as the firmware will find the right place using the preceding code. This file says, "If I'm an STM32F030x6, include the header file for that board; if I'm an STM32F030x8, include the header file for that board," and so on.

The directives used are #if and #elif. The #if tests to see whether the expression that follows is true (in this case, whether STM32F030x6 is defined). If it is, the code following it will be compiled. The #elif is a combination of #else and #if, which says if the expression is not true, then test another expression. The other directive, defined, is true if the symbol is defined.

Predefined Symbols

Finally, the preprocessor itself defines a number of symbols, such as
__VERSION__ (to specify the compiler version) and __linux (on Linux systems).
To see what's predefined on your system, use the following command:

```
$ gcc -dM -E - < /dev/null
```

The __cplusplus symbol is defined only if you are compiling a C++ program. Frequently, you'll see something like this in files:

```
#ifdef    __cplusplus
extern "C"
{
#endif
```

It's part of a song and dance needed by C++ so it can use C programs.
You can just ignore it for now.

Include Files

The #include directive tells the preprocessor to bring in an entire file as if it
were part of the original file. There are two forms of this directive:

```
#include <file.h>
#include "file.h"
```

The first form brings in system header files (files that come with the compiler or system libraries you are using). The second brings in files you create.

One problem with header files is that they can be included twice. If
that happens, you get a lot of duplicate defined symbols and other problems. The solution to this problem is to add a *sentinel* by using the following
design pattern:

```
#ifndef __FILE_NAME_H__
#define __FILE_NAME_H__
// Body of the file
#endif __FILE_NAME_H__
```

The first time through, the __FILE_NAME_H__ symbol (the sentinel) is
not defined, so the entire header file is included. This is good, because we
wanted it included—*once*. The next time through, __FILE_NAME_H__ is defined,
and the #ifndef prevents the code below it from being included until the
#endif is reached at the end of the file. Thus, although the header file is
included twice, the contents of the file appear only once.

Other Preprocessor Directives

A few minor preprocessor directives are also useful, such as #warning, #error,
and #pragma.

The #warning directive displays a compiler warning if seen:

```
#ifndef PROCESSOR
#define PROCESSOR DEFAULT_PROCESSOR
#warning "No processor -- taking default"
#endif // PROCESSOR
```

The related #error directive issues an error and stops your program from compiling:

```
#ifndef RELEASE_VERSION
#error "No release version defined. It must be defined."
#endif // RELEASE_VERSION
```

The #pragma directive defines compiler-dependent controls. Here's an example:

```
// I wish they would fix this include file.
#pragma GCC diagnostic ignored "-Wmissing-prototypes"
#include "buggy.h"
#pragma GCC diagnostic warning "-Wmissing-prototypes"
```

This GCC-specific #pragma turns off warnings about missing prototypes, includes a buggy include file, and turns warnings back on.

Preprocessor Tricks

The preprocessor is a dumb macro processor, and as a result, we've had to adopt a number of style rules, described previously, to keep us out of trouble. The power of the preprocessor also allows us to perform some interesting tricks to make our lives easier. One of them is the enum trick, which we discussed in Chapter 8. In this section, we'll look at commenting out code.

Sometimes, we need to disable some code for testing. One way to do that is to comment out the code. For example, suppose the auditing process is buggy; we can disable it until the audit group gets its act together.

Here's the original code:

```
int processFile(void) {
    readFile();
    connectToAuditServer();
    if (!audit()) {
        printf("ERROR: Audit failed\n");
        return;
    }
    crunchData();
    writeReport();
}
```

And here's the code with the audit removed:

```
int processFile(void) {
    readFile();
//    connectToAuditServer();
//    if (!audit()) {
//        printf("ERROR: Audit failed\n");
//        return;
//    }
    crunchData();
    writeReport();
}
```

Every line that we wanted removed now begins with the comment (//) marker.

Commenting out every line is labor-intensive, however. Instead, we can use conditional compilation to remove the code. All we need to do is surround it with #ifdef UNDEF and #endif // UNDEF statements, like this:

```
int processFile(void) {
    readFile();
#ifdef UNDEF
    connectToAuditServer();
    if (!audit()) {
        printf("ERROR: Audit failed\n");
        return;
    }
#endif // UNDEF
    crunchData();
    writeReport();
}
```

The code inside the #ifdef/#endif block will be compiled only if UNDEF is defined, and no sane programmer would do that. Using #if 0 / #endif does the same thing without depending on the sanity of other programmers.

Summary

The C preprocessor is a simple yet powerful automatic text editor. Used properly, it can make programming tremendously easier. It allows you to define simple numeric macros as well as small code macros. (Actually, you can define large code macros, but you really don't want to do that.)

One of its biggest features is the #include directive, which facilitates the sharing of interfaces between modules. Also, the #ifdef capabilities allow you to write one program that has multiple personalities through the use of conditional compilation.

However, you must remember that the preprocessor does not understand C syntax. As a result, you must remember several style rules and programming patterns to use the system effectively.

For all of its limitations and quirks, the preprocessor can be a powerful tool when it comes to creating C programs.

Programming Problems

1. Write a macro to swap two integers.

2. Advanced: Write a macro to swap two integers of any type. (Read the documentation for GCC's typeof keyword before doing this.)

3. Create a macro called islower(x) that returns true if x is a lowercase letter.

4. Crazy advanced: Figure out how the program *zsmall.c* works (*https://www.cise.ufl.edu/~manuel/obfuscate/zsmall.hint*). This program is a winner of the obfuscated C contest (it won an award for "Best Abuse of the Preprocessor"). All it does is print a list of primes, but all the calculations and loops are done using the preprocessor.

PART II

C FOR BIG MACHINES

So far we've concentrated on embedded programming. With embedded systems, you have limited memory and limited resources. However, C is designed to work on larger machines with operating systems (that we don't have to program ourselves), and it has many features that are useful on these larger machines.

For example, there is a memory region called the *heap* that allows you to allocate and free memory, as needed, to store complex objects. Things like web browsers and XML parsers make extensive use of the heap.

We haven't covered this before because we barely had enough memory for the stack—and dividing memory into a stack and heap would like dividing a drop of water between two glasses. It's possible, but very tricky and not very useful.

We also haven't covered the C I/O system. We've had to do the I/O ourselves, going directly to the hardware. On big machines with an operating system, the C I/O system and the operating system hide all those details from you.

Let's take a look at the differences between embedded and non-embedded programming.

In embedded programming, when you write to a device, you write directly to the device. This means that you must know the details of the device you are using. For non-embedded programming, when you call `write` to write to a device, you tell the operating system to do the work, including buffering to make the I/O more efficient and dealing with the actual device.

In embedded programming, you have limited memory. You need to know where every byte is and how its being used. With non-embedded programming, you have an operating system and memory mapping system, which gives you access to a lot of memory. Most programs can afford to waste memory, and a lot of programs do.

An embedded program is loaded into flash memory by an external loader. In our case, it's called ST-LINK and is hidden inside the IDE, but it's there. The program stays in flash forever and is never unloaded or replaced during the normal operation of the system. Non-embedded systems, on the other hand, have an operating system that loads and unloads programs as needed.

An embedded system runs one program. You barely have enough memory for that. However non-embedded systems can and do run more than one program at a time. The system I'm writing this on is currently running 341 programs, and it's a small system.

Embedded programs never stop, whereas non-embedded ones can exit and return control to the operating system.

Embedded systems store all their data in memory. Non-embedded systems have a filesystem and can read and write file data as well as screens, networks, and other peripherals.

Finally, errors in embedded systems must be handled by your program. For non-embedded systems, you have an operating system that will catch errors not handled by the program and print a warning or stop the program. The operating system keeps a bad program from damaging other resources on the system. In contrast, if an embedded program goes south, you can easily brick the system.

C++ works well on larger systems because, in most cases, the overhead does not significantly affect things. For example, let's suppose you want to write a program to read a bunch of data from a database and write a report. For a report that runs once a day, who cares if the program uses 0.5 seconds of CPU time versus 0.2 seconds?

However, if you are doing high-performance computing, such as gaming, animation, or video editing, you need the performance and precision of C. Even though it's an older language, C still has its place on mainframes.

In this section, you'll learn how to use the heap, which is dynamic memory that can be allocated or freed at will. You will also learn how to deal with the operating system's I/O system—actually, two I/O systems: the buffered I/O system and the raw I/O system.

Finally, you will discover how to use floating-point numbers. Most cheap embedded processors don't have a floating-point unit, so we can't use floating-point numbers in embedded programs. Also, although mainframes have dedicated floating-point hardware, you must use this feature carefully; otherwise, you may get unexpected results.

13

DYNAMIC MEMORY

Embedded systems have very limited random access memory (RAM). So far, we've divided the free memory into a small stack with no space left for anything else. When dealing with bigger systems, we have gigabytes of memory, making it easier to divide the memory into two sections: the stack and the heap.

We talked about the stack in Chapter 7. It's where the program allocates local variables and temporary values for each procedure as it's needed. The heap is a little different. You decide when memory is allocated from the heap as well as when it is returned to the heap. Using the heap, you can create very complex and large data structures. For example, web browsers use the heap to store the structural elements that make up a web page.

This chapter describes how to allocate and deallocate memory. In addition, we'll explore how to implement a linked-list data structure to demonstrate common dynamic memory operations and how to debug common memory problems.

Basic Heap Allocation and Deallocation

We use the malloc function to get memory from the heap. Here is the general form of this function:

```
pointer = malloc(number-of-bytes);
```

This function gets *number-of-bytes* from the heap and returns a pointer to them. The memory is uninitialized, so it contains random values. If the program is out of heap, the function returns the NULL pointer.

The program in Listing 13-1 allocates memory for a structure on the heap and then does absolutely nothing with it.

simple.c
```c
#include <stdlib.h>
#include <stdio.h>

// Singly linked list with name as payload
struct aList {
    struct aList* next; // Next node on the list
    char name[50];      // Name for this node
};

int main() {
    struct aList* listPtr = malloc(sizeof(*listPtr));
    if (listPtr == NULL) {
        printf("ERROR: Ran out of memory\n");
        exit(8);
    }
    return (0);
}
```

Listing 13-1: A simple pointer allocation

To make the program more reliable, we use sizeof(*listPtr) to determine how many bytes to allocate, which is a common design pattern:

```
pointer = malloc(sizeof(*pointer));
```

A common design mistake is to omit the asterisk, like this:

```
struct aList* listPtr = malloc(sizeof(listPtr));
```

There are things and pointers to things. The listPtr variable is a pointer, and the *listPtr expression is a thing. A pointer is small: 8 bytes on a 64-bit system. The size of a thing, in this case, is 56 bytes. The design pattern ensures that you allocate the right number of bytes for the variable, since the variable is repeated in the argument to malloc.

Oftentimes you'll see the structure itself, instead of a pointer to the structure, used in sizeof:

```
struct aList* listPtr = malloc(sizeof(struct aList));
```

That works, but it's slightly dangerous. Suppose someone changes the type of listPtr. For example, the following is incorrect:

```
struct aListImproved* listPtr = malloc(sizeof(struct aList));
```

So what happened? In the beginning we had the following correct but dangerous declaration:

```
struct aList* listPtr = malloc(sizeof(struct aList));
```

Everything worked, because listPtr was a pointer to struct aList. As long as the types matched, everything was okay. Now let's say someone decided to alter the code and made listPtr point to the new and improved version of the aList called aListImproved, *but they didn't change the type in the malloc function*. What's worse, imagine if the code wasn't the simple, obvious one-liner from earlier and instead looked like this:

```
struct aListImproved* listPtr;
// 3,000 lines of dense code

// WRONG
listPtr = malloc(sizeof(struct aList));
```

This code doesn't allocate enough space for the new fields, so every time someone uses the new fields, random memory is overwritten.

A good practice to see if you ran out of memory is to check whether malloc returned a NULL pointer:

```
if (listPtr == NULL) {
    printf("ERROR: Ran out of memory\n");
    exit(8);
}
```

This is vital even if you think malloc will never fail.

NOTE *As a general design rule, I check for error returns on almost every function call that can return an error. The only place I don't check for errors is when I'm writing out the error message, because I haven't figured out where to write the error message telling the user that I can't write error messages.*

Our program has a *memory leak*, meaning that it does not deallocate the memory it uses. When a program deallocates memory, it's returned to the heap for reuse by a later malloc. To do that, we use the free function:

```
free(listPtr);
listPtr = NULL;
```

Setting the listPtr to NULL is a design pattern that makes sure you don't try to use the memory after it's freed. It's not required by the C language.

If we try to use the freed `listPtr` without setting it to NULL first, we'll write into memory that shouldn't have been written to. Here's an example:

```
free(listPtr);
listPtr->name[0] = '\0';  // Wrong, but will execute and
                          // possibly create a strange error
                          // much later in the program
```

When we write to freed memory, something bad may happen later in the program that will be difficult to debug because the relationship between the bug and the preceding mistake will not be obvious.

It's nice if we make our mistakes in an obvious manner, like so:

```
free(listPtr);
listPtr = NULL;
listPtr->name[0] = '\0';   // Program crashes with a good
                           // indication of where and why
```

This is a form of paranoid programming. The idea is to turn a subtle, hard-to-find screwup into one that crashes the entire program and is thus much easier to find.

Linked Lists

Now that we have a heap and can store data in it, we're going to use a primitive data structure called a *singly linked list*, which has several advantages over an array. It does not have a fixed size, and insert and delete operations are much quicker using it than using an array. (Arrays have the advantage of being faster to search.)

Imagine we need to store a number of names for a phone book. The problem is that we don't know how many names. Also, names may be added or removed at any time. For embedded systems, this problem is simple. We create an array in which to store the names. If we run out of room in the array, we tell the users they can't store any more names. A linked list would be better, if we had the memory and if we had a heap. On an extremely limited embedded system, we have neither.

Each element of our list, called a *node*, is allocated from the heap. To keep track of these elements, we have a pointer to the first node. The first node has a pointer to the second node, and so on, until we reach the last node. Its pointer is NULL, indicating the end of the list. There is no fixed number of nodes. If we need another one, we just allocate it from the heap.

Here is the structure for the linked list:

```
#define NAME_SIZE 20    // Max number of characters in a name
/**
 * A node in the linked list
 */
```

```
struct linkedList {
    struct linkedList* next;    // Next node
    char name[NAME_SIZE];       // Name of the node
};
```

The next pointer points to the next node (or NULL), and the name array stores up to 20 characters. Figure 13-1 is a diagram of this list.

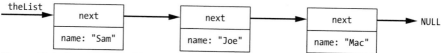

Figure 13-1: A singly linked list

Singly linked lists provide a very simple way of storing a variable number of items in the heap.

Adding a Node

To add a node (say, "Fred") to the list, we must first create one. In the code, we make the newNode variable point to the newly created node. The memory now looks like Figure 13-2.

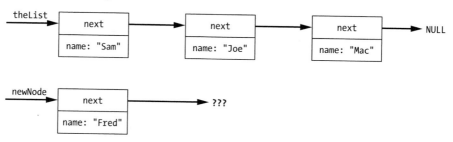

Figure 13-2: New node created

Figure 13-2 shows our linked list (without "Fred") and the new node we've allocated for "Fred." Next, we make the next link of our new node point to the start of the list (see Figure 13-3).

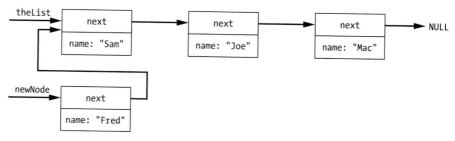

Figure 13-3: The next pointer of the new node points to the start of the list.

The last step is to assign theList = newNode, moving the pointer to the head of our list to our new first node (see Figure 13-4).

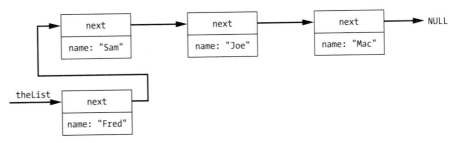

Figure 13-4: Moving the new node to the head of the list

Listing 13-2 shows the code for adding the new node to the start of the list.

```c
static void addName(void)
{
    printf("Enter word to add: ");

    char line[NAME_SIZE];        // Input line

    if (fgets(line, sizeof(line), stdin) == NULL)
        return;

    if (line[strlen(line)-1] == '\n')
        line[strlen(line)-1] = '\0';

    // Get a new node.
    struct linkedList* newNode = malloc(sizeof(*newNode));

    strncpy(newNode->name, line, sizeof(newNode->name)-1);
    newNode->name[sizeof(newNode->name)-1] = '\0';
    newNode->next = theList;
    theList = newNode;
}
```

Listing 13-2: Adding a word to the linked list

We start with a function declaration, and the static keyword indicates that the function is visible only to the code in this file. We first ask for the word to add and get it using the fgets function, which has the following general form:

```c
fgets(array, size, file)
```

This function reads a line from the *file* and puts it in the *array*. The *size* is the number of bytes to stick in the array, including an end-of-string (\0) character. In this case, the array is line (the input line), and the file is stdin (standard in, or in other words, the terminal). If fgets returns NULL, we couldn't read stdin because of an error or running out of data. At that point, we give up and return because we didn't get a word.

The fgets function reads at most *size*-1 characters, because it always puts an end-of-string character (\0) in the array. If the line that's entered is shorter than *size*, the entire line is put in the buffer, including the newline. If it's longer, the input is truncated.

We can't count on a newline being in the buffer, nor do we want one. If the last character in the string (found using the strlen function, which returns the number of characters in the string) is a newline, we delete it by changing it to a null ('\0'). Then we allocate memory for the new node and populate it by copying line into the node's name.

The strncpy function copies the second argument (line) into the first (newNode->name) but copies only the number of characters specified by the third argument. If the data to be copied (line) has more characters than the *size* parameter, it limits the number of characters copied and doesn't insert an end-of-string character (\0) at the end, so just to be safe, we manually add an end-of-string character at the end of the name array.

We make newNode point to the first node, and then we take theList and make it point to the new node, as shown in Figures 13-3 and 13-4.

Printing the Linked List

The rules for printing a linked list are simple. Here's an example:

```
for (const struct linkedList* curNode = ❶ theList;
   ❷ curNode != NULL;
   ❸ curNode = curNode->next){
   printf("%s, ", curNode->name);
}
```

We start with the first node ❶, print it, and then go to the next node ❸. We keep going until we run out of list ❷. In this example, the for loop initializer, end condition, and iteration statement are split over three lines. The code does add an extra comma at the end of the list, but I'm sure you can figure out how to fix that. Figure 13-5 shows how it works.

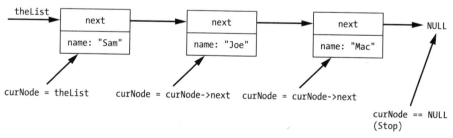

Figure 13-5: Printing the list

Because our list is a simple data structure, printing is simple, and the flexibility of the C for loop makes it easy to go through the list.

Deleting a Node

To delete a node, we first go through the list and find the one we want. Next, we remove the node and then connect the previous node to the next node. The code to go through the list looks like this:

```
static void deleteWord(void)
{
    printf("Enter word to delete: ");

    char line[NAME_SIZE];        // Input line

    if (fgets(line, sizeof(line), stdin) == NULL)
        return;

    if (line[strlen(line)-1] == '\n')
        line[strlen(line)-1] = '\0';

    struct linkedList* prevNode = NULL; // Pointer to previous node
❶ for (struct linkedList* curNode = theList;
        curNode != NULL;
        curNode = curNode->next) {
      ❷ if (strcmp(curNode->name, line) == 0) {
            if (prevNode == NULL) {
              ❸ theList = curNode->next;
            } else {
              ❹ prevNode->next = curNode->next;
            }
          ❺ free(curNode);
            curNode = NULL;
            return;
        }
      ❻ prevNode = curNode;
    }
    printf("WARNING: Node not found %s\n", line);
}
```

We use a for loop, much like we did for printing ❶, but instead of printing the node, we check to see whether it's the one we want with the strcmp function ❷, which returns 0 if the strings are the same. If it's not the one we want, we update the pointer to the previous node ❻ (which we'll need for deleting) and go to the next node using the for loop.

If we do find the node (say, "Joe"), prevNode will point to "Sam" and curNode will point to "Joe," as shown in Figure 13-6.

We next make the link from "Sam" point to "Mac," bypassing the "Joe" node ❹. Then we delete the node by freeing it *and* setting the pointer to NULL ❺, which works as long as prevNode is set. If we want to delete the first node, "Sam," we need to change the pointer to the list to bypass the deleted node ❸.

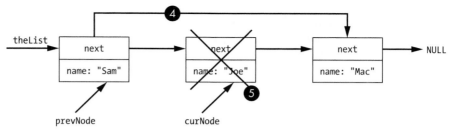

Figure 13-6: Deleting the node "Joe"

Putting It All Together

Listing 13-3 is a small command line program designed to edit and print a linked list interactively.

linked.c
```
/**
 * Demonstrate a singly linked list.
 */
#include <stdio.h>
#include <stdlib.h>
#include <string.h>
#include <stdbool.h>

#define NAME_SIZE 20     // Max number of characters in a name
/**
 * A node in the linked list
 */
struct linkedList {
    struct linkedList* next;    // Next node
    char name[NAME_SIZE];       // Name of the node
};
// The linked list of words
static struct linkedList* theList = NULL;

/**
 * Add a name to the linked list.
 */
static void addName(void)
{
    printf("Enter word to add: ");

    char line[NAME_SIZE];       // Input line

    if (fgets(line, sizeof(line), stdin) == NULL)
        return;

    if (line[strlen(line)-1] == '\n')
        line[strlen(line)-1] = '\0';

    // Get a new node.
    struct linkedList* newNode = malloc(sizeof(*newNode));
```

```c
        strncpy(newNode->name, line, sizeof(newNode->name)-1);
        newNode->name[sizeof(newNode->name)-1] = '\0';
        newNode->next = theList;
        theList = newNode;
}

/**
 * Delete a word from the list.
 */
static void deleteWord(void)
{
    printf("Enter word to delete: ");

    char line[NAME_SIZE];        // Input line

    if (fgets(line, sizeof(line), stdin) == NULL)
        return;

    if (line[strlen(line)-1] == '\n')
        line[strlen(line)-1] = '\0';

    struct linkedList* prevNode = NULL; // Pointer to the previous node
    for (struct linkedList* curNode = theList;
         curNode != NULL;
         curNode = curNode->next) {
        if (strcmp(curNode->name, line) == 0) {
            if (prevNode == NULL) {
                theList = curNode->next;
            } else {
                prevNode->next = curNode->next;
            }
            free(curNode);
            curNode = NULL;
            return;
        }
        prevNode = curNode;
    }
    printf("WARNING: Node not found %s\n", line);
}

/**
 * Print the linked list.
 */
static void printList(void)
{
    // Loop over each node in the list.
    for (const struct linkedList* curNode = theList;
         curNode != NULL;
         curNode = curNode->next) {
        printf("%s, ", curNode->name);
    }
    printf("\n");
}

int main()
```

```
    {
        while (true) {
            printf("a-add, d-delete, p-print, q-quit: ");
            char line[100]; // An input line
            if (fgets(line, sizeof(line), stdin) == NULL)
                break;

            switch (line[0]) {
                case 'a':
                    addName();
                    break;
                case 'd':
                    deleteWord();
                    break;
                case 'p':
                    printList();
                    break;
                case 'q':
                    exit(8);
                default:
                    printf(
                        "ERROR: Unknown command %c\n", line[0]);
                    break;
            }
        }
    }
```

Listing 13-3: A program that implements a linked list

The user inputs commands to add or remove nodes by name, print the list, or quit the program. When the user adds or removes a node, the program dynamically allocates or deallocates memory.

Dynamic Memory Problems

Several common errors can occur when we're using dynamic memory, such as memory leaks, using a pointer after it's freed, and writing data beyond the end of a structure and trashing random memory. Let's look at each error and how to prevent it.

A *memory leak* happens when memory is allocated and never freed. Here's an example:

```
{
    int* dynamicArray;    // A dynamic array
    // Allocate 100 elements.
    dynamicArray = malloc(sizeof(int) * 100);
}
```

Every time the program executes this code, it allocates another 400 bytes of memory. If the program runs long enough, it will consume all available memory and die. (Actually, it will consume enough memory resources to make all the other programs very slow, before using so much memory that the computer is completely useless, runs for a while longer, and finally runs out of memory.)

Using a pointer after it's freed (often referred to as *use after free*) may result in random results or overwriting random memory. Let's look at an example:

```
free(nodePtr);
nextPtr = nodePtr->Next;    // Illegal
```

In this case, the `free` function may write bookkeeping or other data into the node, and as a result `nextPtr` is undefined.

As mentioned earlier in this chapter, a simple design pattern will limit the damage this type of code can do. We always set the pointer to `NULL` after freeing it:

```
free(nodePtr);
nodePtr = NULL;
nextPtr = nodePtr->Next;    // Crashes the program
```

We've exchanged an undefined, random behavior for a reproducible, predictable one. The cause of the crash is easy to find.

The last dynamic memory problem we'll consider is writing data beyond the end of a structure. As you saw earlier, nothing prevents you from writing past the end of an array. You can do the same thing with allocated memory:

```
int* theData;    // An array of data
*theData = malloc(sizeof(*theData)*10);
theData[0] = 0;
theData[10] = 10; // Error
```

There is no good way of preventing or detecting these types of errors using the C language. An external tool or augmented compilation is required.

Valgrind and the GCC Address Sanitizer

Memory errors have become such a problem that many tools have been created to try to detect them, including Valgrind and the GCC address sanitizer.

Valgrind is open source and freely available for Linux and macOS at *http://valgrind.org*. It's designed to find the following: memory leaks, writing past the end of an array or allocated memory block, using a pointer after it's freed, and making a decision based on the value of uninitialized memory.

Valgrind is a runtime tool. You don't need to recompile your code to use it; instead, you compile your program normally and then run Valgrind with the program as an argument.

Listing 13-4 shows a program that leaks memory.

```
/**
 * Leaks memory and uses it badly.
 * Generates warnings when compiled.
 * Generates errors when run.
```

```
 *
 * Please don't program like this.
 */
#include <stdlib.h>

static void leak(void)
{
    char* data = malloc(100);
}

int main()
{
    leak();
    return (0);
}
```

Listing 13-4: A leaky program

Listing 13-5 shows the result of running this program under Valgrind with leak checking set to the maximum.

```
$ valgrind --leak-check=full ./leaker
--snip--
==14500== 100 bytes in 1 blocks are definitely lost in loss record 1 of 1
==14500==    at 0x4C2FB0F: malloc (in /usr/lib/valgrind/vgpreload_memcheck-amd64-linux.so)
==14500==    by 0x10865B: leak (leaker.c:12) ❶
==14500==    by 0x10866B: main (leaker.c:17)
==14500==
==14500== LEAK SUMMARY:
==14500==    definitely lost: 100 bytes in 1 blocks
--snip--
```

Listing 13-5: Valgrind results

From this output, we can see that line 12 is leaking ❶.

The GCC address sanitizer is designed to detect only memory leaks and writing past the end of an array or allocated memory block. Unlike Valgrind, it's a compile-time tool, so you need to compile your code with the –fsanitize=address flag to use it. After that, when you run the program, it automatically generates its report, as shown in Listing 13-6.

```
$ /leaker

=================================================================
==14427==ERROR: LeakSanitizer: detected memory leaks

Direct leak of 100 byte(s) in 1 object(s) allocated from:
    #0 0x7f07c712cb50 in __interceptor_malloc (/usr/lib/x86_64-linux-gnu/libasan.so.4+0xdeb50)
    #1 0x5607aef0b7fb in leak /home/sdo/bare/xx.leaker/leaker.c:15
    #2 0x5607aef0b80b in main /home/sdo/bare/xx.leaker/leaker.c:17
    #3 0x7f07c6c7eb96 in __libc_start_main (/lib/x86_64-linux-gnu/libc.so.6+0x21b96)

SUMMARY: AddressSanitizer: 100 byte(s) leaked in 1 allocation(s).
```

Listing 13-6: Address sanitizer results

Memory problems have plagued programs since the time of the first computer, and they are nasty to try to find. The address sanitizer is one tool that gives us extra help in finding them.

Summary

The heap allows you to add and remove extra memory for your program, as needed. It gives you the ability to create large, complex, and wonderful data structures. A description of the various sorts of data structures and data structure designs could fill an entire book.

This chapter describes the single linked list, which is the "Hello World" of data structures. As you progress, you can learn how to use the heap to store more complex data. For now, you've learned the basics, so where you take it from here is up to you.

Programming Problems

1. Change the program in Listing 13-3, which implements a linked list, so that it always keeps the nodes in order.

2. Given two ordered linked lists, create a function that returns a list of the common nodes. You can do this as a new list or create a list where the body is just a pointer to one of the nodes in the other lists.

3. Change the program in Listing 13-3 to use a doubly linked list. Each node will have a next pointer that points to the next node and a previous pointer that points to the previous node.

4. Write a function to reverse the order of a singly linked list.

5. Write a function that will remove duplicates from a linked list.

14

BUFFERED FILE I/O

In the first part of this book, we struggled to get even the simplest output to the console. But for this part of the book, we have an operating system, and that makes dealing with output and input a lot easier. That's because the operating system hides a great deal of the complexity from you: you just write "Hello World\n", and the operating system sends the data to the appropriate place.

In this chapter you'll learn about C's I/O system, which includes not only the printf function but also functions to read and write disk files in a manner that is both efficient and very flexible.

The printf Function

We've already used the printf function a couple of times for simple output. The basic format of the function is:

```
printf(format-string, argument, ...)
```

The format string tells printf what to print. Any character other than percent (%) is printed. The % character starts a field specification, which tells printf to go to the argument list and print the next argument according to the field specification that follows. For example:

```
printf("Number: ->%d<-\n", 1234);    // Prints  ->1234<-
```

The %d field specification can be modified with a number:

```
printf("Number: ->%3d<-\n", 12);     // Prints  ->.12<- (using . for space)
printf("Number: ->%-3d<-\n", 12);    // Prints  ->12.<- (using . for space)
printf("Number: ->%3d<-\n", 1234);   // Prints  ->1234<-(at least 3 characters)
```

In these examples, %3d tells printf to use at least three characters to print the number. The %-3d field tells printf to print the number with at least three characters and to left-justify it.

So far we've discussed only the d conversion character, which is used to covert an integer argument to text for printing. Table 14-1 lists the major conversion characters.

Table 14-1: Major C Conversion Characters

Conversion character	Argument type	Notes
%d	Integer	The char and short int types are promoted to int when passed as parameters, so this format also works for those three types.
%c	Character	Because of promotion, this conversion character actually takes an integer argument and prints it as a character.
%o	Integer	Prints in octal.
%x	Integer	Prints in hexadecimal.
%f	Double	Works for both float and double types because all float parameters are promoted to double when passed as an argument.
%l	Long integer	The long int type requires its own conversion because the int type is not automatically promoted to long int.

Writing the ASCII Table

Let's write a short program to create a table containing the printable characters with their hex and octal values, which will provide a practical demonstration of the formatting strings. This program (Listing 14-1) gives us a chance to express the same data four different ways and to try out different formats inside a printf statement.

ascii.c
```
/**
 * Print ASCII character table (only printable characters).
 */

#include <stdio.h>

int main()
{
    for (char curChar = ' '; curChar <= '~'; ++curChar) {
        printf("Char: %c Decimal %3d Hex 0x%02x Octal 0%03o\n",
               curChar, curChar, curChar, curChar);
    }
    return (0);
}
```

Listing 14-1: A program to create an ASCII table

First, the %c format string prints out the character as a character. Next, we print out the character as a three-digit decimal number (%3d). To be precise, the type of the argument is a character, and it's promoted to an integer. The number will be three characters long because of the 3 in the argument specification. After that, we print in hexadecimal using the %02x format. The zero (0) tells printf to pad the result with zeros if needed to match the desired width (the width is, of course, 2). Finally, we print in octal with the %03o string.

Listing 14-2 shows the output of this program.

```
Char:   Decimal  32 Hex 0x20 Octal 0040
Char: ! Decimal  33 Hex 0x21 Octal 0041
Char: " Decimal  34 Hex 0x22 Octal 0042
Char: # Decimal  35 Hex 0x23 Octal 0043
Char: $ Decimal  36 Hex 0x24 Octal 0044
Char: % Decimal  37 Hex 0x25 Octal 0045
Char: & Decimal  38 Hex 0x26 Octal 0046
Char: ' Decimal  39 Hex 0x27 Octal 0047
Char: ( Decimal  40 Hex 0x28 Octal 0050
--snip--
```

Listing 14-2: The output of Listing 14-1 (ascii.c)

The printf function is the workhorse of the C I/O system. It helps us get lots of different types of data printed to the console. But that's not the only place we can write, as we'll see in the next few sections.

Writing to Predefined Files

When a program starts, the operating system opens three predefined files:

stdin Standard in, the normal input of the program

stdout Standard out, for normal program output

stderr Standard error, for error output

By default these files are connected to the console, but your command line interpreter can connect them to disk files, pipes, or other things.

The fprintf function sends data to a given file. For example:

```
fprintf(stdout, "Everything is OK\n");
fprintf(stderr, "ERROR: Something bad happened\n");
```

The printf function is merely a convenience function that replaces fprintf(stdout, ...).

Reading Data

The functions that read data are designed to be simple, but unfortunately, they aren't. The printf function has a counterpart called scanf that reads data. For example:

```
// Reads two numbers (do not use this code)
scanf("%d %d", &aInteger, &anotherInteger);
```

First, note the ampersands (&) in front of the arguments, which are used because scanf needs to modify the arguments; therefore, the arguments must be passed by address.

The format string passed to scanf looks a lot like the one for printf, but there is one big problem with scanf: unless you are an extreme expert, you never know how it's going to deal with whitespace. So, we don't use it.

Instead, we use the fgets function to get a single line from the input, and then we use sscanf to parse the resulting string:

```
fgets(line, sizeof(line), stdin);    // Read a line
sscanf(line, "%d %d", &aInteger, &anotherInteger);
```

The general form of fgets is:

```
char* result = fgets(buffer, size, file);
```

where *result* is a pointer to the string that was just read (*buffer*), or NULL if we've reached the end of the file (EOF). The *buffer* is a character array where the line is to be placed, and *file* is a file handle indicating which file to read (stdin is the only file we know about at this point).

The *buffer* will always be null-terminated (\0), so at most *size*-1 characters will be put in *buffer*. (An entire line will be read, even if *buffer* is not large enough to contain it.)

The sscanf function is much like the scanf function, only the first argument is now a string. The rest of the arguments are the same. The sscanf function returns the number of items it converted.

The preceding code assumes that everything works. Let's rewrite it, and this time check for errors:

```
if (fgets(line, sizeof(line), stdin) == NULL) {
    fprintf(stderr, "ERROR: Expected two integers, got EOF\ n");
    return (ERROR);
}
if (sscanf(line, "%d %d", &aInteger, &anotherInteger) != 2) {
    fprintf(stderr, "ERROR: Expected two integers.\n");
    return (ERROR)
}
```

If the first call to fgets returns NULL, something went wrong. We then print an error message to the predefined file for errors (stderr) and return an error code to the caller. Next, we perform an sscanf, which should find two integers. If it doesn't, we again print an error message and return an error code.

The Evil gets Function

The fgets function has a corresponding shorthand function to read data from stdin. It's called gets and has this general form:

```
result = gets(buffer);
```

The gets function reads in a line of data and puts it in the *buffer*, *whether or not the buffer can hold it.*

WARNING   *The gets function is dangerous to use.* Do not use it. *It was created in the very early days of computing when computers were rare, and you assumed anyone who used one was smart and honest. Things have changed since then, and people are a lot less honest. Hackers quickly discovered how to send programs that used gets more data than the buffer could handle, in what was called a* stack smashing attack. *For a time, gets was the most widely available security hole around.*

The current GCC compiler makes gets hard to use. First, *stdio.h* won't define it unless you properly define a conditional compilation macro. When you compile the program, the compiler will warn you, and then when the program is linked, the linker will warn you.

Listing 14-3 shows what happens when you compile a program using gets.

```
$ gcc -Wall -Wextra -o gets gets.c
Agets.c: In function 'main':
gets.c:17:5: warning: 'gets' is deprecated [-Wdeprecated-declarations]
     gets(line);
```

```
        ^~~~
In file included from gets.c:11:0:
/usr/include/stdio.h:577:14: note: declared here
 extern char *gets (char *__s) __wur __attribute_deprecated__;
              ^~~~
/tmp/cc5H1KMF.o: In function `main':
gets.c:(.text+0x1f): warning: the `gets' function is dangerous and should not
be used.
```

Listing 14-3: Attempting to use gets

From the volume of output, you can see how much trouble the GCC compiler goes to in order to persuade you not to use gets.

Now that we've taken a look at a few things we shouldn't use, let's look at some things we should.

Opening Files

The predefined files stdin, stdout, and stdout are file handles. The fopen function allows you to create file handles. Listing 14-4 shows a simple example.

file.c
```
#include <stdio.h>

int main()
{
  ❶ FILE* outFile = ❷ fopen("hello.txt", "w");
    if (outFile == NULL) {
        fprintf(stderr, "ERROR: Unable to open 'hello.txt'\n");
        exit(8);
    }
    if (fprintf(outFile, "Hello World!\n") <= 0) {
        fprintf(stderr, "ERROR: Unable to write to 'hello.txt'\n");
        exit(8);
    }
    if (fclose(outFile) != 0) {
        fprintf(outfile, "ERROR: Unable to close 'hello.txt'\n");
        exit(8);
    }
    return (0);
}
```

Listing 14-4: A file version of "Hello World"

First, the FILE* declaration ❶ declares a new file handle. All file operations require a file handle. Next we have the fopen call ❷, which has this general form:

```
result = fopen(filename, mode);
```

The *mode* can be one of the following:

r Read only

w Write only

r+ Read and write

a Append (write but start at the end of file)

b Used in combination with the other modes for binary files (discussed in the next section)

BEWARE MICROSOFT FILENAMES

Be careful of the Microsoft naming convention that uses the backslash (\) as a separator. If you want to write a file in the top-level directory named *root* with a filename of *file.txt* on Linux or macOS, you would use the statement:

```
FILE* fopen("/root/file.txt", "w");
```

On Microsoft systems, the following does *not* work:

```
// Wrong
FILE* fopen("\root\file.txt", "w");
```

That's because the backslash (\) is the escape character, and since \r is the <return> character and \f is the <form-feed> character, you're trying to write the file:

```
<return>oot<form-feed>ile.txt
```

What you want is:

```
// Right
FILE* fopen("\\root\\file.txt", "w");
```

By escaping the escape character, you get a literal backslash in the path.

Now that we have the files open, we can read and write to them. Text can be written by fprintf and read by fgets. Next, let's take a look at the other type of file: binary files.

Binary I/O

So far we've limited ourselves to text files, but the C I/O system can handle binary files through the use of the fread and fwrite functions. The general form of the fread function is:

```
result = fread(buffer, elementSize, size, inFile);
```

Here, *buffer* is a pointer to the data buffer in which the data will be placed. The *elementSize* is always 1 (see the following box for an explanation). The *size* is the size of the buffer, which is usually sizeof(*buffer*), and *inFile* is the file to read.

The function returns the number of items read, which because *elementSize* is 1 is the number of bytes read. It returns 0 for the end of file and a negative number if there is an I/O error.

ELEMENTSIZE

The original intention was that *elementSize* would be the size of an element in the *buffer* array, and *size* would be the number of elements to read. The result would be the number of elements read. However, as things evolved, almost all programs wanted to read a given number of bytes, not a given number of elements. So, in the real world, *elementSize* is 1, and *size* is the number of bytes to read.

I have seen code where *elementSize* was not 1. Twice. In 40 years of programming. It is extremely rare for this to occur.

The fwrite function has a similar structure:

```
result = fwrite(buffer, elementSize, size, inFile);
```

Everything is the same, except the data is written instead of read.

Copying a File

We'll use fread and fwrite calls to copy a file. Since we don't know how to pass arguments on the command line yet (see Chapter 15), the filenames are hardcoded to *infile.bin* and *outfile.bin*. Listing 14-5 contains the code.

copy.c
```
/**
 * Copy infile.bin to outfile.bin.
 */

#include <stdio.h>
#include <stdlib.h>
#include <stdbool.h>
```

```c
int main()
{
    // The input file
❶ FILE* inFile = fopen("infile.bin", "rb");
    if (inFile == NULL) {
        fprintf(stderr, "ERROR: Could not open infile.bin\n");
        exit(8);
    }
    // The output file
    FILE* outFile = fopen("outfile.bin", "wb");
    if (outFile == NULL) {
        fprintf(stderr, "ERROR: Could not create outfile.bin\n");
        exit(8);
    }
    char buffer[512];   // A data buffer

    while (true) {
        // Read data, collect size
❷      ssize_t readSize = fread(buffer, 1, sizeof(buffer), inFile);
        if (readSize < 0) {
            fprintf(stderr, "ERROR: Read error seen\n");
            exit(8);
        }
❸      if (readSize == 0) {
            break;
        }
❹      if (fwrite(buffer, 1, readSize, outFile) !=(size_t)readSize) {
            fprintf(stderr, "ERROR: Write error seen\n");
            exit(8);
        }
    }
    fclose(inFile);
    fclose(outFile);
    return (0);
}
```

Listing 14-5: Copying a file

First, note the fopen call ❶. We open the file using the rb mode, which tells the system we're going to read the file (r) and that the file is binary (b).

Next, let's take a look at the fread call ❷. The return value for this function is ssize_t, which is a standard type that's big enough to hold the size of the largest object (structure, array, union) that can possibly exist. It also can hold –1 to indicate an error condition.

If we've read all the data from the file, fread returns 0. When that happens, we're done, so we exit the main loop ❸.

Now we come to the fwrite call ❹, which returns a size_t value. This is an unsigned type that holds the size of the largest object you can put in a program, but because it's unsigned, it cannot hold an error value. What happens when fwrite gets an error when writing something? It writes as much as it can and returns the number of bytes written, so it will never return an error code, just a short write.

Note that fread returns an ssize_t result and fwrite returns a size_t result. There are good reasons for this, but it means that if we check to see whether the number of bytes we tried to write is the same as the number we actually asked fwrite to write, we get a compiler warning:

```
35          if (fwrite(buffer, 1, readSize, outFile) != readSize) {
                                    Warning: signed vs. unsigned compare
```

To get rid of the warning, we need to insert a cast, thus telling C, "Yes, I know we are mixing signed and unsigned types, but we have to do it because of the stupid way fread and fwrite are defined":

```
if (fwrite(buffer, 1, readSize, outFile) != (size_t)readSize) {
```

Also note that on the last read we probably won't get a full 512 bytes. That's why we are using *readSize* in the fwrite statement instead of sizeof(*buffer*).

Buffering and Flushing

The C I/O system uses *buffered I/O*, which means that when you do a printf or fwrite, the data may not be sent to the output device immediately. Instead, it will be stored in memory until the system has enough data to make things efficient.

Data going to the console is *line buffered*, which means that if you print part of a line, it might not go out until the rest of the line is sent. Let's see how this can get us into trouble with the program in Listing 14-6.

```
/**
 * Demonstrate how buffering can fool
 * us with a divide-by-zero bug.
 */

#include <stdio.h>

int main()
{
    int zero = 0;     // The constant zero, to trick the
                      // compiler into letting us divide by 0
    int result;       // Something to put a result in

    printf("Before divide ");
    result = 5 / zero;
    printf("Divide done\n");
    printf("Result is %d\n", result);
    return (0);
}
```

Listing 14-6: Dividing by zero

When running this program, you would expect to see the following output:

```
Before divide Floating point exception (core dumped)
```

But what you actually see is this:

```
Floating point exception (core dumped)
```

Your first thought might be that printf did not execute, but it did. The data went into a buffer and was sitting in the buffer when the program aborted, giving a false indication that printf did not work.

NOTE *Integer divide by zero results in a floating-point exception (core dumped) and aborts the program. Floating point divide by zero causes a NaN value to be assigned to the result, and the program will not abort. There's a lot of history around this behavior. The term* core dumped *is a holdover from when computer memory actually consisted of ferrite cores. As to the floating-point exception for integer divides, it was an old oddity when I started programming, and I still don't know why things were done this way.*

To fix this problem, we need to tell the I/O system "write the buffered data out now," which is done with the fflush function:

```
printf("Before divide ");   fflush(stdout);
```

Flushing out the data ensures that we can see it. On the other hand, we don't want to flush after every write, as that would defeat the purpose of buffering, which is to make I/O more efficient.

Closing Files

Finally, after we're done with a file, we need to tell C that we're finished with it. We do this using the fclose function:

```
int result = fclose(file);
```

where *file* is the FILE* to close and *result* is 0 if it worked or nonzero if it didn't.

Summary

In the embedded world, I/O is difficult because you have to write code to deal directly with the device, and you need to write different code for every different type of device.

The C I/O system is designed to hide all those details from you. It also provides a lot of nice features, such as formatting, buffering, and device independence. The buffered I/O system works well for most general applications.

Programming Problems

1. See what happens when you put too many or too few parameters in a printf statement. What happens when you put the wrong type (for example, double instead of int)?

2. Write a program that asks the user for a temperature in Centigrade and converts it to Fahrenheit.

3. Write a program that counts the number of words in a file. Be sure you document the definition of "word," as some people's idea of a word may be different from yours.

4. Write a program that compares two files line by line and writes out the lines that differ.

15

COMMAND LINE ARGUMENTS AND RAW I/O

In this chapter, we explore how command line arguments allow the operating system to pass information to a program when the program is invoked. We also take a look at another feature that's close to the operating system: the raw input/output (I/O) system. This system lets us precisely control how a program performs I/O. Done right, it can be a tremendous asset to a program.

We'll use the raw I/O system to perform a high-speed file copy. This program will also use command line arguments to specify the source and destination files, so we don't need to hardcode them into the program.

Command Line Arguments

Operating systems give the user the ability to provide a program with a number of command line options when the program is run:

```
$ ./prog argument1 argument2 argument3
```

C passes in these arguments through two parameters, argc and argv, to main:

```
int main(const int argc, const char* const argv[])
```

The first parameter, argc, contains the number of arguments. For historical reasons, it is an integer and not an unsigned integer. The second parameter, argv, is an array of strings representing the actual arguments.

If you run a program with an invocation like this:

```
./prog first second third
```

the argv and argc parameters will contain the following:

```
argc     4
argv[0]    ./prog
argv[1]    first
argv[2]    second
argv[3]    third
```

The first argument is the name of the program. The next argument is the *first* parameter on the command line, and so on.

Listing 15-1 contains a short program designed to print the command line arguments.

echo.c
```
/**
 * Echo the command line arguments.
 */
#include <stdio.h>

int main(const int argc, const char* argv[])
{
    for (int i = 0; i < argc; ++i) {
        printf("argv[%d] = %s\n", i, argv[i]);
    }
    return (0);
}
```

Listing 15-1: Printing command line arguments

You don't have to name the argument count argc and the argument vector argv, nor do you have to declare argv and argc const, but it's conventional to do so.

Raw I/O

The two major file I/O systems available to C programmers are *buffered I/O* and *unbuffered I/O*. The standard I/O system (printf), which we discussed in Chapter 14, uses buffers. In this chapter, we'll work with unbuffered I/O.

To show the differences between the two, let's consider an example. Say you want to clean out your closet, and you have 500 old power cords to throw away. You could do the following:

1. Pick up a power cord.
2. Walk outside to the trash can.
3. Throw it away.
4. Repeat 500 times.

This method would be like using unbuffered I/O to get rid of the power cords. The *throughput* (speed at which you are doing the work) is terrible.

Let's add a buffer—in this case, a garbage bag. The procedure now looks like this:

1. Put a power cord in bag.
2. Keep putting cords in the bag until it is full. (It holds 100 cords.)
3. Walk outside to the trash can.
4. Throw the bag away.
5. Repeat five times.

Buffering makes the repetitive process more efficient, so when would you want to use unbuffered I/O? You would use it in cases where it would be more efficient to walk out to the trash can for each item. Say you had to throw away five refrigerators. You wouldn't want to put five refrigerators in a trash bag and then throw them away. Instead, you'd throw away each one individually.

Using Raw I/O

If we wanted to copy a file, we could use the buffered I/O system to do it, but that would mean we would need to let the buffered I/O system choose the size of the buffer. Instead, we want to set our own buffer size. In this case, we know that a size of 1,024 bytes is optimal for the device we are using, so we create the program shown in Listing 15-2 to use raw I/O to copy a file using a 1,024-byte buffer.

copy.c
```
/**
 * Copy one file to another.
 *
 * Usage:
 *      copy <from> <to>
 */

#include <stdio.h>
#include <stdbool.h>
#include <stdlib.h>

#include <unistd.h>
```

```
#include <sys/types.h>
#include <sys/stat.h>
#include <fcntl.h>

#ifndef O_BINARY
#define O_BINARY 0      // Define O_BINARY if not defined.
#endif // O_BINARY

int main(int argc, char* argv[])
{
  ❶ if (argc != 3) {
        fprintf(stderr, "Usage is %s <infile> <outfile>\n", argv[0]);
        exit(8);
    }

    // The fd of the input file
  ❷ int inFd = open(argv[1], O_RDONLY|O_BINARY);

  ❸ if (inFd < 0) {
        fprintf(stderr, "ERROR: Could not open %s for input\n", argv[1]);
        exit(8);
    }

    // The fd of the output file
  ❹ int outFd = open(argv[2], O_WRONLY|O_CREAT|O_BINARY, 0666);
    if (outFd < 0) {
        fprintf(stderr, "ERROR: Could not open %s for writing\n", argv[2]);
        exit(8);
    }

    while (true)
    {
        char buffer[1024];     // Buffer to read and write
        size_t readSize;       // Size of the last read

      ❺ readSize = read(inFd, buffer, sizeof(buffer));
      ❻ if (readSize < 0) {
            fprintf(stderr, "ERROR: Read error for file %s\n", argv[1]);
            exit(8);
        }
      ❼ if (readSize == 0)
            break;

      ❽ if (write(outFd, buffer, readSize) != readSize) {
            fprintf(stderr, "ERROR: Write error for %s\n", argv[2]);
            exit(8);
        }
    }
  ❾ close(inFd);
    close(outFd);
    return (0);
}
```

Listing 15-2: A program to copy one file to another using raw I/O

To use the program in Listing 15-2, we must specify an input file and an output file:

```
$ ./copy input-file output-file
```

The program first checks to see that the proper number of arguments is supplied ❶. Next, it opens the input file ❷. The general form of the open function is *file-descriptor* = open(*filename, flags*). The flags indicate how the file is to be opened. The O_RDONLY flag opens the file read-only, and the O_BINARY flag indicates that the file is binary. The O_BINARY flag is a funny one (I'll explain it in the next section).

The open command returns a number called a *file descriptor*. If there is an error, it returns a negative number, which means the next step in the program is to check for errors ❸.

Then we open the output file using the O_WRONLY (write only) and O_CREAT (create the file if needed) flags ❹.

The additional 0666 parameter means that if the file is created, it's in protection mode. It's an octal number, with each digit representing a protection user set and each bit representing a protection type:

4 Read

2 Write

1 Execute

The digits are in the following order: *<user>*, *<group>*, *<other>*. The 0666 parameter tells the system to create the file so that the user can read and write it (6), so that accounts in the same group as the user get read/write access (6), and so that anyone else gets the same read/write permission (6).

NOTE *If we had used 0640, the user would have read/write access (6), the group would have only read access (4), and everyone else would have no access (0).*

Once the files are open, we do the copy ❺. The read function has the general form:

```
bytes_read = read(fd, buffer, size);
```

where *fd* is the file descriptor, *buffer* is the buffer that receives the data, and *size* is the maximum number of characters read. The function returns the number of bytes read (*bytes read*), 0 to indicate the end of the file (EOF), or a negative number indicating an error.

After reading, we check for an error ❻. Then we check to see whether we have reached the end of the file ❼. If so, we're done transferring data.

At this point we're sure to have some data, so we write it ❽. The write function has the general form:

```
bytes_written = write(fd, buffer, size);
```

where *fd* is the file descriptor, *buffer* is the buffer that has the data, and *size* is the number of characters to write. This function returns the number of bytes written or a negative number to indicate an error. Once the write is completed, we close the file descriptors ❾.

Using Binary Mode

Unfortunately, text files are not portable across operating systems because different operating systems use different characters to indicate the end of a line. C was originally written for Unix, which inspired Linux. Both operating systems use line feed (character number 0x0a) as the line ending.

Say you open a text file with no O_BINARY flag and want to write to it. If you write out a string to a file using:

```
// Bad style; 3 should be a named constant.
write(fd, "Hi\n", 3);
```

on Linux, you'll get a file with three characters in it:

```
48  69  0a
H   i   \n
```

Other operating systems have to translate the end-of-line sequence into their native line ending. Table 14-1 lists the various line endings.

Table 15-1: File Line Endings

OS	Line ending	Characters	Translation
Linux	Line feed	\n	None
macOS	Carriage return	\r	Replace \n with \r on output
Windows	Carriage return, line feed	\r\n	Insert \r before each \n

If you are running a C program on Windows and execute this:

```
// Bad style; 3 should be a named constant.
write(fd, "Hi\n", 3);
```

which is the same code as before, four characters are written:

```
48  69  0d  0a
H   i   \r  \n
```

There will be times, however, when you're writing a binary file and want byte 0a to be written as 0a without translation. On Linux, that's easy, because Linux never does translation. However, other operating systems do, so they added a new O_BINARY flag to tell the library that a binary file is being used and to skip the file translation.

Linux does not have the O_BINARY flag since it makes no distinction between binary and text files. In fact, you can have a half-binary/half-text file. (I don't know why you'd want to do that, but Linux will let you.)

I included the O_BINARY flag in Listing 15-2 because I wanted the copy program to be portable. We need to supply an O_BINARY mode when using Apple and Microsoft systems, but if we compile the program on a Linux system, O_BINARY is undefined.

Thus, the hack is to define it if it is not already defined by the operating system in the header files:

```
#ifndef O_BINARY
#define O_BINARY 0      // Define O_BINARY if not defined.
#endif // O_BINARY
```

If the operating system has an O_BINARY defined, the #define will not be compiled. If we are using a Linux-like operating system with no O_BINARY, #define O_BINARY 0 will be compiled, and O_BINARY will be assigned the value of 0, which does nothing—and doing nothing is exactly what we need on Linux.

ioctl

In addition to reading and writing, the raw I/O system provides a function called ioctl that performs I/O control. Its general form is:

```
result = ioctl(fd, request, parameter);
```

where *fd* is the file descriptor, *request* is the device-specific control request, and *parameter* is the parameter to the request. For most requests, the function returns 0 if the request worked and a nonzero value otherwise (some ioctl calls return something different).

You can use ioctl to eject removable media, rewind or fast-forward tape drives, set the speed and other parameters of a serial device, and set the address information for a network device. Because the ioctl specification is open-ended, a lot of functionality has been crammed into this interface.

Summary

The raw I/O system provides the best control over what your I/O operations actually do. There is minimal editing or interference from the operating system, but this control comes with a price. The buffered I/O system helps limit your mistakes, whereas the raw I/O system does not. Still, if you know what you're doing, it can be a tremendous asset.

Programming Problems

1. Write a program that takes one argument: the name of the person running the program. It then says Hello `<name>`. Here's an example:

   ```
   ./hello Fred
   Hello Fred

   ./hello
   Hello stranger
   ```

2. Write a program that scans the argument list and, if -d is an argument, prints Debug mode. If the -d is missing, it prints Release mode. Add other options as well.

3. Time how long it takes the copy program in Listing 15-2 to copy a large file. Now change the buffer size to 1. See how fast the program is. Change the buffer size to 16384. See how fast it runs. Try 17000. Note: almost every disk reads and writes in 512-byte blocks. How does this fact explain the timings you are seeing?

4. Research the getopt function and use it to parse the command line arguments you invented for problem 1.

16

FLOATING-POINT NUMBERS

In this part of the book, we work through some C features that aren't typically useful in embedded programming but that you may encounter in mainframe programming. Floating-point numbers aren't common in embedded programming because a lot of low-end processor chips can't handle them. Even when you have a CPU that does work with them, floating-point arithmetic is slow, inexact, and tricky to use.

However, because you will occasionally encounter these numbers in scientific or 3D graphic programs, you should be prepared. This chapter covers the basics of floating point, why floating-point operations are so expensive to compute, and some of the errors that can occur while using them.

What Is a Floating-Point Number?

A *floating-point number* is one in which the decimal point floats. It can occur in different places in the number, such as 1.0, 0.1, 0.0001, or 1000.0. Strictly speaking, having a digit after the decimal point isn't required. For example, 1.0 and 1. are the same number. However, floating-point numbers are easier to read and more obvious if they have digits on both sides of the decimal point.

We can also write floating-point numbers using exponent notation, such as 1.0e33, which represents the number 1.0×10^{33}. (You can use an uppercase E or lowercase e, but the lowercase version is more readable.)

Floating-Point Types

In C, the floating-point types are float, double, and long double. The double type is supposed to have twice the precision and range of the float (single-precision) type. The long double has a greater precision and range than the other two types.

All floating-point constants are of the double type unless you tell C differently. Adding an F suffix to the end of a number makes it a single-precision float, and adding an L at the end makes it a long double.

The decimal point is required for floating-point numbers. Consider the following code:

```
float f1 = 1/3;
float f2 = 1.0 / 3.0;
```

The first assignment does not assign f1 the value 0.3333. Instead, it assigns it the value 0.0, because 1 and 3 are integers. C performs an *integer divide* (which results in integer 0), promotes it to floating point, and makes the assignment. The second line does what we want and assigns the value 0.3333.

Automatic Conversions

C does some automatic conversions behind your back. If one operand of an expression is a floating-point number, C automatically converts the other to a float. Here's an example:

```
f = 1.0 / 3;    // Bad form
```

In this case, the 3 will be turned into 3.0 before the division operation. This example is considered bad form because you don't want to mix integers and floating-point constants if you can help it. Also, if you assign a floating-point number to an integer, it is converted to an integer.

Problems with Floating-Point Numbers

One of the problems with floating-point numbers is that they're not exact. For example, 1/3 in decimal floating point is 0.333333. No matter how many digits you use, it still is not exact. Rather than show what happens with binary floating point (used by a computer), we're going to use a decimal floating point (familiar to humans). Everything that can go wrong with our decimal floating point can go wrong with the binary version. The only difference is that with decimal floating point, the examples are easier to understand.

Decimal floating point is a limited version of scientific notation. Here's an example:

```
+1.234e+56
```

This number has a sign (+), a fraction (four digits), and an exponent. This is not a problem for humans, but representing numbers like this in a computer is tricky.

Computers use a similar format, except the exponent and fraction are in binary. Also, they mix up the order and store the components in the order sign, exponent, and then fraction. For more details, see the IEEE-754 floating-point specification, which is used by almost all computers currently.

Rounding Errors

You know that 1 + 1 is 2, but 1/3 + 1/3 is not 2/3. Let's take look at how this works. First, let's add the numbers:

```
+3.333e-01      // 1/3 in our notation
+3.333e-01      // 1/3 in our notation
+6.666e-01
```

However, 2/3 is the following:

```
+6.667e-01
```

This is an example of a rounding error. There is a small error between +3.333e-01 and 1/3. Because of the standard rounding rules we are using, we round down. When we compute 2/3, we get 6.67e-1. In this case, the rounding rules cause us to round up, so although 1 + 1 = 2 (integer), 1/3 + 1/3 != 2/3 (floating point).

We can use some tricks to minimize rounding errors here. One trick most computers use is to add guard digits during calculations. A *guard digit* is an extra digit added to the number while the calculations are being done. When the result is computed, the guard digit is dropped.

One of the early programs I wrote was an accounting program. In spite of the fact that I should have known better, I used floating point for money. It worked well for about three months of transactions, but then my balance disagreed with the bank's by one penny ($0.01). The cause was a floating-point roundoff error. Never use floating point for money. Use integer cents instead.

Digits of Precision

Single-precision floating point (float) should give you about 6.5 digits of precision, but that's not always true. How many digits can you trust? In the previous example, we might be tempted to say that the first three digits of our decimal floating point are accurate, but we can't rely on that.

Let's compute $2/3 - 1/3 - 1/3$:

```
+6.667e-01    // 2/3
-3.333e-01    // 1/3
-3.333e-01    // 1/3
+0.001e-01    // Result unnormalized
+1.000e-04    // Result normalized
```

How many digits are correct? The first digit of our result is 1. (*Normalization* means that we change the number so that there is a digit in the first location. All floating-point numbers are stored normalized, except for a few edge cases that we'll cover later.) The correct first digit should be 0.

A number of problems are inherent in the design of floating-point arithmetic. Mainly they boil down to the fact that most numbers are inexact, which can result in computational errors and problems with exact comparisons.

If you are doing a limited amount of floating-point operations, they probably won't bite you, but you should be aware of them. If you are doing a lot of floating-point operations, you should check out the branch of computer science called *numerical analysis* that's devoted to dealing with floating-point issues and how to get stable results out of them, but that's beyond the scope of this book.

Infinity, NaN, and Subnormal Numbers

The IEEE floating-point format has a few bit patterns that make no sense as numbers. For example, consider the number $0*10^5$. Since 0 times anything is 0, we can use the exponent in this case to indicate a special value. In this section, we'll look at a few of these, as well as the edge cases of the floating-point format.

Let's consider the following expression:

```
float f = 1.0 / 0.0;
```

If this were an integer, dividing it by zero would abort your program. However, because it's floating point, the result is that f is assigned the value INFINITY (this constant is defined in the #include <math.h> header file).

Similarly, the statement:

```
float f = -1.0 / 0.0;
```

assigns f the value -INFINITY.

The numbers INFINITY and -INFINITY are not floating-point numbers (they have no digits and no decimal point), but the IEEE floating-point specification has defined several of these special numbers. Since you are likely to encounter these types of numbers (especially if your program contains bugs), it's important to know what they are.

You also may encounter a NaN (for Not a Number), which is generated when an operation cannot produce a result. Here's an example:

```
#include <math.h>
float f = sqrt(-1.0);
```

Newer versions of the C standard include complex numbers, but the sqrt function always returns a double, so sqrt(-1.0) always returns NaN.

HISTORICAL NOTE

The statement:

```
float f = 1.0 / 0.0;
```

results in the program assigning f the value INFINITY, and the operation continues normally.

On Linux, the statement:

```
int i = 1 / 0;
```

results in the program being aborted with the following error:

```
Floating point exception (core dumped)
```

This message is wrong for a number of reasons. First, it's an integer exception that causes the problem, not a floating-point exception. Second, core memory went away about 40 years ago. Third, memory dumps are disabled by default on almost all current Linux distributions.

Now, what's the tiniest number we can represent in our floating-point scheme? You might be tempted to say it's the following:

```
+1.0000e-99
```

The fraction 1.0000 is the smallest fraction we can create. (If we used 0.5000, it would get normalized to 5.0000.) And −99 is the smallest exponent we can get with two digits.

However, we can get smaller:

```
+0.1000e-99    // -99 is the limit on the exponent.
```

And smaller still:

```
+0.0001e-99
```

Up to this point, the numbers we've been discussing have been normalized, which means a digit is always in the first position. Those numbers are considered to be *subnormal*. We've also lost some significant digits. We have five significant digits with the number +1.2345e-99, but only one for +0.0001e-99.

In C, the isnormal macro returns true if a number is normalized, and the issubnormal macro returns true if the number is subnormalized.

If you encounter subnormalized numbers, you've reached into the darkest corners of the C floating point. So far, I've not seen any real program that's made use of them, but they exist and you should be aware of them.

Implementation

Floating points can be implemented in a variety of ways. Let's start with the STM chip we've been using. Implementation is simple: you can't have floating point. The hardware doesn't do it, and the machine doesn't have enough power to do it in software.

Lower-end chips generally have no floating-point unit. As a result, floating-point operations are done through the use of a software library, which comes with a cost. Floating-point operations in general take about 1,000 times longer than their integer counterparts.

Once you get into the better chips, you'll find native floating-point support. The operations are still expensive; a floating-point operation will take roughly 10 times longer than an integer operation.

Alternatives

One of the best ways to deal with floating point is to not use it. As mentioned previously, one example is when working with money. If you store money as a float, rounding errors will eventually cause you to generate incorrect totals. If instead you store money as an integer number of cents, you'll avoid floating point and all its ills.

Let's define a simple fixed-point number with the number of digits after the decimal fixed at 2. Here are some examples and an integer implementation:

```
Fixed point    Implementation
12.34          1234
00.01             1
12.00          1200
```

To add or subtract fixed point, just add or subtract the underlying implementation:

```
 12.34           1234
+22.22          +2222
------          -----
 34.56           2346

 98.76           9876
-11.11          -1111
------          ------
 87.65           8765
```

To multiply fixed-point numbers, multiply the two numbers and divide by 100 to correct for the placement of the decimal point:

```
  12.00            1200
x 00.50          x 0050
                  60000 (Uncorrected)
------           ------
x 06.00            0600 (After 100 correction)
```

To divide, you do the opposite: divide the underlying numbers and multiply by a correction.

Listing 15-1 contains a program demonstrating the use of fixed-point numbers.

fixed.c

```c
/**
 * Demonstrate fixed-point numbers.
 */
#include <stdio.h>

/**
 * Our fixed-point numbers have the form
 * of xxxxx.xx with two digits to the right
 * of the decimal place.
 */
typedef long int fixedPoint;            // Fixed-point data type
static const int FIXED_FACTOR = 100;    // Adjustment factor for fixed point
/**
 * Add two fixed-point numbers.
 *
 * @param f1 First number to add
```

```
 * @param f2 Second number to add
 * @returns f1+f2
 */
static inline fixedPoint fixedAdd(const fixedPoint f1, const fixedPoint f2)
{
    return (f1+f2);
}
/**
 * Subtract two fixed-point numbers.
 *
 * @param f1 First number to subtract
 * @param f2 Second number to subtract
 * @returns f1-f2
 */
static inline fixedPoint fixedSubtract(
    const fixedPoint f1,
    const fixedPoint f2)
{
    return (f1-f2);
}
/**
 * Multiply two fixed-point numbers.
 *
 * @param f1 First number to multiply
 * @param f2 Second number to multiply
 * @returns f1*f2
 */
static inline fixedPoint fixedMultiply(
    const fixedPoint f1,
    const fixedPoint f2)
{
    return ((f1*f2)/FIXED_FACTOR);
}
/**
 * Divide two fixed-point numbers.
 *
 * @param f1 First number to divide
 * @param f2 Second number to divide
 * @returns f1/f2
 */
static inline fixedPoint fixedDivide(
    const fixedPoint f1,
    const fixedPoint f2)
{
    return ((f1*FIXED_FACTOR) / f2);
}
/**
 * Turn a fixed-point number into a floating one (for printing).
 *
 * @param f1 Fixed-point number
 * @returns Floating-point number
 */
static inline double fixedToFloat(const fixedPoint f1)
{
    return (((double)f1) / ((double)FIXED_FACTOR));
```

```
}
/**
 * Turn a floating-point number into a fixed one.
 *
 * @param f1 Floating-point number
 * @returns Fixed-point number
 */
static inline fixedPoint floatToFixed(const double f1)
{
    return (f1 * ((double)FIXED_FACTOR));
}

int main()
{
    fixedPoint f1 = floatToFixed(1.2);  // A fixed-point number
    fixedPoint f2 = floatToFixed(3.4);  // Another fixed-point number

    printf("f1 = %.2f\n", fixedToFloat(f1));
    printf("f2 = %.2f\n", fixedToFloat(f2));
    printf("f1+f2 = %.2f\n", fixedToFloat(fixedAdd(f1, f2)));
    printf("f2-f1 = %.2f\n", fixedToFloat(fixedSubtract(f2, f1)));
    printf("f1*f2 = %.2f\n", fixedToFloat(fixedMultiply(f1, f2)));
    printf("f2/f1 = %.2f\n", fixedToFloat(fixedDivide(f1, f2)));
    return (0);
}
```

Listing 16-1: Using fixed-point numbers

This is not a perfect implementation. Rounding errors occur in some places, such as the multiply and divide operations, but if you're really into fixed point, you should be able to spot them easily.

Summary

Understanding the underlying implementation and the limitations of floating-point numbers is important. As mentioned previously, you should never use floating point for money. Accountants like exact numbers, and rounding errors can result in incorrect answers. The numerical analysis branch of computer science deals with analyzing how computations are made and figuring out how to minimize errors. This chapter shows you the basics. If you're going to use floating-point numbers extensively, you should have a working knowledge of numerical analysis. However, the best way of using floating point is to avoid it altogether, so make sure you understand that alternatives to floating point, such as fixed point, exist.

Wikipedia has a good article on the IEEE floating-point standard with links to lots of online reference material: *https://en.wikipedia.org/wiki/IEEE_754.*

Programming Problems

1. Write a function that computes the sin of an angle. How many factors do you need to compute to get an accurate answer?

2. Using a float, compute pi to as many digits as possible. How many digits more will you get if you change the data type to double? How many for long double?

3. Say you want to find the number of bits in the fraction part of a floating-point number. Write a program that starts with $x = 1$ and keeps dividing x by 2 until $(1.0 + x = 1.0)$. The number of times you divided by 2 is the number of bits in your floating-point calculations.

17

MODULAR PROGRAMMING

So far we've been working with small, simple one-file programs, which is fine if all you're going to do is write sample programs for a book. In the real world, however, you're probably going to encounter programs with more than 50 lines in them.

The Linux kernel has 33,000 files and 28 million lines of code (and those numbers are increasing as you are reading this). You can't deal with that amount of information without organizing it by dividing up the code into *modules*.

A module ideally is a single file containing a collection of data and functions that does one thing well with minimum interaction with other modules. We've already used the STM HAL collection of modules earlier in this book, including the module containing the HAL_Init function. It does a lot of work internally, but we never see it. We see only a simple module that does one thing well: it initializes all the stuff needed to get the hardware to work.

Simple Modules

Let's create a program that uses two files. The main program will be called *main.c* (see Listing 17-1) and will call a function in the *func.c* file (see Listing 17-2). We'll use a makefile (see Listing 17-3) to compile the two files into one program.

main.c
```
/**
 * Demonstrate the use of extern.
 * @note: Oversimplifies things.
 */
#include <stdio.h>

❶ extern void funct(void);        // An external function

int main()
{
    printf("In main()\n");
    funct();
    return (0);
}
```

Listing 17-1: The main program

The first thing to notice is the declaration of funct ❶ in *main.c*. The extern keyword tells C that the function is defined in another file, named *func.c*. Listing 17-2 contains that file.

func.c
```
/**
 * Demonstration of a function module
 */
#include <stdio.h>
/**
 * Demonstration function
 */
❶ void funct(void)
{
    printf("In funct()\n");
}
```

Listing 17-2: The file that defines the function

The funct function is defined ❶ in the *func.c* file, and the makefile in Listing 17-3 handles the compilation.

```
main: main.c func.c
    gcc -g -Wall -Wextra -o main main.c func.c
```

Listing 17-3: simple/Makefile

The first line of the makefile tells make that the target main must be rebuilt if *main.c* or *func.c* changes. The second line tells make that when one of those files changes it should compile both files and use them to make the program.

In this example, we've taken a function and a main program and put them in two different files. Then we told make to tell the compiler to combine them into one program. This is an oversimplified version of modular programming, but these basic principles are used with more complex programs with larger and more numerous modules.

Problems with the Simple Module

The previous example has a few problems. The first one is that the same information is repeated twice.

In *main.c*, we have the following:

```
extern void funct(void);        // An external function
```

And in *func.c*, we have this:

```
void funct(void)
```

which means that if we change one file, we must change the other.

Worse, *C does not check types across files*, which means it's possible to have the lines:

```
// File a.c
extern uint32_t flag;    // A flag
```

and:

```
// File b.c
int16_t flag;      // A flag
```

in two different files. Suppose file *a.c* decides to set flag to zero. The program is going to deposit 32 bits worth of zero into flag, which is defined in file *b.c* as being only 16 bits long. What will actually happen is that 16 bits will go into flag, and 16 bits will go into something else. The result is that unexpected, surprising, and difficult-to-debug things will happen to your program.

It is possible to declare a variable extern in a file and later declare it without the extern. C will check to make sure that the type in the extern definition matches the type in the actual declaration:

```
#include <stdint.h>
extern uint32_t flag;     // A flag
int16_t flag;             // A flag
```

Compiling this will result in an error:

```
16.bad.c:3:9: error: conflicting types for 'flag'
 int16_t flag;  // A flag

16.bad.c:2:17: note: previous declaration of 'flag' was here
 extern uint32_t flag; // A flag
```

Concerning the second problem, suppose we want to use our external function funct in several different files. Do we want to add an extern statement to each of them? That would mean the definition of funct would be duplicated in many different places (and not checked by the compiler).

The solution is to create a header file to hold the extern definition. Listing 17-4 contains this file.

func.h
```
#ifndef __FUNC_H__
#define __FUNC_H__
❶ extern void funct(void);
#endif // __FUNC_H__
```

Listing 17-4: The file that defines the function

Along with the function definition ❶, this file also contains *double inclusion protection*. The #findef/#endif pair prevents problems that might occur if your program does something like this:

```
#include "func.h"
#include "func.h"
```

This will cause the definitions in *func.h* to be defined twice, which is not a problem for extern declarations, but it will upset the compiler if multiple instances of #define are involved.

This example looks a bit silly, because in real programs, the problem is not so obvious. You may have a case where the code looks like:

```
#include "database.h"
#include "service.h"
```

but the *database.h* file includes the *direct_io.h* file, which includes *func.h*, and the *service.h* file includes the *network.h* file, which includes *func.h*. You then get *func.h* included twice, even though you took the long way to do it.

The format of the #include statement has changed slightly in these examples as well. Instead of:

```
#include <file.h>
```

it's this:

```
#include "file.h"
```

The quotation marks indicate that the file to be included is a user-generated file. The compiler will search for it in the current directory instead of searching through the system files.

Listing 17-5 contains an improved *main.c* that uses the include file to bring in the extern declarations.

good/main.c
```
/**
 * Demonstrate the use of extern.
 */
#include <stdio.h>
```

```
#include "func.h"

int main()
{
    printf("In main()\n");
    funct();
    return (0);
}
```

Listing 17-5: Improved main.c

Listing 17-6 contains the improved *func.c* that includes *func.h*. The extern functions defined in *func.h* are not really needed to compile *func.c*, but by bringing them in, we make sure that the extern matches the actual function declaration.

good/func.c
```
/**
 * Demonstration of a function module
 */
#include <stdio.h>
#include "func.h"
/**
 * Demonstration function
 */
void funct(void)
{
    printf("In funct()\n");
}
```

Listing 17-6: Improved func.c

By including the *func.h* file twice, we've solved the problem that can occur when the extern does not match the actual declaration. Including it in *func.c* lets the compiler check the definition of the function, while in *main.c*, the inclusion provides us with the definition of the function.

Making the Module

The makefile for this program has changed as well (see Listing 17-7).

```
CFLAGS = -g -Wall -Wextra

OBJS = main.o func.o

❶ main: $(OBJS)
        gcc -g -Wall -Wextra -o main $(OBJS)

main.o: main.c func.h

func.o: func.c func.h
```

Listing 17-7: Improved Makefile

The first line defines a macro called CFLAGS, which is a specific name used to compile C programs. The next line defines another macro called OBJS (there is nothing significant about that name), which contains a list of the objects we use to make our program. In this example, we're going to compile *main.c* into the *main.o* object file and compile *func.c* into the *func.o* object file.

NOTE   *Object files on macOS and Linux systems end in .o. On Windows systems, object files end with .obj.*

We're using a macro here simply to avoid having to write the list twice in the next rule ❶, which tells make to create *main.o* from *main.c* and *func.h*. However, this rule isn't followed by a rule telling make *how* to do this. When make doesn't have a rule for something, it falls back to its list of built-in rules. When we create a *.o* (or *.obj*) file from a *.c* file, that built-in rule is:

```
$(CC) $(CFLAGS) -c file.c
```

where CC is the macro containing the name of the C compiler (in this case, cc, which is an alias for gcc).

This example demonstrates a simple modular program, but the design pattern works when programs have additional modules.

What Makes Good Modules

The following list outlines some rules for making good modules:

- Each module should have a header file with the same name as the module. That file should contain the definitions of the public types, variables, and functions in that module (and nothing else).
- Every module should include its own header file so that C can check to make sure the header file and the implementation match.
- Modules should contain code used for a common purpose, and they should expose the minimum amount of information to the outside world. The information they do expose through extern declarations is global (seen by the entire program), and as described in the next section, sometimes that can be a problem.

Namespaces

One problem with C is that it does not have namespaces. In C++, for example, you can tell the compiler that all the symbols in a given module belong to the db namespace, so you can create a module with entries like insert, delete, and query that are visible to other people as db::insert, db::delete, and db::query, respectively.

In C, if you define a public function called Init, no one else can define a function called Init in any module. If this does happen, the linker will complain about a duplicate symbol. Since there may be more than one item that needs initialization, that can be a problem.

Most programmers solve this issue by adding a module prefix to the name of each public function, type, or variable. You can see this in action with the HAL library that gets added automatically to your Nucleo projects. For example, as shown in Listing 17-8, all the functions that manipulate the UART begin with the UART_ prefix.

```
HAL_StatusTypeDef UART_CheckIdleState(UART_HandleTypeDef *huart);
HAL_StatusTypeDef UART_SetConfig(UART_HandleTypeDef *huart);
HAL_StatusTypeDef UART_Transmit_IT(UART_HandleTypeDef *huart);
HAL_StatusTypeDef UART_EndTransmit_IT(UART_HandleTypeDef *huart);
HAL_StatusTypeDef UART_Receive_IT(UART_HandleTypeDef *huart);
```

Listing 17-8: An excerpt from stm32f0xx_hal_uart.h

The key point here is that a public symbol in the HAL library starts with HAL_, which makes it easy to determine whether a function belongs to the library. It also ensures that you don't accidentally use a name already in use by the HAL library.

Libraries

Listing every file that goes into a program is not too bad when there are fewer than 20 files. After that, it gets a little tedious, but it's manageable until the number gets really big. The mainframe programs we've been writing use the standard C library functions. The C library has more than 1,600 files. Fortunately, we don't need to list them all when we compile a program.

The standard C library is a file named *libc.a*, and it's automatically loaded when your program is linked. The library is a collection of object files in a simple archive format (hence the *.a* extension).

Let's create our own library containing several modules to square various types of numbers. Listing 17-9 shows a function to square a floating-point number.

square_float.c
```
#include "square_float.h"

/**
 * Square a floating-point number.
 *
 * @param number Number to square
 * @returns The square of the number
 */
float square_float(const float number) {
    return (number * number);
}
```

Listing 17-9: A function to square a floating-point number

Listing 17-10 is the header for that module.

```
#ifndef __SQUARE_FLOAT_H__
#define __SQUARE_FLOAT_H__
extern float square_float(const float number);
#endif // __SQUARE_FLOAT_H__
```

Listing 17-10: The header file for the square_float.c module

Listing 17-11 defines a function to square an integer.

```
#include "square_int.h"

/**
 * Square an integer.
 *
 * @param number Number to square
 * @returns The square of the number
 */
int square_int(const int number) {
    return (number * number);
}
```

Listing 17-11: A function to square an integer

Listing 17-12 defines its header file.

```
#ifndef __SQUARE_INT_H__
#define __SQUARE_INT_H__
extern int square_int(const int number);
#endif // __SQUARE_INT_H__
```

Listing 17-12: The header file for square_int.c

Next, Listing 17-13 is a similar function to square an unsigned integer.

```
#include "square_unsigned.h"

/**
 * Square an unsigned integer.
 *
 * @param number Number to square
 * @returns The square of the number
 */
unsigned int square_unsigned(const unsigned int number) {
    return (number * number);
}
```

Listing 17-13: A function to square an unsigned integer

Listing 17-14 defines the header file.

```
#ifndef __SQUARE_UNSIGNED_H__
#define __SQUARE_UNSIGNED_H__
extern unsigned int square_unsigned(const unsigned int number);
#endif // __SQUARE_UNSIGNED_H__
```

Listing 17-14: The header file for square_unsigned.c

We are going to put our three functions in a library. If users want to use this library, they will have to include all those header files. That's a lot of work.

To make things easier, we'll create a header file called *square.h* for the library. This file consolidates the individual headers for each of the preceding library components (modules). As a result, people who use this library just need to include *square.h* (see Listing 17-15) instead of a bunch of individual headers.

square.h
```
#ifndef __SQUARE_H__
#define __SQUARE_H__
#include "square_float.h"
#include "square_int.h"
#include "square_unsigned.h"
#endif // __SQUARE_H__
```

Listing 17-15: The header file for the library

We've now followed our style rule of one header per program file, as well as the style rule that says the interface to a library should be as simple as possible.

Next, let's create a small test program for our library (see Listing 17-16).

square.c
```
/**
 * Test the square library.
 */
#include <stdio.h>

#include "square.h"

int main()
{
    printf("5 squared is %d\n", square_int(5));
    printf("5.3 squared is %f\n", square_float(5.3));
    return (0);
}
```

Listing 17-16: A test program for the library

Notice that we don't test all the members of the library (this will matter later).

Now that we have the source files for our library, we need to turn them into an actual library. As mentioned previously, a library is a set of object files in an archive format, sort of like a *.zip* file, only without the compression.

In this case, we'll create the *libsquare.a* file (the library itself) from the *square_float.o, square_int.o,* and *square_unsigned.o* files.

The make program is quite intelligent and has the ability to update an archive's components. For example, one of the components of *libsquare.a* is *square_int.o*. The following rule makes this a component of the library:

```
libsquare.a(square_int.o): square_int.o
        ar crU libsquare.a square_int.o
```

The first line tells make that we are creating or updating the *square_int.o* component in the *libsquare.a* library. This component depends on the *square_int.o* object file.

The second line is the actual command to add the library. The c option tells ar to create the archive if it does not exist. The r causes ar to create or replace the *square_int.o* component in the archive. The U flag tells ar to run in nondeterministic mode, which stores the creation time of the file in the archive (we'll discuss deterministic versus nondeterministic mode later in this chapter). Following that command is the name of the library (*libsquare.a*) and the name of the component to add or replace (*square_int.o*). The linker sets the naming convention. It must begin with *lib* and end with *.a* (more on this naming convention later).

Next, with the following directives, we tell make what components should make up the *libsquare.a* library:

```
libsquare.a: libsquare.a(square_int.o) \
        libsquare.a(square_float.o)

libsquare.a(square_unsigned.o)
        ranlib libsquare.a
```

The first two lines tell make what components to make *libsquare.a* out of. The third line, ranlib libsquare.a, tells make to run a program called ranlib on the archive after installing all the components to create a table of contents for the archive.

ranlib and Library Linking

The reason we use ranlib is due to some of the early linkers. Suppose that we had an archive with the components *a.o* (defines a_funct), *b.o* (defines b_funct), and *c.o* (defines c_funct) and that the program needed a function in *b.o*. The linker would open the archive and go through it serially, looking at each member to see whether it was needed. The decision process goes like this:

1. Look at the list of undefined symbols (the program uses b_funct, so it's undefined).

2. Open the archive.

3. Look at *a.o*. Does it define a needed symbol? No. Do not load it.

4. Look at *b.o*. Does it define a needed symbol? Yes. Load it.

5. Look at *c.o*. Does it define a needed symbol? No. Do not load it.

Now suppose that *b.o* needed the a_funct function. The linker would not go back and reexamine the archive. It would continue on and look only at *c.o*. Since *c.o* does not define the symbol, it would not be loaded. The linker would reach the end of the archive and abort because it did not find an object file to satisfy the need for a_funct.

Because of the way the linker worked, sometimes you needed to specify the same library two or three times. To solve that problem, a table of contents was added to the archive so the components could be loaded in random order (thus the name ranlib).

Now the algorithm to load components is as follows:

1. Look at the list of undefined symbols (the program uses b_funct, so it's undefined).
2. Open the archive.
3. Do we have an undefined symbol that's in the table of contents?
4. If so, load it.
5. Repeat until we have no more symbols that can be satisfied by this library.

This process solves the ordering problem because the table of contents makes everything accessible.

The following command actually links the library with our program:

```
square: square.o libsquare.a
        $(CC) $(CFLAGS) -o square square.o -L. -lsquare
```

The -L. flag tells the linker to search the current directory (.) for library files. Otherwise, only the system library directories are searched. The library itself is specified with the -lsquare directive. The linker looks for a library called *libsquare.a*, first in the current directory (because of the -L.) and then in the system directories.

Listing 17-17 shows the full makefile for this project.

```
CFLAGS=-g -Wall -Wextra

all: square

square: square.o libsquare.a
        $(CC) $(CFLAGS) -o square square.o -L. -lsquare

libsquare.a: libsquare.a(square_int.o) \
        libsquare.a(square_float.o) libsquare.a(square_unsigned.o)
        ranlib libsquare.a

libsquare.a(square_int.o): square_int.o
        ar crU libsquare.a square_int.o

libsquare.a(square_float.o): square_float.o
        ar crU libsquare.a square_float.o

libsquare.a(square_unsigned.o): square_unsigned.o
        ar crU libsquare.a square_unsigned.o

square_int.o: square_int.h square_int.c

square_float.o: square_float.h square_float.c
```

```
square_unsigned.o: square_unsigned.h square_unsigned.c

square.o: square_float.h square.h square_int.h square_unsigned.h square.c
```

Listing 17-17: The full makefile

Because our test program does not call square_unsigned, the *square
_unsigned.o* module will not be linked into our program. (The test for
square_unsigned was omitted to demonstrate how the linker will not link
in unneeded object files.)

Deterministic vs. Nondeterministic Libraries

Ideally, if you run a make command, the resulting binary should be the same,
no matter when the command was executed. For this reason, originally the
library files did not store information on who created the components or
when they were created.

However, that causes some difficulties for the make program. How can
it determine whether the version of *square_int.o* in the archive is newer or
older than the version you just compiled if the archive doesn't store the
modification date?

The ar command was modified to store this information. Because this
feature broke legacy functionality, the ar maintainers decided to make storing this information optional. If you specify the D option, the modification
times are not stored and you get a *deterministic archive* (the same binary every
time). If you specify U for *nondeterministic*, you get a different binary each time,
but one that the make program likes better. The default is D, the legacy format.

Weak Symbols

So far, we've defined modules with functions and variables that are always
loaded. In other words, if a module defines a doIt function, that's the only
definition of the function that's loaded. An extension to the C language
provided by GCC and most other compilers allows for *weak symbols*. A weak
symbol tells the linker, "If no one else defines this symbol, use me."

One example of where weak symbols are used is in the STM interrupt
table. You *must* define functions to be called for every possible interrupt;
the hardware requires it. So you have to write an interrupt route for interrupts that never occur. Since the function is never going to be called, that
should make things simple.

However, the STM firmware is designed around the idea that although
interrupt routes for disabled interrupts *should* never be called, that doesn't
mean that they will *never* be called. The STM firmware defines interrupt
handlers for all interrupts that brick the system. If they ever do get called,
your system stops and you get a chance to go in with the debugger and try
and figure out why.

The only way a default interrupt handler will be called is if you turn on interrupts and don't provide your own interrupt handler. In that case the default interrupt knows something went wrong and just sits there waiting for you to figure out what.

The STM interrupt handler from the USART2 interrupts is the function USART2_IRQHandler, which is defined as follows:

```
void USART2_IRQHandler(void) {
    while(true)
        continue;
}
```

However, if we define our own, the one in the firmware library disappears, in spite of the fact that the other 40 or so interrupt functions in the same module will be loaded.

Let's see this in action with our own code. In Listings 17-18 and 17-19 we have sub1 and sub2, and sub2 is defined twice (once in *main.c* and once in *sub.c*). When the linker looks at those two files, it says, "There are two sub2 functions here. Should I raise an error? No. One of them is weak, and I can throw it away." The sub2 in *main.c* will get linked in and the one in *sub.c* will not.

Let's first define a main program whose job is to call our two subroutines (see Listing 17-18).

main.c
```
#include "sub.h"

int main()
{
    sub1();
    sub2();
    return (0);
}
```

Listing 17-18: The main program to call the two subroutines

In Listing 17-19, we tell the compiler that sub2 in *sub.c* is weak through the GCC extension.

sub.c
```
#include "sub.h"

void sub2(void) __attribute__((weak));

void sub1(void) {}
void sub2(void) {}
```

Listing 17-19: Tells the compiler sub2 is weak

Next, we need a header file, so let's produce one (see Listing 17-20).

sub.h
```
#ifndef __SUB_H__
#define __SUB_H__
extern void sub1(void);
```

```
extern void sub2(void);
#endif // __SUB_H__
```

Listing 17-20: The header file

Finally, we define our own `sub2` function in Listing 17-21.

sub2.c
```
#include <stdio.h>
#include "sub.h"

void sub2(void) {
    printf("The non-weak sub2\n");
}
```

Listing 17-21: Defining the sub2 function

If we link *main.c* and *sub.c*, the weak `sub2` will be linked in. If we link *main.c*, *sub.c*, and *sub2.c*, the non-weak version defined in *sub2.c* will be used.

This is useful for cases like interrupt routines where you have to define one whether you use it or not. It allows you to supply a fallback or default version.

Summary

Modules enable you to split up large programs into manageable units. Good design means a large program does not need to have large parts. Multiple modules can be organized into a library. The advantage of a library is that it can include a large number of specialized modules, and the linker will only link in the needed ones.

Good programming is all about organizing information, and modules and libraries let you organize a huge programming mess into manageable-sized units.

Programming Problems

1. Write a library to compute the area of geometric shapes (`rectangle_area`, `triangle_area`, and so on). Each function should be in its own object file, and all the area functions should be combined into a single library. Write a main program to perform a unit test on the functions.

2. Rewrite one of the serial output programs created in previous chapters so that all of the UART-related code is in a module of its own.

3. Test to see what happens when:

    a. You define two weak symbols and one strong one.

    b. You define two weak symbols and no strong one.

    c. You define two strong symbols.

AFTERWORD

This book should give you a good start with embedded C programming, but there's a whole world outside *Bare Metal C* waiting for you to explore it. In closing, here are some helpful tips for starting down the road to professional programming.

Learn How to Write

By far, the most important skill a professional programmer can have is being able to write well, as the programming process includes writing several types of documents, such as proposals, requirements, design documents, user documentation, and sales literature.

Take a creative writing course where your work is reviewed by others in your class. The feedback I got from the San Diego Writing Workshop was some of the most valuable training I've received in my life.

Here's a pro tip: if you're writing the design or requirements for a project, you have great power in steering the direction of the project.

Learn How to Read

You can learn a lot by "reading" technical documentation. I've put "reading" in quotation marks because you don't read most technical documents in their entirety. You scan them to find the information you need at the time.

Here's a list of the documents I've used in preparation for this book:

- ISO/IEC9899:2017, "Programing Languages: C" (500 pages)
- RM0360 reference manual, "STM32F030x4/x6/x8/xC and STM32F070x6/xB Advanced ARM®-based 32-bit MCUs" (800 pages)
- ARM® Developer Suite Assembler Guide Version 1.2, *https://developer .arm.com/documentation/dui0068/b* (400 pages)
- "Using the GNU Compiler Collection" (GCC documentation, 1,000 pages)
- GNU Make Manual, *https://www.gnu.org/software/make/manual* (225 pages)

I did not read all these documents cover to cover. I probably used about 0.5 to 15 percent of them. I've become proficient at using the `find` command to locate the portion of the documentation I'm interested in.

Collaboration and Creative Theft

No matter how experienced you are, you are only one person. By getting together with other people and reviewing each other's work, you can expand your own knowledge and the knowledge of others. A good example of where this has worked well is the Linux kernel. Thousands of people have shared their code, received feedback, improved their code, and then collected it into the most powerful operating system in the world.

Looking through publicly available code to see how other programmers do things is also helpful. One example is the HAL firmware that comes with the STM32 Workbench. It is professional code that provides great internal documentation. (See the upcoming "Doxygen" section.) The bad news is that it's designed to be used on a whole set of different chips, so you have to deal with the land of 200 `#ifdefs`. Lots of good source is available. Browse through some and see what you pick up.

Useful Open Source Tools

The open source community has a long history of developing quality tools to aid in program creation and editing. These free tools are created by the people who want to use them, as opposed to commercial programs that add features that help sell the programs but might not be useful. This section describes a few helpful open source tools.

Cppcheck

The Cppcheck program is a static program checker. In other words, it looks for problems in your program that the compiler didn't find, which is getting tough these days as the compilers have become quite sophisticated.

This program was responsible for finding my favorite bit of C code. This was the error message:

```
Detect matching 'if' and 'else if' conditions
```

In other words, the body of the `if` and the body of the `else` contained the same code. There's no need for the condition if the computer does the same thing when the condition is true or false.

Here's the code in question:

```
if (flag) {
    //(removed) processMessage()
} else {
    //(removed) processMessage()
}
```

That's right, the body of the `if` was one commented-out procedure call, and the body of the `else` was the same commented-out procedure call!

I prefer Cppcheck over most commercial static program analyzers because it generates a minimum number of false positives. If Cppcheck flags a line in your code, it's a good idea to look at that code.

Doxygen

Ever since the first program grew to be longer than 50 lines, people have tried to make programming languages that are self-documenting. So far, they've failed. The people behind Doxygen created a system where through structured comments in your program, you can create documentation for it (at least in theory).

The first difficulty is that you have to put the comments in the code, and many engineers fail to comment their code at all. Another issue is that the documentation looks like it was automatically generated. Although it's actually very good for automatically generated documentation, it's still automatically generated documentation.

The Cppcheck program mentioned in the previous section uses Doxygen for its internal documentation.

Valgrind

The Valgrind project is a suite of tools designed to look at your program to check for errors dynamically. One of the most popular tools in the suite is memcheck, which looks for memory errors such as array overflows, pointers being used after they are freed, and so on. It's very effective at detecting most simple runtime errors.

SQLite

SQLite is an embedded database library that's good for small databases (up to 100,000 records). It's not the fastest database in the world, but for small embedded systems where you don't want the overhead of a major database, it works well. You'll need to learn SQL to use it, but it's a valuable skill to learn.

Never Stop Learning

Computer technology is changing at an amazing rate. That one little 38¢ STM microchip we use in this book has more power than all the computers in the world had in 1950. The technology will never stop changing, so you should never stop learning. You never know what new discovery you'll find around the corner.

APPENDIX
PROJECT CREATION CHECKLIST

Native C Project

For programs that run on the PC, start the STM32 Workbench, select a workspace if needed, and then complete the following steps:

1. In the main window, select **File ▸ New ▸ C/C++ Project**.
2. In the C/C++ Project window, select **C Managed Build** and click **Next**.
3. In the C Project window:
    a. Fill in the name (no spaces or funny characters).
    b. In the Project Type column, select **Executable ▸ Empty Project**.
    c. In the Toolchains column, select the one for your native system. For example, if you are on Windows with Visual C++, you would choose Visual C++. If you're on Linux, you would select the Linux C compiler, GNU gcc.
    d. Click **Next**.

4. In the Configurations window:
   a. Uncheck **Release**.
   b. **Debug** should remain checked.
   c. Click **Finish**.

5. In the main window:
   a. In the Project Explorer (left column), select the project.
   b. Select **File ▸ New ▸ Source File**.

6. In the Source File window:
   a. In the Source File field, enter the name of your program file (ends with *.c*).
   b. Click **Finish**.

7. Back in the main window (with the file shown in the editing pane):
   a. Enter the program.
   b. Select **File ▸ Save All**.
   c. Select **Project ▸ Build Project.**
   d. Select **Run ▸ Run Configuration**.

8. In the Create, Manage, and Run Configurations window:
   a. In the left column, select **C/C++ Application**.
   b. Click **New**.
   c. Under C/C++ Application, click **Browse**.

9. In the File dialog:
   a. Go to your workspace and open the project folder.
   b. In the project folder, open the *Debug* directory.
   c. Select the executable for your program.
   d. Click **OK**.

10. Back in the Create, Manage, and Run Configurations window:
   a. Click **Apply**.
   b. Click **Close**.

You can now run and debug your program.

STM32 Workbench Embedded Project

For programs that run on the Nucleo board, start the STM32 Workbench, select the workspace if needed, and then complete the following steps:

1. In the main window, select **File ▸ New ▸ C Project**.
2. In the C Project window:
   a. Fill in the name (no spaces or funny characters).
   b. In the Project Type column, select **Executable ▸ Empty Project**.
   c. In the Toolchains column, select **Ac6 STM32 MCU GCC**.
   d. Click **Next**.

3. In the Configurations window:
   a. Uncheck **Release**.
   b. **Debug** should remain checked.
   c. Click **Finish**.

4. In the Target Configuration window:
   a. For the series, select **STM32F0**.
   b. For the board, select **NUCLEO-F030R8**.
   c. Click **Next**.

5. In the Project Firmware Configuration window:
   a. Click **Hardware Abstraction Layer (Cube HAL)**.
   b. Download the target firmware (needed only once).
   c. Click **Finish**.

6. Back in the main window:
   a. In the Project Explorer (left column), select the project.
   b. Select **Project ▸ Properties**.

7. In the Properties window:
   a. Expand **C++ Build**.
   b. Go to **Settings**.
   c. Go to the **Tool Settings** tab.
   d. Select **MCU GCC Compiler ▸ Debugging**.
   e. Debug level: **Maximum (-g3)**.
   f. Select **MCU GCC Compiler ▸ Miscellaneous**.

g. Other flags: -fmessage-length=0 OWa,adhls=$(@:%.o=%.lst).

h. Turn on **Listings**.

i. Click **Apply**.

j. Click **OK**.

8. In the main window:

a. In the Project Explorer (left column), select the project.

b. Expand the project.

c. Expand the *src* directory.

d. Click *main.c* to edit it.

e. Enter the program.

f. Select **File ▸ Save All**.

g. Select **Project ▸ Build Project**.

h. Select **Project ▸ Run** or **Project ▸ Debug**.

INDEX

NOT operator (~), 68, 69
NUCLEO-F030R8, xix, 32–51
    setup, 35
NUL character (\0), 101
NULL pointer dereference, 169
numbers, 53
    fixed-point, 263–265
    floating-point, 257–265
    magic, 93
    representation, 59
numerical analysis, 260
NVIC_EnableIRQ, 167, 168, 176

O

O as variable name, 55
O_BINARY, 252–255
objcopy (arm-none-eabi-objcopy), 46
object file, 11, 184
    absolute, 192
    relocatable, 192, 193
O_CREAT, 252, 253
octal, 59
    printf, 238
one-character version of Hello World,
    142–143
open flags
    O_BINARY, 252–255
    O_CREAT, 252, 253
    O_RDONLY, 252, 253
open function, 252, 253
opening files, 242
open mode, file, 243
    rb, 245
    wb, 245
open source tools, 282–284
operating system, 222
operations, bit, 67
operator
    ++, 65
    +=, 65
    --, 66
    address of (&), 94
    AND (&), 68, 69, 74
    decrement (--), 66
    dereference (*), 94
    equals (==), 78
    exclusive OR (^), 69
    greater than (>), 78

greater than or equal (>=), 78
    increment (++), 65
    left shift (<<), 69–70
    less than (<), 78
    less than or equal (<=), 78
    NOT (~), 68, 69
    not equals (!=), 78
    OR (|), 67, 68
    right shift (>>), 70
    shorthand, 65
optimizer, 3
O_RDONLY, 252, 253
OR operator (|), 67, 68
Outline window, 28
output.map, 47
overflow, 63–64
    array, 98–100
oversampling (serial), 149

P

PA2 pin, 149, 150
PA3 pin, 149, 150
packed attribute, 125, 126, 135
parameter, pointer, 128, 129
parameterized macros, 210
parentheses warning, 79
permanent memory (flash), 195
perspective, debug, 27, 28, 48
phony target, make, 16
PIC processor, 170
pin
    analog, 41
    floating, 85
    GPIO, 41, 42
    PA2, 149, 150
    PA3, 149, 150
    pulldown, 85
    pullup, 85
pointer, 91
    arithmetic, 97
        scaling, 98
    assign from array, 97
    debugger, 96
    declaration, 94
    function, 136
        typedef, 136
    parameters, 128, 129
    printf (%p), 95

Bare Metal C is set in New Baskerville, Futura, Dogma, and TheSansMono Condensed. The book was printed and bound by Sheridan Books, Inc. in Chelsea, Michigan.

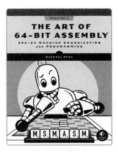

Never before has the world relied so heavily on the Internet to stay connected and informed. That makes the Electronic Frontier Foundation's mission—to ensure that technology supports freedom, justice, and innovation for all people— more urgent than ever.

For over 30 years, EFF has fought for tech users through activism, in the courts, and by developing software to overcome obstacles to your privacy, security, and free expression. This dedication empowers all of us through darkness. With your help we can navigate toward a brighter digital future.